Shakespeare and the Story

Shakespeare and the Story

Aspects of Creation

by

JOAN REES

UNIVERSITY OF LONDON
THE ATHLONE PRESS
1978

Published by
THE ATHLONE PRESS
UNIVERSITY OF LONDON
at 4 *Gower Street London* WC1

Distributed by Tiptree Book Services Ltd
Tiptree, Essex

USA and Canada
Humanities Press Inc
New Jersey

ISBN 0 485 11179 9

Printed in Great Britain by
WESTERN PRINTING SERVICES LTD
Bristol

Contents

Note

All references to quotations from Shakespeare are to the edition by Peter Alexander (London and Glasgow, 1951), though alternative readings of the text have sometimes been preferred.

For my father

I

The Work of Creation

The aim of this book is to observe Shakespeare's handling of his stories for the light this may throw on the creative imagination engaged in his plays. Story and narrative may not be ideal terms to apply to drama but there are no others readily available to denote the series of events which Shakespeare chooses to treat, the sequence in which he takes them, and the methods he adopts in ordering and developing them. Any single approach has inevitable limitations but the present one gives entry into the plays, and illuminates them, on a number of levels and at every point it tends to sharpen realisation of the immense creative vitality pouring into these extraordinary works.

In the existing state of Shakespeare studies the procedure adopted and the rewards it offers seem to have a special usefulness. Shakespeare's creative imagination is the source from which spring not only his own works but also all the critical activities which centre upon him. The vitality and quality of this imagination provide the justification of the most pedantic enquiry and the most ambitious study but, as rivers sometimes travel a long way from their source, so critical studies sometimes lose sight of the reason for their existence. It is useful, from time to time, to remind ourselves of the fount from which all else springs lest priorities become confused and critical pedantry and ambition come to be regarded, or regard themselves, as self-supporting and self-justifying. It is with this in mind that the present book is offered, for the approach to Shakespeare via his handling of story development makes possible a description of the plays in which emphasis falls firmly upon the creative imagination whence they derive their life and power.

Others have commented, more or less extensively, upon Shakespeare's treatment of the story in his plays. In the examples which follow, 'plot', 'action' and 'story' are interchangeable terms since what all the writers are concerned with is the events of the plays and the way in which Shakespeare works with, or upon, them.

'. . . strip the poetry from a play of Shakespeare and what is left but a rather haphazard story about a set of vaguely outlined and incredibly "stagey" characters?', asks S. L. Bethell,[1] making a divorce of elements which few would condone. For E. E. Stoll, the dynamic of Shakespeare's plays exists in the disparity between the action, or story, and the characters. In *Julius Caesar*, he writes, 'even as in the dramatist's greater work, the action is not the legitimate issue of the character'.[2] For him, to use Virginia Woolf's words in *Between the Acts*, 'The plot is only there to beget emotion': the excellence of Shakespeare's dramatic writing is to show characters acting under stress, the stressful situation itself being a given condition, something contrived or imposed from without, requiring no psychological motivation in the character itself. The exhibition of the resulting behaviour constitutes the heart of the drama and it is all the more striking because its causes are *not* lodged in the psyche of the protagonists. This is in some ways a valuable but also a very vulnerable thesis. J. I. M. Stewart has taken issue with Stoll and, in his *Character and Motive in Shakespeare* (1949), argued that action and character are in fact interwoven. He claims that Shakespeare is a subtle-souled psychologist, anticipating in his positing of Leontes' jealousy, for example, or Othello's, the findings of Freud and his followers. According to this reading, when we come upon difficulties in the story we explain them, by whatever resources lie to hand, as so many devices employed by Shakespeare to make a profound observation upon human nature.

H. T. Price makes an equally comprehensive, but different, approach:

> Shakespeare had an eminently constructive mind. Shakespeare's work is a strict intellectual construction developed from point to point until he brings us to the necessary and inevitable conclusion. He interrelates part to part, as well as every part to the whole. His inner idea is manifested in an action, with which it is intimately fused, so that the crises in the action which move us most deeply reveal at the same time most clearly the inner core of Shakespeare's thought.[3]

[1] In *Shakespeare and the Popular Dramatic Tradition* (London, 1944), p. 16.
[2] *Art and Artifice in Shakespeare* (Cambridge, 1933), p. 145.
[3] *Construction in Shakespeare* (University of Michigan Contributions in Modern Philology, no. 17, May, 1971).

This approach has been a fruitful one. The coherence and significance of image patterns and other characteristics of the plays have been traced and described, often illuminatingly, as aspects of the interrelation of part to part and of every part to the whole. Yet when Price writes that 'the crises in the action which move us most deeply reveal at the same time most clearly the inner core of Shakespeare's thought', this, though a stimulating proposition, seems to point to a central weakness in the approach. If a scattering of competent persons were asked to define the inner core of Shakespeare's thought as clearly revealed in the death of Cordelia, or the suicide of Othello, it is not likely that the answers would show a high degree of unanimity. Price takes it that Shakespeare starts from an 'inner idea' which he then manifests in action, action and idea being 'intimately fused', so that the crises of the action lead to the ultimate revelation of the idea: but this is to make a feature of the plays which is indisputably there i.e. the action, subservient to a feature of which we have no independent knowledge—the idea. We are then in a region where few controls operate.

Dr Johnson has also written of Shakespeare's stories, as usual incisively. In the Preface to his edition of Shakespeare, he comments:

> The plays are often so loosely formed, that a very slight consideration may improve them, and so carelessly pursued, that he seems not always to comprehend his own design. He omits opportunities of instructing or delighting which the train of his story seems to force upon him, and apparently rejects those exhibitions which would be more affecting for the sake of those which are more easy.
>
> It may be observed, that in many of his plays the latter part is evidently neglected. When he found himself near the end of his work, and in view of his reward, he shortened the labour, to snatch the profit. He therefore remits his efforts where he should most vigorously exert them, and his catastrophe is improbably produced or imperfectly represented.

Johnson here, unlike the other commentators quoted, is talking about Shakespeare's behaviour as a story-teller as such, and not about his stories in relation to his poetry or his characters or to an inner core of thought. In so far as he is commenting on the articulation of events and the handling of episodes in a narrative structure his example is followed in the present book more nearly than that of any of the other critics cited, for the linear development of the plays and their narrative techniques will form the basis of the discussions. The advantage of looking at the plays in this way and leaving aside for the time being other considerations, is that some highly interesting features are thrown into sharp relief. Some plays, for example, seem very strikingly to change course or to alter their emphases during the process of writing, and there are some which set a pace in early Acts which creates problems in the latter parts of the plays. Dr Johnson, when he talked about 'carelessness' and 'neglect' was responding to the unevennesses that he found but, though he put his finger (as usual) on a crucial quality, he interpreted what he found by too narrow a code. These unevennesses, as this book will attempt to show, are properly to be seen as the signatures of creative imagination, working with irresistible vigour within the chosen story, bursting it open, perhaps, or distorting it, but producing in the end a singular and astonishing work of art. We should always be astonished by Shakespeare and it is a serious charge against many critical accounts that by over-intellectualising and schematising his work they misrepresent the leaping life that is in it.

Because of the unexpected development, the unlooked-for dimension added to the action, the sheer depth and intensity of imaginative creation, Shakespeare is the most exciting of writers and to read him is always a discovery. What his processes of creation were we shall not now know but D. H. Lawrence, speaking for himself, conveys an experience which may very well be nearer to Shakespeare's than the calculation implied in Professor Price's 'strict intellectual construction developed from point to point'. Lawrence's poem is called 'The Work of Creation' and it compares the work of the artist to the work of God:

> Even an artist knows that his work was never in his mind,
> he could never have *thought* it before it happened.
> A strange ache possessed him, and he entered the
>   struggle,
> and out of the struggle with his material, in the spell of
>   the urge
> his work took place, it came to pass, it stood up and
>   saluted his mind.

The artist, like God:

> knows nothing beforehand.
> His urge takes shape in flesh, and lo!
> it is creation! God looks himself on it in wonder,
>   for the first time.
> Lo! there is a creature formed! How strange!
> Let me think about it! Let me form an idea.

To Dr Johnson it was a fault in Shakespeare that he seemed 'not always to comprehend his own design'. For Lawrence it is a characteristic of the creative act that the imagination working at full pressure may be beyond the reach of the conscious intelligence. The mind recognises what it has done after it has done it and may be surprised at what has been produced: 'How strange it is! Let me think about it! Let me form an idea'. The ideas of the artist are equivalent to the ideas of the critic: that is to say, they relate to the completed work and they may have little to do with the impulses and energies engaged in the creative process.

Following the progress of the story holds the promise of arriving for ourselves at that moment when we can say 'lo it is creation!' but we shall not find it always in the unpremeditated. Shakespeare was a busy, prolific and professional dramatist. He sought many kinds of material, he tried many methods, he made many experiments. Sometimes he rehearsed the same basic situations or the same kinds of approach more than once, trying out new presentations and variations, and the work of creation may take place in these circumstances as in others. He gave a great deal of attention to the making of his plays, the kinds of material they could be made from, and the kinds of effect which could be achieved. In particular, he gave a great deal of attention to stories and the way they could be managed. As time went on he gained abundant experience of what could be done with them and where their limitations lay. It will be useful to give some general consideration to the background against which this experience was acquired before proceeding further.

Of course there are important distinctions between the art of the dramatist and that of the non-dramatic narrator. A play must take account of the physical properties of the theatre and of the talents and the physical and temperamental qualities of the actors. There are restrictions on time, place and event but, to offset these, an actor, given the opportunity, can make a gesture speak volumes or can bring the house down in laughter. Lighting, costume, grouping, can create effects beyond the scope of the written word. Nevertheless, there is a good deal of similarity between non-dramatic narrative and the dramatic methods of Shakespeare's theatre. Numerous descriptive passages in the plays serve instead of elaborate scenic effects and the soliloquy, to explain motive or make situations clear to the audience, was a well-accepted convention. When he uses a narrative source, Shakespeare sometimes dramatises the material into a lively and natural scene (the opening scene of *As You Like It* is a case in point), but in *Cymbeline*, for example, he is content with straightforward exposition.

Some plays—there are outstanding modern examples—reduce the story element to the barest minimum. Sequence of events is whittled away almost out of existence and another kind of dramatic structure takes its place. By contrast, Shakespeare's plays have stories at their core, stories which can be extracted and retold, as he himself extracted them from his sources and retold them. Stories may delight but, inevitably, they also falsify. The imposition of a beginning and ending belies the unbroken continuum of life which has no beginning but the creation of the world and will have no ending till its destruction. The material of a story can be no more than a handful, more or less large or small, of the influences, ideas, memories, experiences, out of which the words and gestures and actions of individuals arise. Yet the degree to which artificiality obtrudes itself varies greatly and, according to the skill or predilection of the teller, the organisation of experience which a story offers can be very simple or very subtle. At its simplest, as a string of sequential episodes, it is capable of giving pleasure because there is order and point of some sort, even if only rudimentary, in the sequence; at its most complex, it may gather in so much of the sub-soil of action that the sequential thread is of minimal importance. Modern literature again offers the most obvious examples: Virginia Woolf's novel, *The Waves*, for instance. The pleasures to be derived from a story of this kind are more sophisticated than those offered by the simpler form. Story, nevertheless, there still is.

In their book, *The Nature of Narrative*, Scholes and Kellogg[4]

[4] R. Scholes and R. Kellogg, *The Nature of Narrative* (Oxford, 1966), p. 250.

write of '. . . the miserable state of English narrative in the fifteenth and early sixteenth centuries: a state of moribundity so profound that it required the introduction of Spanish picaresque, of Italian literary epic, and the revival and translation of Greek romance before signs of life began to re-appear'. The narrative zest, when it had found matter to feed on, proved to be vigorous and by the end of the sixteenth century was drawing its material from many sources. As narrative materials were assembled, so also grew the wish to make complex structures of them. Sidney and Spenser were tale-tellers on a large scale and within very complicated structures: Sidney, in his revised *Arcadia*, seeking to assemble narrative corre-latives for a comprehensive philosophy of love, war and statecraft, and Spenser, in his *Faerie Queene*, compounding stories drawn from all aspects of the cultural heritage of his time, to illuminate and nourish the inner life of man.

Sidney himself marks the gap between the narrative style of a sophisticated literary culture and more primitive methods when he includes in *Arcadia* the story told by Mopsa, the country girl, to the princess Pamela. '. . . so being her time to speak', Sidney writes:

(wiping her mouth, as there was good cause) she Mopsa thus tumbled into her matter. In time past (sayd she) there was a king, the mightiest man in all his country, that had by his wife, the fairest daughter that ever did eat pappe. Now this king did keepe a great house, that everybody might come and take their meat freely. So one day, as his daughter was sitting in her window, playing upon a harpe, as sweete as any Rose; and combing her head with a combe all of precious stones, there came a Knight into the court, upon a goodly horse, one hair of gold, and the other of silver; *and so* the Knight casting up his eyes to the win-dow, did fall into such love with her, that he grew not worth the bread he eate; till many a sorry day going over his head, with Dayly Diligence and Grisly Grones, he wan her affection, so that they agreed to run away togither. *And so in May*, when all true hearts rejoyce, they stale out of the Castel, without staying so much as for their breakfast. Now forsooth, as they went togither, often all to-kissing one another, the Knight told her, he was brought up among the water Nymphes, who had so bewitched him, that if he were ever askt his name, he must presently vanish

The Work of Creation

8   *The Work of Creation*

away: and therefore charged her upon his blessing, that she never
aske him what he was, nor whether he would. *And so* a great
while she kept his commandement; til once, passing through a
cruel wilderness, as darke as pitch; her mouth so watred, that she
could not choose but aske him the question. And then, he making
the greevousest complaints that would have melted a tree to have
heard them, vanisht quite away: and she lay down, casting forth
as pitifull cries as any shrich-owle. But having laien so (wet by
the raine and burnt by the Sun) five dayes, and five nights, she
gat up and went over many a high hill, and many a deepe river;
till she came to an Aunts house of hers; and came, and cried to
her for helpe: and she for pittie gave her a Nut, and bad her never
open her Nut, til she was come to the extremest misery that ever
tongue could speake of. *And so* she went, and she went, and
never rested the evening, where she went in the morning; til she
came to a second Aunt; and she gave her another Nut.

Pamela interrupts Mopsa at this point, recognising that the end of
the story is likely to be very long in coming. Obviously Sidney is
making fun of a primitive kind of narrative technique, one which
'tumbles into the matter' without any preliminary artistic shaping
of the material and which jumbles together, quite uncritically,
assorted motifs and formulae from romance and fairy tale. Mopsa's
method of ensuring sequence for the middle passages of her story is
the crudest possible but, although Sidney mocks, Mopsa's tale shows
plenty of awareness of what 'a good yarn' requires. The superlatives
with which she describes her characters indicate her recognition
that interest has to be aroused in them, and she knows, furthermore,
like Pooh-Bah, how important corroborative detail may be in
enlivening an otherwise bald and uninteresting narrative. The
princess of the story is sitting in her window playing the harp when
she first sees her knight and if she is also, at the same time apparently, combing her hair with a comb of precious stones, a combination of activities which seems difficult to achieve, this only goes to
show that Mopsa has observed how much incidental detail can
contribute to a story, and she will overdo it rather than leave it out.
She also knows that even the most exotic tale needs to be brought
nearer home from time to time if the audience is to become really
engaged with it, and so she records that the knight and the princess

stole away from the castle 'without staying so much as for their breakfast'. She adventures into the symbolic mode when she makes irresistible temptation beset the princess while 'passing through a cruel wilderness, as dark as pitch', but after five days and five nights of lamentation, the action moves briskly with little pause for comment as she goes from aunt to aunt, and from nut to nut. Mopsa is also provident in laying up material for the ending of her story. There will be a trail of nuts to pick up, leading eventually, no doubt, to the explanation of the knight's mystery and to reconciliation of the happy pair with the king, and at last Mopsa will reach her final 'and so': 'And so they lived happily ever after'.

Mopsa's story, then, is one end of a spectrum whose other extreme will take in some very accomplished examples. Sidney well knew that a tale 'holdeth children from play, and old men from the chimney corner' and he adds, in this passage from the *Apologie for Poetry*, that most men 'are childish in the best things, till they be cradled in their graves'. Yet he makes it clear that narrative interest in itself appeals only to an unsophisticated taste. He himself was a young and highly educated aristocrat, writing for a literary and cultivated audience, and when he wrote narrative he had multifarious interests in mind. Shakespeare's social and educational background was different and the preconceptions which Sidney brought to bear on his thinking about literature, Shakespeare did not necessarily share. Since he wrote for the popular stage, he might be expected to have more sympathy with Mopsa's enthusiasm for the story-as-story than Sidney did but, as it happens, among his earliest works are two non-dramatic poems with which he hoped to attract the attention of just that aristocratic and cultivated world to which Sidney belonged, and the treatment of the story in these is, consequently, strongly influenced by other than narrative considerations.

In the circumstances, an examination of the handling of the story material in *Venus and Adonis* and *The Rape of Lucrece*, and of Shakespeare's attitude to his story in plays written at about the same time, is likely to shed some useful light on his early experiences as story-teller and how he reacted to them.

Venus and Adonis and *The Rape of Lucrece* are sophisticated examples of narrative, as *Arcadia* and *The Faerie Queene* are, but whereas Sidney and Spenser work by a combination of many stories, Shakespeare in these poems works by amplification of a few episodes merely. In his use of amplification he is following a favourite practice of Elizabethan narrators, in verse and prose alike. This is not a matter of circumstantial detail used to give life to the scene around character and event but a rhetorical skill, used to open out suggestions arising in the narrative for the purpose of developing a topic which may be only slightly related to the main story line or for the sake of adding decorative ornament. Both poems have this feature but Shakespeare does not succeed equally well with both.

They are patronage poems, bids, that is, for the interest and support of the young Earl of Southampton and Shakespeare chooses Ovid, a fashionable poet, to provide his ground plan. The stories were very familiar to an educated audience and this being so everything depended on the poet's treatment of them. With *Venus and Adonis* Shakespeare was very clever indeed. He fused several episodes from the *Metamorphoses* and by doing so gave himself a point of view from which to approach the well-known tale and make it piquant and new. That Venus, the goddess of Love, should woo, and woo unsuccessfully, a callow boy is a situation capable of many ironies. Venus's victory over Mars, contrasted with her frustration by Adonis, is one of them; the behaviour of Adonis, as against that of the stallion who responds with forthright male vigour to the invitation of the mare, is another; but the poem concentrates particularly on the comic implications of the reversal of sexual roles.

'Thrice fairer than myself', Venus begins, '. . . more lovely than a man' and within a few lines she has lifted the boy down from his horse and 'Backward she pushed him, as she would be thrust'. Her arguments and her blandishments are the traditional strategy of the male lover but Adonis's total lack of response and Venus's physical incapacity to take what she wants give the seduction speeches a comic context which Shakespeare takes every opportunity to emphasise. The courser's conduct contrasts with that of Adonis but it contrasts also with that of Venus for she is trying, unsuitably and ineffectually, to play the courser's role. On several occasions when her wooing is in full flow, Shakespeare deliberately breaks the tone of the writing so as to expose the essential comic indignity of the situation. Venus 'sweats' with heat and effort (l.175), she pleads with Adonis in the imagery of lovers' exchange of hearts, but in reply:

'For shame', he cries, 'let go, and let me go;
My day's delight is past, my horse is gone,
And 'tis your fault I am bereft him so'. (ll.379–81)

Once the point of view has been found, some effects of the poem
are guaranteed: it can be salacious, farcical, and witty on this theme
at will. But Shakespeare is free to have his cake and eat it too, for
within the overall comic ironies he can deploy his arguments for love
and generation, he can display his richest and most luxurious
language, and he can invoke true feeling, especially in Venus's fears
when she hears the noises of the boar hunt and comes suddenly
upon Adonis's body.

In its treatment of the material *Venus and Adonis* may be said to
be entirely successful, sustaining interest brilliantly from the swift
launching of the poem in the opening stanza, which presents, without preamble, the characters and the situation, to the last moment
when Venus, weary of the world, flies through the skies, drawn by
her doves to Paphos. The episodes of the narrative are few and most
of them are slight. Adonis ducks out of the way of Venus's kiss
(ll.84–90), Venus cries in frustration (ll.217–22), Adonis smiles
(ll.241–6). The discovery of his body is dramatic because it is
preceded by Venus's fears and then by her reassurance, so that she
comes upon him when she is hurrying, as she thinks, to greet him:

As falcons to the lure away she flies;
The grass stoops not, she treads on it so light;
And in her haste unfortunately spies
The foul boar's conquest on her fair delight (ll. 1027–30).

But most of the poem is sustained by resourceful invention on a
limited narrative base. It is incidentally interesting that at the two
points where 'amplification' becomes most nearly 'digression',
Shakespeare draws attention to the fact, as if to forestall criticism.
The first occasion occurs with the splendid description of the hunt-
ing of 'poor Wat' and the second with Adonis's unexpectedly
mature distinction between love and lust. 'Unlike myself thou
hear'st me moralise', Venus says of her sympathetic evocation of the
hunted hare, and Adonis comments on his own eloquence: 'The
text is old, the orator too green.'

In October 1817, John Keats wrote to his friend Bailey, telling
him about his projected new poem, *Endymion*. 'It will be a test, a

trial of my powers of imagination and chiefly of my invention which is a rare thing indeed—by which I must make 4,000 lines of one bare circumstance and fill them with poetry.' Though neither *Venus and Adonis* nor *The Rape of Lucrece* separately runs to 4000 lines, they offered Shakespeare a similar test of invention. *The Rape of Lucrece* is longer than *Venus and Adonis* and Shakespeare does not come so successfully out of the trial. The poem plunges us directly into action, as *Venus and Adonis* does, and it encompasses the sensational events of rape and suicide, both of which are made into fully developed scenes. It might seem that the opportunities for development of the story material are greater than in *Venus and Adonis*, but instead of a successful blending of elements such as we have in the earlier poem, *Lucrece* presents, rather, a succession of set pieces—on Night, on Time, on Opportunity, on the grief of Hecuba and the treachery of Sinon. The story of the rape and suicide of Lucrece needed, perhaps, for its fullest development, a psychological treatment which Shakespeare at this stage could not supply. Tarquin's struggles with himself before he goes to Lucrece's bedroom approach it, but little individuality is conveyed as he balances the urgency of present desire against the certainty of future remorse. The very 'normality' of the situation, a male lover attempting to win a woman, makes severer demands on the poet's capacity to 'make it new' than *Venus and Adonis* did. The comic-ironic point of view from which Shakespeare chose to view the situation in *Venus and Adonis* gave him a great deal of freedom and he was able to impart edge and élan to the telling of the story. But with the tale of Lucrece no liberties can be taken; it must be told 'straight'. There are strong moments as, for example, when Tarquin tells Lucrece that he is fully aware of the ill consequences which are likely to follow his deed but nevertheless he means to indulge his will—this clear-sightedness makes the scene more appalling than a rash and hot-blooded act might do. Again, the lassitude and nausea that overcome Tarquin as he leaves Lucrece's room, 'sweating with guilty fear', are also strongly evoked. In general, however, the eloquent and interesting passages gain little from their context and are not bound so intimately with all other parts as the material of *Venus and Adonis* mostly is.

'This same invention', Keats goes on in the letter already quoted, 'seems indeed of late years to have been forgotten as a poetical excellence.' There was no danger of forgetting it in the late 1590s.

Amplification, and the development of new variations on old themes, gave to poets of the time an impulse for writing which did not need to be reinforced by the intensity of personal emotion. The eloquence which was released when Spenser and Sidney unlocked the tongues of English poets produced the excitement and offered all the challenge of a new discovery. Shakespeare was exploring his capacity in this line when he wrote his narrative poems, just as Keats was trying out his own powers when he wrote *Endymion*.

It was a severe test that Shakespeare set himself for both poems are founded on one and the same basic situation, that of sexual attack, and the two together total something near Keats's 4000 lines. How rigorous the self-imposed conditions were can readily be seen if *Venus and Adonis* and *The Rape of Lucrece* are compared with poems in the same mode, Marlowe's *Hero and Leander*, for example, and Daniel's *Complaint of Rosamond*. Daniel's *Rosamond* makes a particularly apt comparison because in its 742 lines it includes many of the motifs of *Venus and Adonis* and *The Rape of Lucrece*, including the appeal to youth, beauty and erotic pleasure contained in Shakespeare's earlier poem, and the theme of sexual chastity in the later. Henry's unexpected meeting with Rosamond's funeral procession and his grief for her parallel Venus's coming upon the dead body of Adonis and her mourning for him. *Rosamond* is organised as a lament for lost innocence and a warning to others to beware of temptation and, with its movement and variety of material, its composition can have offered relatively few problems compared with the virtuoso task which Shakespeare imposed on himself in writing his pair of poems.

Keats's words to Bailey about making 4000 lines out of one bare circumstance and filling them with poetry suggest that the narrative element in his conception of *Endymion* was minimal. The same is true of Shakespeare's approach to *Venus and Adonis* and *The Rape of Lucrece*. Narrative opportunities offered by the story material are, in fact, eschewed by him. He could have made more of the boar-hunt in *Venus and Adonis* but did not. He could have made more of the banishment of Tarquin and the ending of the monarchy in *The Rape of Lucrece* but he did not, limiting himself strictly to 'invention' out of 'one bare circumstance' in each case.

On the evidence of these poems then, it would seem that Shakespeare took Elizabethan courtly disdain of narrative even further than others; but if we turn to the plays he was writing at the same time, we find a quite different situation. In them, the story's the thing. If he had already written *The Comedy of Errors* and *The Taming of the Shrew* when he turned to *Venus and Adonis*, the composition of the poems must have challenged him deeply. The Latin prologue to *Menaechmi*, which provides the basis of *The Comedy of Errors*, promised lavishness of plot 'measured not by the peck or bushel, but by the barnful',[5] and Shakespeare takes care to see that there is no want of episode in either of these early comedies. In both, material from several sources is dovetailed, so that the *Amphitruo* of Plautus and an episode from Gower's *Confessio Amantis* help to develop the possibilities of 'pleasant error' for which the *Menaechmi* provides the basic suggestion. Gascoigne's *Supposes* is similarly fed into the material of *The Taming of the Shrew*, and the *Amphitruo* is called upon again. In the poems Shakespeare was working to extract as much as possible from a deliberately limited story line. In the plays he takes pains to gather together plenty of material to ensure that the action is kept going and that his characters are busy. Clearly he thought that a play requires action where a poem need not, but whether he preferred working within one set of conditions rather than another the evidence will not positively show. There are signs, however, that the tightly-schemed story of *The Comedy of Errors*, which he had taken pains to work out, pinched him a little. It is required by the story that Adriana be a shrew and justly reproved as such by Luciana in Act II, sc. i and by the Abbess at the end, but Shakespeare's imagination presents to him, even this early, two sides to a case, and Adriana's dependence on the love she fears she has lost makes an appeal for sympathy which runs across the bias of the play.

Shakespeare's experience at this point in his career appears, then, to have offered him two views about the function of the story. In a non-dramatic poem it was possible to do with very little narrative action and attempt to maintain interest by deploying other resources. In drama it was safer to have plenty although this might unfortunately result in some bruising of characters who start to grow out of the situations in which they are placed. *The Two Gentlemen of Verona* and *Love's Labour's Lost* show him experimenting with the

[5] *Narrative and Dramatic Sources of Shakespeare*, ed. G. Bullough, vol. i, p. 5.

proportions in which the ingredients might be mixed and the two kinds of experience are brought into splendidly successful combination with the writing of *Romeo and Juliet*. There Shakespeare had, ready-made, a good and strongly constructed story in Brooke's poem of *The Tragical History of Romeo and Juliet*. It was a story, moreover, which provided opportunity for the lyrical and rhetorical powers of his non-dramatic work and one which gave him freedom to develop characters—notably, the Nurse and Mercutio, who were not tightly constricted by the story-line though they contributed to it. The combination of conditions produces a masterpiece of his early career.

Shakespeare's early experience of narrative contains the seeds that are to germinate in his later work. The techniques of amplification and variation that he learnt from contemporary practice and theory and that he exercised in his two narrative poems will be called into the service of his mature drama. He tended always to favour a firm narrative framework and often announced in his text, by prophecy, instruction, or some other kind of anticipatory statement, the major developments to follow. This gave him useful support while leaving him free to develop the circumstances and implications of events rather than being pressed by the need to insist continuously on action. But the tendency, faintly present in *The Comedy of Errors*, for character to challenge story, asserts itself on later occasions in a notable way. This is the point to which Professor Stoll and Mr Stewart addressed themselves in commentaries quoted earlier and pursuit of the story-line will lead back to it more than once in the following chapters.

Character study is in itself a less popular critical activity now than it used to be but it still exerts a hold, and rightly so, for recognition of Shakespeare's superb insight into an immense variety of character is one of the most rewarding 'ideas' that has been formed about his plays. Yet even the best of ideas can lead astray, as the Arden edition note to the beginning of *Othello*, Act IV, sc. i, will illustrate:

I have never understood [the editor writes] why Shakespeare makes Iago—and that rather clumsily—recall Othello to the handkerchief which he seems to have forgotten. The handkerchief was earlier useful as a piece of (potentially) ocular proof which Othello was demanding. But it is highly dangerous for Iago, since it may at any moment provoke a challenge from Othello to Cassio, if they meet, on a point of refutable detail, not on general guilt. And Iago's courage, though undoubted, is not the kind that takes *needless* risks. And he has reduced Othello to such a condition of unthinking rage that the risk is now useless.

Mr Ridley's puzzlement derives, it appears, from the assumption that Shakespeare intends in *Othello* to give an insight into human characteristics as they are exposed by the situation he is treating. Shakespeare has, in fact, given enough information on these lines to supply possible answers to the question in the terms in which it is put: for example, that Iago takes a fiendish delight in playing his fish, Othello has risen to this bait once and Iago revels in his power to make him do so again; the fact that Othello says 'I would most gladly have forgot it' indicates how painfully the story planted by Iago has affected him, and Iago's forcing him into full conscious acknowledgement of it once again adds to his torments and is instrumental in weakening still further his power to resist Iago's manipulations. But the assumption about Shakespeare's 'intentions' which has dictated the form of the question may be groundless and a more pertinent explanation of why Iago recalls the handkerchief at this point relates to Shakespeare's method of handling his story. Two scenes in particular in *Othello* embody crucial moments in the action and both of them set severe problems. One is Act III, sc. iii, in which Iago arouses Othello's suspicions of Desdemona, and the other is Act V, sc. ii, when all Iago's machinations are exposed. At the beginning of Act III, sc. iii, Othello is saying to Desdemona, 'I will deny thee nothing', and at the end he is saying to Iago, 'Damn her, lewd minx; O damn her'. The change requires masterly management and is brilliantly accomplished. Successive comings and goings create the impression of time passing in which Iago's suggestions can fructify, and his reputation for honesty, insisted on just before and in the early part of this scene, increases his credibility. Desdemona's innocent pleadings for Cassio and the unfortunate dropping of the handkerchief all contribute to the development of the situation, which is carried through with extraordinary economy and power.

The climax of the story, like the development of it, needs to be swifter, more economical and more urgent than in the Cinthio story on which the play is based, and, in Act V, sc. ii, the unweaving of

Iago's tissue of lies and hints and suggestions presents another difficult piece of business to carry through. Othello murders Desdemona
and Emilia knocks at the door. When Othello tells her to apply to
her husband for confirmation of Desdemona's guilt she is stunned.
Her denials at this point that Desdemona was unfaithful amount to
no more in fact than her denial in Act IV, sc. ii, which Othello
brushed aside. They *seem* to have more weight here than they did
earlier because, with the murder of Desdemona, the situation has
been pushed to its extreme, and also because Emilia now knows that
it is her husband who is the 'wretch' who poisoned Othello's mind.
In Cinthio's story, Emilia knows of Iago's activities from the beginning and there is no rapid dénouement after the death of Desdemona. By making Emilia the first to discover Iago's true nature
and at the same time to enlighten Othello, Shakespeare gives
dramatic excitement to the business of the unravelling and propels
the play forcefully towards Othello's suicide. But protestations are
not enough. Emilia needs one piece of substantial evidence to support
her case, as Iago did in the earlier scene, and when Othello mentions
the handkerchief she has her cue. The taking of the handkerchief by
Iago is a matter of fact, not of opinion, and it functions here to
convince Othello of Iago's guilt as earlier Iago's story had convinced
him of Desdemona's. The handkerchief is a vitally important aid in
the manipulation of the story and for this reason it needs to be
recalled by Iago in Act IV, sc. i. It is the bond which pulls together
the protracted original narrative into a tightly-knit whole. The
audience is kept alert to its importance without, *pace* Mr Ridley,
damaging violation of the psychological situation, but Shakespeare's
artistry is more manifest if one watches the handling of the story
first, rather than seeking to read the story in terms of character.

Shakespeare's early experiences with narrative are indicative of
developments to come. He pursued its possibilities with zest and
almost infinite variety for perhaps twenty-five years. He found ways
of making the narrative package more malleable as he had more
and more experience to put into it and as his imagination extended
and deepened. In the end he carried the possible relationships of
story to play to lengths of audacity and originality that the early
writing could not be expected to foreshadow. If *The Comedy of
Errors* and *The Tempest*, the first and last plays, share a neo-classical
structure, the common feature only serves to emphasise what worlds

away in other respects they are. To observe Shakespeare's handling of his stories is to see in some part the career of his imagination.

The following chapters discuss aspects of his narrative experience under broad headings and with reference to groupings of plays. In two final chapters, *Hamlet* and *King Lear* are treated separately in discussions which build on the preceding studies of other plays. To those who cannot accept, even for the sake of exploration, the hypothesis that Shakespeare was, to an important extent, Lawrentian rather than Pricean,[6] a comment of A. C. Bradley's may perhaps serve as sufficient basis for the examination of the plays which is here undertaken: 'Whether Shakespeare has this clearly in his mind is a question neither answerable nor important; this is what came out of his mind.'

[6] Accredited philosophers—Susanne Langer, for instance—could be cited in support of the generative view of form which this book takes; but Lawrence's poem makes a useful reference point since in its pithy and provocative way it brings out sharply some of the points I want to make in contrast to Price's emphasis upon 'intellectual construction'.

2

Growth and Change (i)

Narrative situations of particular interest are presented by the plays to be considered in this chapter and the next. The problems and solutions they embody are different but there are relationships between them and, moreover, they illuminate Shakespeare's methods and attitudes in other plays. Dame Helen Gardner claims 'a flash of genius' for Bradley when he 'pointed to the curious analogy between the early stages of dramatic composition and those soliloquies in which Iago broods over his plot, drawing at first only an outline, puzzled how to fix more than the main idea, and gradually seeing it develop and clarify as he works upon it or lets it work'.[1] This is an interesting idea which can be taken further for we do not need to depend only on Iago to see something of stages of composition in Shakespeare's plays which precede the completed work. As we study the way Shakespeare works upon his plot 'or lets it work', we soon find that 'development' and 'clarification' are to be understood in rather special senses. The developments which take place are not always those which seem naturally lodged in the initial situations and the clarification of the material sometimes involves, paradoxically, ambiguity or, in Keats's words, 'uncertainties, mysteries, doubts'. *The Merchant of Venice* provides some early illustrations of these findings.

In *The Merchant of Venice* three stories are interwoven. One is started in the opening scene when Bassanio explains his plans to get out of debt by marrying a wealthy wife and Antonio promises to raise money on credit in order to finance the wooing. The second scene introduces the second story—that is, the choice of caskets demanded of Portia's suitors by her father's will. Scene iii of Act I pushes the first story a stage further as Antonio negotiates his loan with Shylock the Jew and the audience is made aware of the deep animosity which exists between the two. Act II is very busy. We are

[1] '*Othello*: A Retrospect, 1900–67', *Shakespeare Survey*, 21 (1968), pp. 1–11.

first reminded of the casket story by the arrival of the Prince of Morocco at Belmont. Launcelot Gobbo appears (and his father) for no particular reason except to be taken with Bassanio to Belmont, and Gratiano also adds himself to the expedition. Thus in the first two scenes of the Act possibilities for comic exploitation at Belmont are being gathered together and very little, if any, plot movement takes place while this is done. In scene iii a quite different story is added to the material already assembled and the Jessica-Lorenzo plot is introduced. This story, once started, moves very rapidly and its development is complete by scene vi. Jessica and Lorenzo elope together, Jessica helping herself to a dowry from her father's coffers on the way. Two more episodes in the casket story follow in scenes vii and ix and at the end of scene ix a messenger brings news that Bassanio has arrived: in other words, the climax of the casket story is approaching. In scene viii, meanwhile, we have heard the Venice gossip about Shylock's two-fold distress on account of Jessica's elopement and we have been told of the rumours that all is not well with Antonio's fleet. Act III brings us to the end of the casket story. Bassanio makes the right choice and the marriage of the two pairs of lovers, Bassanio and Portia, Gratiano and Nerissa, is arranged. Jessica and Lorenzo come from Venice to join them.

The traditional comic resolution is thus fully prepared. The successful passing of a test and a romantic elopement in spite of a hostile parent have been accomplished and no further development of this material appears to be possible. All interest is now centred on story one, Antonio's bond to Shylock. Act III begins with this, before it moves on to dispose of the lovers, and scene i introduces a new character, Tubal, for the purpose of drawing out the elements of the situation as it affects Shylock. In scene iii, Antonio is arrested and by the end of the Act Bassanio and Gratiano and Portia and Nerissa have all gone away from Belmont leaving Jessica and Lorenzo in charge. Act IV is devoted to the climax and completion of the Shylock-Antonio story. There is nothing of the original material left over for Act V but a tiny thread of a new story line is thrown out by Portia at the end of Act IV when she plans the ring business.

On this analysis, it is evident that Shakespeare has used up a great deal of story material very quickly and, if we look again, we see that even the first four Acts have contained a proportion of 'unnecessary' or 'filling' material. Launcelot Gobbo has no necessary function in any of the stories, and neither has his father. Act III, sc. v, when the principals have left Belmont, is equally without story function. Launcelot expresses his grave doubts to Jessica about the possibility of her salvation, because of her Jewish blood, and when Jessica answers that her husband has made her a Christian he reproaches Lorenzo for his thoughtlessness: 'This making of Christians will raise the price of hogs'. If we ask why Shakespeare wrote it, the answer may be that he wanted another scene for Launcelot. If we ask similarly why he wrote the first part of Act V, sc. i, in which again Jessica and Lorenzo are the actors with Launcelot making a brief and funny appearance, the answer is more interesting but the point to be made here is that it does not directly forward any story but rather marks time till Portia and Bassanio severally return to Belmont. It also provides some of the most splendid poetry of the play. Jessica and Lorenzo have never been fully defined figures so that they can be used for 'filler' scenes without their personalities causing unwanted complications. Their usefulness derives from their not being very interesting in themselves, but to be left at the beginning of the last act with two negative characters who have nothing to do seems an unhappy position for a dramatist: Shakespeare makes them speak divinely and a potentially awkward gap in the action is superbly filled.

The story, or stories, of *The Merchant of Venice* would seem then not to be well-paced. With so much action on hand it might have been relatively simple to spread it evenly throughout, but what happens here is characteristic of other plays too. Shakespeare, once engaged with his characters and situations, drives on with an energy which imparts liveliness and dramatic interest but the sheer momentum generated by this treatment leaves problems in filling out a full-length play. Act V, as a result, is an appendage, developing a little story of its own with an independent resolution. The play offers an example also of the unpredictability of Shakespeare's imaginative engagement with his material as he worked on it. There is nothing in the situation of Jessica, for example, which disqualifies her for a much fuller treatment than she receives: on the contrary, her story would seem to afford interesting opportunities which Shakespeare does not explore. As for Antonio, the play begins with him and sets him up as a complex and enigmatic figure but as things turn out he might well complain, like the son in Pirandello's *Six Characters in*

Search of an Author: 'I am a dramatically unrealised character'. The crux of the matter is that he comes into collision with Shylock and it is Shylock who touches the spring of special creative power in this play. There is no inherent need in the bond story for Shylock's point of view as a member of a persecuted race to be represented. The bond story would indeed run more smoothly without it and there is enough plot interest of various kinds before Shylock asks his dreadful questions in Act III, sc. i: 'Hath not a Jew eyes? . . . If you prick us do we not bleed?' and so on. At this moment Shakespeare becomes caught up in Shylock's experience and the bond plot and Antonio and perhaps the whole Christian company never looks quite the same again.

Shylock's disturbing effect on the play is well known. He may not be the first of Shakespeare's characters to burst the bounds of the story in which he is placed (Richard III is a possible predecessor) but he is the most striking of the early non-conformists. Any claims that Mercutio, in *Romeo and Juliet*, may be thought to have are not really of the same order for he serves the purposes of the central story in a way which Shylock does not. It has been suggested that he also grows too big for his role in the story, even that Shakespeare had to kill him off in order to save his play; but there is no strong case for this view since the various aspects of Mercutio's personality have readily definable functions in the story. The lyric beauty of the love of Romeo and Juliet has to be protected from the scepticism and ridicule which their immaturity may provoke and both Mercutio and the Nurse stand between them and the audience's cynicism until the point is reached when it is both necessary and safe to leave the young lovers to make their tragic appeal alone. The Queen Mab speech, which suggests a side of Mercutio's character not otherwise displayed, helps to ensure that his death makes a deep impression on the audience and effectively subdues them in preparation for the tragic events to come.

The development of the character and situation of Shylock does not by any means help the affairs of the principal characters as the treatment of Mercutio does though Shakespeare, having created him, adopts various means to assimilate him into the texture of a comedy. The scene between Jessica, Lorenzo and Launcelot at the end of Act III, with its jokes about Jews and pork, palliates by its good humour and its comic references the severity of the opposition between Jews and Christians in the court scene which follows. The participation of the partners in the Christian/Jewish marriage in the last Act and their role in setting its key-note has the same effect, and in fact, the whole of the last Act with its development of the ring story functions to smoothe over the disturbance caused by Shylock. Shylock, with his pride, his passion, his lust for vengeance and his final humiliation, is too disconcerting an element to be absorbed within the framework of romantic comedy, whereas the non-serious misunderstandings contrived by Portia and Nerissa can be thoroughly resolved. By these means Act V brings the play round again to the happy ending which was prepared for in Act III, sc. iii, with the additional happiness that Antonio's ships have come safely to port; but no one speaks again of Shylock or his fate. It was resourceful to find fresh matter for the fifth Act when the original material had run out and clever to turn it to good service so that all may seem well at the end and the play may be saved for comedy in spite of the shadows which gathered earlier and were not dispersed. Such resourcefulness and seizing of opportunity are characteristic of Shakespeare's handling of narrative. In *The Merchant of Venice* he may do no more than cover up the problems caused by the development of Shylock but, in other plays, this kind of difficulty, and others which arise as he lets his story work, spur him to a higher reach of creativity than the lyricism and the comedy, beautiful and entertaining as they are, of Act V.

The Merchant of Venice stands at the beginning of the great central period of Shakespeare's career. As he widened his scope and ventured further, he grew more familiar with sorts of crisis which might arise in animating the body of his narrative materials and his flexibility in dealing with them also grew. The problem of Shylock is one of super-abundant creative vitality and it is one which is encountered again, a few years and many plays later, in *Measure for Measure*. *The Merchant of Venice* has always been a popular play, whereas *Measure for Measure* appeals to a more sophisticated taste. Both plays have their triumphs, both, from a narrative point of view, their flaws. The action does not run evenly to the end of *The Merchant of Venice* and we are disturbed when Shylock drops out of view at the close of Act IV and is never heard of again. In *Measure for Measure* we cannot help but notice the lurch in the action when Mariana is unexpectedly introduced into Act III and the story is thereby enabled to move forward again. The two plays illustrate an aspect of the limitations of narrative. Committed to a narrative structure, as in these plays he is, Shakespeare cannot simply set his characters arguing and leave them to it (as a Shavian treatment of *Measure for Measure* might), nor could he have contrived a genuinely open-ended conclusion for *The Merchant of Venice* with the Christians, perhaps, looking at themselves in a mirror and wondering what sort of people they saw reflected there. He had to drive on to a resolution at the final curtain. This he does, but to see what seduces him on the way and how and to what extent he recovers himself is to see something of the colossal imagination at work and to glimpse also the tension which exists between this great force and the medium within which it works. *Measure for Measure* will be dealt with more fully in the next chapter.

A second kind of narrative problem which leaves a notable mark on Shakespeare's plays is closely linked to the first in that the solution to it may involve a change or modification of direction; but its nature is different. It arises not because 'too much' creative excitement is aroused by one aspect of the material but because too little is generated by another. *The Merchant of Venice* has been taken as a specimen of the first kind of situation, *Much Ado About Nothing* offers an example of the second kind. That Beatrice and Benedick take over the centre of attention from the ostensible leads, Hero and Claudio, is a commonplace of criticism and it is worth enquiring further both into the handling of the story materials which produces this situation and into what flows from it.

A play with *Much Ado About Nothing* as its title will need to be conducted very dexterously if it is to arouse and retain the audience's interest. Nothing will come of nothing unless some extraordinary means are adopted to produce something. A mischief-maker who determines to make something of nothing for the discomfort of others will be a useful figure in such a plot and may, moreover, be material for an interesting study in malicious and evil machinations. *Othello* might be called *Much Ado About Nothing*, with Iago as the operator who 'creates' death and despair out of 'nothing'—a non-existent situation. Don John is scarcely a figure of his stature, though, like Iago, he is jealous of a 'young start-up' who has usurped, as he sees it, the position rightfully his. Don John has the role of Iago but without the depth of his characterisation and he is not a big enough figure, consequently, to carry the major interest of the play. An alternative focus of interest is the victim of the intrigue. *Othello* gives full attention to both the mischief-maker and the victim and is doubly rich because of this. *Cymbeline* shows us the victim of a plot similar in kind to both Don John's in *Much Ado About Nothing* and Iago's in *Othello* and adds a new element to this situation— Posthumus's remorse at his condemnation of the supposedly unfaithful wife, even while he still believes her guilty:

> Gods! if you
> Should have ta'en vengeance on my faults, I never
> Had liv'd to put on this; so had you saved
> The noble Imogen to repent; and struck
> Me, wretch more worth your vengeance . . .
> (V, i, 7-11)

The friar in *Much Ado* expects that Claudio, when he believes Hero dead, will similarly repent, even though he still believes the accusation true; but Claudio gives no sign that this is likely. Claudio speaks an epitaph at Hero's tomb but Posthumus offers his own life in atonement for his act of vengeance on Imogen:

> For Imogen's dear life take mine; and though
> Tis not so dear, yet 'tis a life . . .
> (V, iv, 22-3)

Claudio's grief at Hero's fall and remorse at her supposed death never cut as deep as Posthumus's experiences do, and Claudio like Don John is disqualified from bearing the main burden of the play.

If the natures and reactions of neither contriver nor victim are to be explored to any depth, a third possibility seems to be left—to throw the emphasis of the plot on to the 'ado' itself and treat it with liveliness and bustle; in other words to go for activity above all. Shakespeare sets to work on this with energy, bringing together his assortment of lords and ladies in Messina all fit and ready to strike sparks off one another. To increase the amount of action and keep it going smartly, he tells two stories, one after another. The first hinges on confusion about Don Pedro's intentions with regard to Hero and, when that is disentangled early in Act II, the second and major story is started at once. This will produce a big set-piece in the church scene, a revelation inducing penitence, a second betrothal and a dramatic unmasking followed by reconciliation. These are good scenes providing strong theatrical material and perhaps it hardly matters if on analysis one cannot quite make the ends of the plot tie up, any more than one can see how the confusions of the first story are supposed to have occurred.

To help the *Much Ado* plot along, Shakespeare invents Dogberry and Verges and the watch, and very funny, as well as very useful, they are. Dogberry is clearly connected on the one side with Elbow in *Measure for Measure* and on the other with the representative of a higher branch of the same family, Justice Shallow of *Henry IV* part ii. A Jack's obeyed in office, even when his derangement of epitaphs is as extreme as Dogberry's, and Conrade, Borachio and Don John are circumvented by the 'shallow fools' of the watch.

Dogberry and his company enliven the main plot as well as bring it to a happy conclusion and their assistance, in both functions, is very welcome. The disadvantage of having only lightly sketched characters is that as soon as the 'ado' abates for a moment the characters are likely to seem dull or foolish for being deluded as they were, or self-righteous for rushing to judgement on the slightest of evidence. The only hope of their keeping our interest is for us to see as little as possible of them in between their big moments. That Hero and Claudio are given little to say in their last 'big moment', their reunion in the final scene, is itself a recognition of the tact which needs to be exercised in dealing with characters with as little depth as they have. The actors can safely be left to present them as attractive and happy young people, whereas nothing that Claudio has hitherto said indicates that he would rise to the occasion now; as for Hero, it is rather too late for her to reveal an independent character. Hermione, in *The Winter's Tale*, also suffers a public repudiation because of baseless jealousy but in the later play Shakespeare realises her more fully (as he has also by then realised Iago and Othello and Posthumus). Hero swoons in the church; Hermione speaks for herself nobly at her trial.

There are other points to be made about Shakespeare's treatment of the main plot in *Much Ado About Nothing*. The story of the innocent bride unjustly maligned and the lover deceived by appearances is an old and well-worked one. Shakespeare could have known a number of versions of it which gave him plenty of material to choose from, but, in the event, he made little of it. He even omits

the crucial scene in which Don John 'proved' to Claudio and Don
Pedro that Hero is unfaithful although, as Professor Bullough
points out, the scene is given in all the analogues.[2] In *Much Ado* the
scene is merely reported, the reporter being Borachio, who, as he
himself cheerfully remarks, tells the tale vilely (Act III, sc. iii). The
audience may very well have forgotten by this time the details of the
plot which Borachio outlined rapidly to Don John in Act II, sc. ii
but if they have it does not matter. They know that the watch are
listening to every word that Borachio says in III, iii and that, whatever the particular nature of the villainy perpetrated may be, it will
be exposed; so that they can thrill to the tensions of the church scene
and laugh when the opportunity presents itself, without worrying
themselves very much about the precise details of the events by
which the situations are produced. It speaks a great deal, however,
for the confidence of the playwright in other aspects of his material
that he can afford to deal 'vilely' with a pivotal point in his main
story, and it also suggests that the main story as such did not much
interest him.

Beatrice and Benedick are Shakespeare's own inventions and
Professor Bullough argues for unity of design in the play as a whole.
Shakespeare, he writes, 'enjoyed novelle, fabliaux, histories, as
material affording a wealth of action which he could reweave into
an elaborate design of balance, parallelism, symmetry, contrast and
organic development . . . The whole play is a pattern of contrast
worked out on the themes of false report and deception which link
the story of Hero and Claudio with that of Beatrice and Benedick'
(p. 81).

It is difficult quite to accept these terms. Balance, parallelism,
symmetry etc. are to be found in the play but 'a pattern of contrast
worked out on the themes of false report and deception' seems
rather an abstraction derived from the play than a description of the
play itself. In fact, we are able to see *Much Ado* growing and
changing under Shakespeare's hands. A wife to Leonato, Imogen,
appears in the early stage directions, and Claudio is endowed with
an uncle in Act I, sc. i. Leonato's Imogen has no role in the play as
it stands, perhaps because, as the character of Beatrice grew, the
younger woman proved strong enough to make a mother for Hero
dispensable. If Shakespeare originally intended to put most of the

[2] *Narrative and Dramatic Sources of Shakespeare*, vol. ii, p. 76.

weight of the play on the main story, he might have felt that Hero needed the support of a mother in the masculine world which surrounds her but, as matters turn out, Beatrice proves able to stand up for her sex in general and for Hero in particular without the need of other assistance. Similarly, a near relative for Claudio might well have appeared to be useful if Shakespeare was thinking initially of developing more of the source material for the Hero/Claudio story. Family relationships have some importance in the play as it is. Hero has her father, whose affection for his daughter is touching, and Beatrice has two uncles. In this relationship also, Leonato is an attractive figure. Claudio claims Beatrice as 'cousin' in Act II, sc. i after his betrothal to Hero, and Benedick and Claudio bandy claims to cousinship in the marriage scene at the end of the play.

Not only does Act I, sc. i provide Claudio with a mysterious uncle but Antonio has an even more mysterious son, referred to in Act I, sc. ii, and even seen then, but never heard of again and evidently quite disposed of by Act V, sc. i, when Leonato is able to tell Claudio that Antonio has a daughter who is sole heir to both brothers. Since this daughter will turn out to be really Hero, it does not appear that Antonio by this time has any children of his own at all. The provision of extra characters and the multiplication of uncle-cousin-nephew relationships which the extra characters involve, suggest that Shakespeare had possibilities in mind when he began the play which he afterwards discarded. In fact, Beatrice and Benedick become so interesting, growing so splendidly out of and beyond the first bouts of wit, that Hero's mother and Claudio's uncle and Antonio's somewhat pathetic son are never missed.

Considering the treatment of the main plot of *Much Ado About Nothing*, we may conclude that at this stage in his career Shakespeare had not yet developed the insight which he later had into the manifold revelations of character a tortured situation may produce; but though this may very well be true, it is not necessarily the right explanation of the relative shallowness of the treatment of the main plot in the play. *Much Ado* is, after all, a comedy and can never have been intended to be an exclusively romantic one since Beatrice and Benedick are present from the beginning. Clearly these two are meant to act as foils to Hero and Claudio. Claudio appears as a model of what a young hero should be, handsome, brave and a lover; and Hero is an ideal conventional heroine, quiet, gentle, and docile.

By contrast Beatrice and Benedick are noisy and assertive and they woo by friction rather than by consonance. The plot devised by their friends to bring them together and overcome their mutual resistance works with the maximum of comic effect. The device of the two contrasted pairs of lovers is a good one and the sub-plot might be expected to throw the affairs of the principal pair into sharper relief, making their griefs more poignant, their joys more touching. But this hardly happens. Though the main plot of the play with its jealousy and vengeance motifs provides one or two theatrically exciting scenes, Hero and Claudio seem to have no principle of growth in them and they remain to a large extent unproductive dramatic material. Beatrice and Benedick, on the other hand, who insist on asserting that they are too clear-sighted and clear-headed to fall in love and who yet are to be brought to confess love for each other, offer all kinds of potential. The surface of the action concerning them can itself be made amusing while at the same time a depth below the surface can be revealed in which are to be found qualities of character only imperfectly known even to Beatrice and Benedick themselves. Comic irony, as well as more moving effects, lies in this situation.

Shakespeare's realisation, as his play grows, of the limitations of one aspect of his material and the strength of another is reflected in the way in which the creative energy, which finds no scope to work in Hero and Claudio, flows with increasing vigour into Beatrice and Benedick. The climax of this process occurs in Act IV, sc. i, the church scene. The part of this scene which begins when all the characters except Beatrice and Benedick have left the stage sets a special stamp on the play and exerts its influence on what comes after and on our reactions to what has gone before.

The scene begins with the public repudiation and disgracing of Hero by Claudio at the altar. This is a highly dramatic episode and Claudio's language is appropriately passionate. At the culminating point, Hero swoons, Leonato would be glad to be released by death from the disgrace, and the bridegroom's party turn and leave the church. When they have gone, Benedick speaks first:

BENEDICK: How doth the lady?
BEATRICE: Dead, I think. Help Uncle!.
Hero! why Hero! Uncle! Signor Benedick! Friar!

This is the first time we have seen Beatrice and Benedick together since Don Pedro mooted the scheme to make them fall in love with each other. We have seen them both swallowing the bait offered by their friends and each has had a later scene in which the effects of new love have been exhibited. The obvious development of the situation would be a comic scene in which they meet and try out their new roles in their new relationship; but Don John's plot concerning Hero and Claudio intervenes and instead they meet in circumstances of dismay and distress. Benedick's action in staying behind with Leonato's family instead of leaving with his friends, Claudio and Don Pedro, declares his new feelings without any need of words and he at once tries to make himself useful to his new party, calming Leonato and attempting to work out an explanation of events. At line 254, he and Beatrice are left alone together and at this point a series of fine modulations begins, between the comic and serious aspects of the situation, which gives to reader and audience a new insight into the characters of Beatrice and Benedick and gives also another dimension to the play.

Tragic and comic are terms which describe not so much events as points of view. A man slipping on a banana skin is comic to the spectator but the fall is painful and humiliating to the man who slips. King Lear's torments may be sport to wanton gods though his suffering seems to embrace the whole world. It is not always true that our sincerest laughter with some tears is fraught but the line which separates comedy and tragedy is a thin one and this fact constitutes a well-known hazard for all story-tellers. It is one of the remarkable features of Shakespeare's handling of his materials that, far from avoiding the risks, he goes out to meet them and he plays, dangerously sometimes, with the comic/tragic ambivalence of experience. In early plays he makes use of relatively simple juxtaposition. Thus, *The Comedy of Errors* has a 'tragic' framework of disaster, loss and threatened death. In *Love's Labour's Lost,* the stylised courtly world is confronted at the end with grief and misery. Later, in a more daring mingling of modes, the beery voice of the porter breaks into the horrors of Duncan's murder, and King Lear mistakes a joint stool for his daughter. Finally, in the romances, Shakespeare explores a new kind of formal synthesis of tragedy and comedy. He experiments throughout his career with the interplay between the comic and the tragic spirit but nowhere in comedy is the possibility of shifting points of view played with more subtly than it is in this scene of *Much Ado About Nothing*.

The audience's acquaintance with Beatrice and Benedick up to this point leads them to expect comedy. Their appearances have been marked by battles of words and wits and Beatrice keeps up the old style briefly here. But Benedick speaks seriously from the beginning and with his declaration of faith that Hero is innocent, he draws a heart-felt exclamation from Beatrice: 'Ah! how much might the man deserve of me that would right her!' This is sincere at its face value but it is also partly an invitation to Benedick to declare his love. When he does so, it is with a certain objective sense of the comedy of the situation: 'I do love nothing in the world so well as you. Is not that strange?' It certainly is strange considering that not long before he had exclaimed on seeing Beatrice: 'Oh God . . . here's a dish I love not. I cannot endure my Lady Tongue.'

Both Beatrice and Benedick feel some embarrassment in the newness of their feelings and Beatrice especially hesitates to commit herself until Benedick has protested his love a second time. She responds then completely and unreservedly: 'I love you with so much of my heart that none is left to protest'. This ought to be a breath-taking moment in the theatre, for each has made a gesture of trust and surrender whose magnitude has to be measured against their former independence and their claims to invulnerability. The awkwardness of Benedick's position, divorcing himself from friends who might expect his support, to ally himself with the other party; Beatrice's and Benedick's consciousness of the change that has taken place in their feelings since they last saw each other; these things, together with the uncertainties of their new relationship, combine with the anxieties of the Hero-Claudio situation to produce a capacity for sympathy and tenderness for which the rest of the plot provides no opportunities. Beatrice's surrender is an exquisite moment that ought to have its full value in the scene before the more usual and less intimate aspects of personality begin to assert themselves again.

High in spirits and extravagant, Benedick urges her to bid him do anything for her and she replies 'Kill Claudio'. From the sweetness of her confession to this violence is a startling leap. It is often laughed at in the theatre, but that is because the actors have not been able to convey the full range of the emotions involved in the scene. Shakespeare's dialogue here plays over a complex of inter-woven feelings and the changes of tone reveal first one strand, then another. The defensive prevaricating of Beatrice is one element, the self-mockery of Benedick's 'Is not that strange?' is another. His leap of high spirits after she has said she loves him shows his usual gay spirit, and her 'Kill Claudio' recalls us to her passionate involve-ment in Hero's suffering and her more robust and militant spirit. 'Wherefore sink you down?', she asks when Hero faints before her accusers. Beatrice is for resistance, not passive suffering, and her defence of Hero takes the form of aggression towards Claudio. 'Kill Claudio' is a speech from tragedy and Beatrice is a tragic heroine, demanding revenge for an intolerable wrong which, so long as it persists, will make happiness impossible. The revenge itself, if successfully carried out, will also damage their future and lay the stain of a friend's blood upon their new love. There is no happy issue from the situation.

To Benedick, at this point, things do not look quite like this. Though he is sorry for Hero, he is not deeply concerned about her as Beatrice is. Beatrice's avowal of love is the most important element in the situation for him. As for Claudio, he has up to this time been his close friend, though he believes him now to have been misled. His reaction—'Ha! not for the wide world'—brings together in sharp contrast his view of the situation with Beatrice's and they strike against each other with comic effect. For Beatrice it is not funny but deadly serious and Benedick gradually begins to see this and asks a sober question 'Is Claudio thine enemy?'; and then the scene suddenly and unexpectedly lifts off into comedy again.

The substance of Beatrice's account of Claudio's villainy, begin-ning at line 297, is serious enough but the manner which Shake-speare gives her for her statement of it is not. We are not now invited to see her as a deeply distressed young woman who moves our own sympathy by the strength of her feelings, but instead we are shown her as excited, partly incoherent, partly absurd as she sweeps onward on a torrent of words to sensational extravagances: 'O God, that I were a man! I would eat his heart in the market place!' This is a classic broad-comedy situation, the woman ranting and the man vainly trying to stop the flood. But the pace slackens and the tone modulates again into the voice of true feeling:

BEATRICE: I cannot be a man with wishing; therefore I will die a
woman with grieving.

BENEDICK: Tarry, good Beatrice. By this hand, I love thee.

BEATRICE: Use it for my love some other way than swearing by it.

BENEDICK: Think you in your soul that Count Claudio hath
wronged Hero?

BEATRICE: Yea, as sure as I have a thought or a soul.

BENEDICK: Enough, I am engaged; I will challenge him.

This is absolutely serious and returns us again to the tragic situation.
The scene has played between the tragic and the comic modes
throughout, and what has been achieved is a remarkable extension
of the characters of Beatrice and Benedick. Without forfeiting or
denying their comic aspects, Shakespeare has revealed depths in their
natures which their roles hitherto have not suggested. Our knowledge of these colours our whole attitude to them in retrospect and
they dominate our interest and our sympathy in a way which Hero
and Claudio never do.

The effects of this scene having been created, they are not allowed
to lapse. The new note which has been introduced here sounds again
in the scenes which follow.

Act IV, sc. ii, comes immediately after with the splendid and
uncomplicated comedy of Dogberry's and Verges' examination of
Borachio and Conrade. Then comes a second remarkable scene in
which Shakespeare sways the mood to and fro across the tenuous
line between tragedy and comedy. It begins with a recall of the
direst threat that hangs over the play, the threat of death. Hero is
thought to be dead when she swoons in the church scene; Beatrice
thinks that she will die with grieving unless Benedick avenges Hero
by killing Claudio; Antonio opens Act V, sc. i, with warning
Leonato: 'If you go on thus you will kill yourself.' He urges him to
have patience but Leonato insists that his griefs are too deep for
patience: 'I will be flesh and blood', and he goes on

> For there was never yet philosopher
> That could endure the toothache patiently.
> However they have writ the style of gods,
> And made a push at chance and sufferance.

This is a noble and traditional vein and Leonato is a figure of dignity
and real grief. He has recovered from his first shock at the accusation

and the immediate impulse to believe it, and now his soul, like Beatrice's, tells him that Hero is maligned. Yet the scene may remind us of another kind of 'suffering' in the play. 'Gallants, I am not as I have been', says Benedick in Act III, sc. ii, showing evident signs of some disturbance of spirits. Don Pedro and Claudio and Leonato know very well that they have infected him with love for Beatrice, but they tease him as though ignorant of this.

DON PEDRO: If he be sad, he wants money.
BENEDICK: I have the toothache.
DON PEDRO: Draw it.
BENEDICK: Hang it!
CLAUDIO: You must hang it first and draw it afterwards.
DON PEDRO: What! Sigh for the toothache?
LEONATO: Where is but a humour or a worm.
BENEDICK: Well, everyone cannot master a grief but he that has it.

The earlier scene is entirely comic. Shakespeare in Act V seems deliberately to be transposing its material into a different key.

After the preliminary dialogue between Antonio and Leonato, ending with Leonato's threat to make known to Don Pedro and Claudio his conviction that they dishonour Hero unjustly, the prince and the young man enter. This is their first appearance since they left Hero for dead in the church scene and since then we have seen Beatrice's grief and Benedick's resolution, for love of her, to repudiate his friendship with Claudio. We are unlikely to be sympathetically disposed to Don Pedro and Claudio at this point. The encounter with Leonato is bound to be difficult for them and they try to avoid it, but the old men insist on speaking to them. Leonato speaks with dignity, pathos and courage:

> Know Claudio, to thy head,
> Thou hast so wronged mine innocent child and me
> That I am forced to lay my reverence by
> And, with grey hairs and bruise of many days
> Do challenge thee to trial of a man.
> I say thou hast belied mine innocent child;
> Thy slander hath gone through and through her heart,
> And she lies buried with her ancestors.

Don Pedro tries gently to reconcile him to what he thinks is the truth but Claudio grows impatient:

CLAUDIO: Away! I will not have to do with you!
LEONATO: Canst thou so daff me? Thou hast killed my child.
If thou kill'st me, boy, thou shalt kill a man.

This is serious and, as in the incipient tragedy of the Beatrice–Benedick scene earlier, the situation seems fraught with disastrous possibilities. Then, exactly as in the earlier scene, the dialogue suddenly lifts off into comedy. Just as we have been drawn to sympathise with Beatrice in her deep distress at her cousin's ill treatment and then all at once been obliged to detach ourselves from her and watch with amusement as she grows voluble and vehement and Benedick tries in vain to restrain her, so here, when our sympathies have been engaged for Leonato, we are given the indignant but comic caperings of Antonio. Taking up Leonato's last, utterly serious speech, he goes on:

He shall kill two of us, and men indeed;
But that's no matter; let him kill one first,
Win me and wear me; Let him answer me.
Come, follow me, boy; come, sir boy, come, follow me;
Sir boy, I'll whip you from your foining fence;
Nay, as I am a gentleman, I will.

This comic exaggeration of the dignified challenge of Leonato goes on to name-calling, just as Beatrice vents her wrath on Claudio with a string of disparaging descriptions. Antonio lays it on thick:

Boys, apes, braggarts, Jacks, milksops!
. . .
Scambling, outfacing, fashion-monging boys
That lie and cog and flout, deprave and slander.

And as Benedick tries to interrupt to stem the flow of Beatrice's eloquence, so Leonato endeavours without success to quieten his brother. The comic effort of the earlier scene is repeated with the variation that in one episode the participants are a young man and woman and in the other two old men. In both, the comedy in the scene rises from a ground-work of deep feeling full of tragic potential: Antonio's comic defiance is aroused by sympathy with and desire to protect his brother; the whole incongruous situation of the two old men challenging the two retreating younger ones is a consequence of certain hardness and self-involvement in Don Pedro and Claudio, and, on Leonato's and Antonio's part, their commitment to bonds of affection which enable them to feel for each other and for Hero.

The rest of Act V, sc. i, continues to play between tragedy and comedy though not so delicately. Don Pedro and Claudio jest weakly about their encounter with Leonato and Antonio and receive sombre answers from Benedick who has come to deliver his challenge to Claudio. They tease him about Beatrice, jests quite without savour, since Benedick and Beatrice have met and they know each other much better than their friends suspect. Don Pedro and Claudio appear in their most unfavourable light in this scene with heartless references to 'two old men without teeth' and 'the old man's daughter' (Hero). But Benedick knows that hearts may be broken, and his parting speech sets the whole situation on a different level from that which they acknowledge: 'My lord, for your many courtesies, I thank you', he says to Don Pedro. 'I must discontinue your company . . . You have among you killed a sweet and innocent lady.' The exposure of Don John's plot then takes place and tensions are relaxed. There is a jet of rich comedy in Dogberry's two final speeches but before this a serious reproof has been dealt to Don Pedro and Claudio in Leonato's words when Borachio takes on himself all the blame for Hero's supposed death:

> No, not so villain, Thou beliest thyself;
> Here stand a pair of honourable men,
> A third is fled, that had a hand in it.
> I thank you, princes, for my daughter's death;
> Record it with your high and worthy deeds;
> 'Twas bravely done, if you bethink you of it.

The rich inspiration of the Beatrice–Benedick part of Act IV, sc. i carries through, then, to give a similar humanity to the Leonato/ Antonio episode in Act V, sc. i. In both scenes, sympathy does not preclude amusement, nor a sense of comedy destroy respect. The comic airs play over the near-tragic bass in both scenes and the effect is enormously enriching to the play—though it must be confessed that one effect of these scenes is to depress the stock of the never-very-substantial Claudio. His encounters with the old men and with Benedick since the church scene have exposed very plainly the shallowness of his character and we may think that his reacceptance into the family circle at the end is a good deal beyond his deserts.

The building up of the parts of Beatrice and Benedick does not produce the kind of major difficulty with the flow of the story which the growth of Shylock did in *The Merchant of Venice* or which the growth of Isabella in *Measure for Measure* will do. On the contrary, it serves to give a life and interest which are wanting elsewhere. The meeting in church, nevertheless, has an effect on what follows and so, consequently, on how we estimate the earlier behaviour of the characters. In other words, the story grows and subtly changes in the course of the play. Having opened out as it has, it could have gone further but, again as in *The Merchant of Venice*, Shakespeare cuts the line of development, restores Claudio to Hero, sets Beatrice and Benedick at comic odds again and finishes with a care-free dance. His play has its neatly concluded story but there is a germ of life within it which is far more satisfying. That it has been able to develop as fully as it does within the limits which are set is one of the joys of *Much Ado About Nothing* and makes the play one of the warmest-hearted of Shakespeare's comedies as well as one of the best triumphs of his art in that kind.

3
Growth and Change (ii)

The plays to be treated in this chapter have narrative problems akin to those of *The Merchant of Venice* and *Much Ado About Nothing*. With *All's Well that Ends Well* we come to another work in which a fresh infusion of energy saves a play whose main plot is in danger of being drained of life, though the situation arises from a different set of circumstances from those which influenced *Much Ado*. In *Measure for Measure* we have a play which shares with *The Merchant of Venice* the problem caused by a release of creative vigour in excess of the scope provided by the framework of the story. Identified in this way, the narrative problems of *All's Well* and *Measure for Measure* are evidently different from each other but it is in fact profitable to treat them together because of a major feature which they have in common.

The stories of *All's Well that Ends Well* and *Measure for Measure* draw attention to themselves and have given rise to difficulties to a degree which is exceptional in Shakespeare's work. Many kinds of description of what happens and many accounts of why it happens have been offered. In both plays the principal character is a young woman of strongly marked individuality. In one, the crux of the action consists in the fact that Helena's husband imposes on her a set of conditions, meant to be impossible, which have to be fulfilled before he will acknowledge her as his wife. In the other, the Duke's deputy imposes on Isabella an intolerable condition which must be fulfilled if her brother's life is to be spared. It has commonly been found that the statement of the situation, leading up to the crucial moment, is powerful in both plays but that there is a change and, many would say, a loss in the working out of the dilemmas. All except her singleness of purpose is squeezed out of Helena by the need to arrange for the fulfilment of Bertram's conditions. Isabella loses independence when the Duke takes matters over and she becomes a passive instrument of his plans.

The stories of both plays involve the same obvious difficulty, that whereas the initial situation lends itself to characterisation and subtle psychological treatment, the resolution does not. The question then is, why did Shakespeare choose such stories? W. W. Lawrence's answer in *Shakespeare's Problem Plays*[1] is that Shakespeare made use of old and well-tried narrative formulae (in *All's Well*, the folk-lore motifs of the fulfilment of tasks and the healing of the king) because 'he could count on their acceptance, confident that his audience would go as readily with him into the land of make-believe as men of past generations had done' (p. 28). In other words, we should accept the stories simply as made up of narrative conventions and not disturb ourselves about their details. We should also, Lawrence suggests, bear in mind that Shakespeare 'was a man of his own time, that he shared its inconsistencies and contradictions, and that he must have been far less disturbed than we are by habits of thought accepted by his age' (p. 77). As for *Measure for Measure*, there are real-life counterparts to the crucial situation consisting of the bargain offered to Isabella, that she should exchange her chastity for her brother's life, but many elements in the play, particularly the roles of the Duke and Mariana, Lawrence argues, derive, like those of *All's Well that Ends Well*, from 'conventional story-telling, and are thoroughly artificial'. Although the play 'seems real through the brilliancy and veracity of the portraiture of most of its characters, and through the intensely human struggle of the basic plot, it never-theless exhibits improbabilities and archaisms which must be judged in the light of early traditions and social usages' (p. 114).

Lawrence's work is valuable but his conclusions do not follow inevitably from the evidence he collects. They depend on a number of assumptions about Shakespeare's attitudes and about the attitudes of his contemporaries which can hardly be proven. They seem also to take the plays out of the range of critical response. Moreover, though it can be argued that a convention—courtly love, for example, or pastoralism—gives a poet freedom to express his own apprehensions of life in all the fulness he can command, the narrative conventions which Professor Lawrence finds in these plays do not appear to serve this purpose. The weight of critical judgement is, on the contrary, that they inhibit, they do not release, expression.

E. M. W. Tillyard's comments in his *Shakespeare's Problem*

[1] First published 1931. References here are to the Penguin Shakespeare Library edition (1969).

Plays[2] are related to Lawrence's. He argues that Shakespeare was especially interested in subtle characterisation in *All's Well that Ends Well*: 'All the greater therefore was his difficulty in dealing with folk-lore material where psychological subtlety is least to the point' (p. 95). Considering the possibility of allegorical or symbolic interpretations of *Measure for Measure* as a way of resolving its difficulties, he writes: 'The simple and ineluctable fact is that the tone in the first half of the play is frankly, acutely human and quite hostile to the tone of allegory or symbol' (p. 123). When the Duke takes charge of events, significant action is denied to Isabella: 'Shakespeare must have seen that to carry the play through in the spirit in which he began it was impossible' (p. 132). 'The play is not of a piece but changes its nature half-way through' (p. 123). These comments, together with a general observation on Shakespearean comedy, provoke again the question of why Shakespeare chose the stories he did: 'One of Shakespeare's recurrent problems as a comedy writer was how to combine the romantic and improbable and fantastic plots he usually chose with a vitality and a realism of characterisation which his own inclinations insisted on' (p. 93). Why did he court this problem by choosing plots so uncongenial, apparently, to his inclinations?

Professor Lawrence invokes the potency of old tales as his answer to the question, at least as it arises with reference to *All's Well* and *Measure for Measure*. An alternative possibility is provided by an incidental remark of F. W. Bateson in a review, to the effect that Shakespeare almost always borrowed his plot 'because, it sometimes seems, he found human *action* of so little interest in itself'.[3] But if we are prepared to grant that story is a matter of minor importance to Shakespeare and to speculate that action may be for him only a transparent (and disposable) envelope through which we are enabled to see the inner life of his characters, then our difficulty with *All's Well* and *Measure for Measure* still remains, since the tendency of the action in these plays appears to be to *conceal* rather than to reveal the natures of the characters concerned.

The various comments and speculations demonstrate how important and interesting Shakespeare's choice and treatment of story in these plays are. Since we cannot reconstruct the process of choice,

---

[2] (London, 1950).
[3] *Times Literary Supplement*, 30 August 1974, p. 921.

our only recourse in attempting to pursue the matter is once again to consider the *treatment* of the stories to see if any further light is to be gained.

The use of contrasting or similar groups or individuals was an early part of the planning of *Much Ado About Nothing* and it is a common Shakespearean device, employed again in *All's Well that Ends Well*. At the beginning of the play we are presented with two hopeless situations: Helena's love for Bertram and the King's illness. "'twere all one', says Helena:

> That I should love a bright particular star
> And think to wed it, he is so above me,

and the King accepts that he is beyond medical care:

> labouring art can never ransom nature
> From her inaidable estate . . .

Her diagnosis of her own situation and the King's of his are equally conclusive to Helena when they are first stated, but quite soon a sudden vigour seizes her and determines her to defy the impossible and create hope of success in a hopeless case: 'What I can do can do no hurt to try' (II, i, 133).

Her first *volte-face* comes after her exchanges with Parolles in Act I, sc. i. This conversation provides an interval between her expression of hopelessness and her new resolution at the end of the scene to seek to influence events rather than accept them passively as they occur. Moreover Parolles' arguments against virginity—''tis against the rule of nature'—find an echo in Helena's own heart. 'How might one do, sir, to lose it to her own liking?' is the question that occupies her, and Parolles' ''Tis a commodity will lose the gloss with lying; the longer kept, the less worth' gives a note of urgency to her dilemma. Her change of mind in Act II, sc. i, with the King, is less prepared. She seems to accept her dismissal in lines 124-7, but in line 133 she begins to urge her case with an unexpected new force. The duplicated situation perhaps makes preparation the second time unnecessary; we are willing then to accept that Helena is not the kind of person easily to acknowledge defeat. It will not be surprising later when she sets her mind to accomplish the *impossibilia* that Bertram sets her, though what comes of her determination in that instance may be disappointing.

Character and situation are thus established at the beginning of the play by a clever doubling of the theme of hopelessness, with Helena as a common factor in both episodes. Character is established also by the pairing of Helena and Parolles as objects of Bertram's misjudgement. Though others speak most highly of Helena throughout the play, Bertram can see nothing in her which should win his regard; and in a matching situation, whereas others quickly recognise the false façade of Parolles, Bertram takes him as companion and adviser. The correcting of these wrong estimates is the major business of the play. From another aspect the patterning of material relates Parolles and Bertram to each other since they are both guilty of deception and self-delusion. Parolles deceives, or attempts to deceive, others and at least partially deludes himself that he is a fine fellow. Bertram deceives Diana about his intentions towards her, but mainly he is self-deluded, jealous of honour, and yet unable to see where it really resides.

> . . . That is honour's scorn
> Which challenges itself as honour's born
> And is not like the sire,

as the King says, in words directly applicable to Bertram (Act II, iii, 131–3). Both are brought by humiliation to discard their false pretences, Parolles in the camp scene, Bertram in the last scene when he is driven from lie to lie, dealing treacherously with Diana and Parolles by the way. Reduced to truth, finally, both receive the kindness beyond their deserts which is pure charity' '. . . though you are a fool and a knave you shall eat', Lafew promises Parolles; 'Will you be mine, now you are doubly won?' asks Helena, ready to forgive all.

The nature of Helena herself is built up of a pairing. Avowing her love of Bertram to the Countess in Act I, sc. iii, she invokes the Countess's sympathy by reminding her of her own youth:

> if yourself,
> Whose aged honor cites a virtuous youth,
> Did ever in so true a flame of liking
> Wish chastely, and love dearly that your Dian
> Was both herself and love . . . (200–4)

That Helena herself is both Diana and Venus appears in Act I, sc. i in her conversation with Parolles. She is not afraid of, or embarrassed by, sexual love. She agrees in her heart that virginity should be lost but she will keep it for the man she loves. Her speech, beginning at line 154, is in essence a description of a complete love relationship:

> There shall your master have a thousand loves,
> A mother, and a mistress, and a friend,
> A phoenix, captain and an enemy,
> A guide, a goddess, and a sovereign,
> A counsellor, a traitress, and a dear . . .[4]

She is physically and emotionally mature and in her well-blended nature, frank sexual passion exists alongside a chastity which keeps her faithful and devoted to one man.

The dual nature of Helena represents part of the patterning of the play and aspects of the duality appear in other characters. The clown is a Venus man and his confession of his wish to marry Isobel immediately precedes the revelation to the Countess of Helena's love for Bertram — in fact, the clown with his story interrupts the steward's narration. 'Tell me the reason why thou wilt marry?' the Countess commands, and he replies: 'My poor body, madam, requires it'; but his passions are more easily aroused than fixed and after he has been to court he loses interest in Isobel. Diana of Florence, on the other hand, is so far untouched by passion. She participates in the affairs of Helena, but is emotionally uninvolved. She receives Bertram's wooing with some contempt and promises herself:

> Since Frenchmen are so braid,
> Marry that will, I live and die a maid.
>   (IV, ii, 73–4)

Considering the troubles which followed upon his previous attempt at match-making, the King at the end may seem unwise to urge Diana to choose a husband; but he is only attesting one pattern in a play in which it is proper that Diana should be 'both herself and Love'.

---

[4] The Arden edition takes the speech to be about the court 'and its cult of love'. It reads to me far more like a rhapsody of Helena's on the 'infinite variety' of the love she longs to be allowed to give to Bertram. As such, it is a piece of very intimate self-revelation as she suddenly realises when she catches herself up at l. 163. The court then enters her mind as a threat to her dream. Parolles, not unnaturally, is puzzled at the turns the conversation is taking.

Act I is totally successful with its establishment of the story, and the situation in particular of Helena, chaste and yet full of desire, hopelessly disqualified by birth from the marriage she wishes and yet believing that somehow circumstances may be made to yield to her. Act II also is full of narrative interest as Helena cures the King and is married to and at once deserted by Bertram. All this is conducted rapidly and vigorously and is full of life and invention. Helena is evidently veiled when she comes to offer her father's cure to the King and there is a little theatrical shock when the King's saviour is presented to the unsuspecting Lafew, Parolles and Bertram as the familiar Helen. The scene of the marriage choice is written for maximum effectiveness as Helena passes from one young man to another till finally she stops at Bertram, and her characteristic acknowledgement of both Diana and 'imperial Love' expresses itself in her blend of boldness and modesty:

> I dare not say I take you; but I give
> Me and my service, ever whilst I live,
> Into your guiding power. This is the man.
>   (II, iii, 100–2)

The initial situations have been productive of great interest in character and episode. Even Bertram, though so much less mature than Helena, may create sympathetic attention. His young self-centred arrogance is understandable enough and so is his resistance to being tied to a wife—and this particular wife with all her associations with the home he has just left—as soon as he has escaped from the domestic scene to make his place in a man's world.

Now comes the crux of the story, Bertram's letter to Helena setting out the conditions, on the face of it impossible, on which she can become his wife in more than name. Since Bertram has sworn not to return while his wife lives, Helena leaves France. Her announced intention is to undertake a pilgrimage to the shrine of Saint James of Compostella and to die abroad, but she is next seen in Florence (rather out of the way, surely) where Bertram (as she knows) also is; and there she meets Diana and the Widow and arranges to save Bertram from his worst self by deceiving him. In the last scene she again arranges the situation so that the whole range of Bertram's perfidy will appear in the full light of day before she herself appears in person to claim him as her own, 'doubly won'.

Whether in all this she is to be properly described as a schemer or contriver, or whether it is more appropriate to consider that events show humble patience being rewarded by favourable opportunity—these are debatable matters. The treatment of Helena does not make the answer clear, for instead of the revealing intimacy of our contacts with her earlier in the play (as, for instance, in I, i, 73–92, when she lays bare to the audience in soliloquy the real cause of her grief which others on stage misinterpret)—instead of that frankness of presentation which involved us with her feelings and fortunes, she is now an opaque character whose feelings and reactions can only be guessed at. We know less of her and she also seems to be less of a person. It is typical of the changed situation that the consummation of her marriage, for which she longed tenderly and passionately, becomes not the hoped-for acknowledgement of love, but a mating in which she herself is unrecognised:

> O strange men!
> That can such sweet use make of what they hate,
> When saucy trusting of the cozened thoughts
> Defile the pitchy night. So lust doth play
> With what it loathes for that which is away.
> (IV, iv, 21–5)

The substitution of Helena for Diana in Bertram's bed offends against the expectations which the play has in the earlier Acts encouraged and frustrates the interest which has been aroused by the character and situation of Helena. The girl who was so full of life and aflame with her womanhood in the early Acts passes out of the play when the scene moves to Florence, for the story as it has developed has no longer any room to accommodate her.

With the Florence scenes there comes altogether a change. New characters are introduced, but we do not know them as we knew the earlier ones. Bertram seems to have changed from a boy to a hardened man but we know very little about him save that he invariably behaves badly. We do not see how he can have grown to love Helena, though we are told he has, and we notice that he no more addresses Helena directly, when he accepts her as his wife at the end, than he had done when first obliged by the King to take her hand. 'Take her by the hand', says the King in Act II, sc. iii, 'And tell her she is thine.' 'I take her hand', says Bertram registering by the third person pronoun that he obeys the King but does not commit himself to Helena. In Act V, sc. iii, he again addresses the King:

> If she, my liege, can make me know this clearly,
> I'll love her dearly, ever, ever, dearly.

On a narrative level this is undeniably disappointing. A marvellous situation has failed to develop the potentialities it appeared to have. The various false starts and ambiguous revelations of the last scene create some interest in the dénouement but can scarcely restore the full involvement in character and personal situation which we experienced earlier.

The barrier to development is Bertram's letter. With such a rubric as that to work from, what could become of the vibrant girl of the first two Acts? And Helena being trapped by the story, the heart goes out of the play. Let us then consider the letter as a narrative device.

The task-to-be-fulfilled motif has some clear attractions. It generates curiosity about how the seemingly impossible is to be accomplished and may by this means stimulate enough interest to keep the attention of reader or audience to the end of the story. It also offers a paradigm of the triumph of virtue over apparently insuperable odds and this is always a satisfying narrative pattern. It is doubtful, however, whether these qualities of the device would be enough by themselves to attract Shakespeare. There are plenty of other narrative models which fulfil the same or similar functions and which do not carry the same disadvantages. The main attraction of this one for Shakespeare may, in fact, have been quite different.

A noteworthy feature of Shakespeare's narrative procedure in his plays is his use of a programme. *Richard III* provides an early example. The historical material in that play is very largely patterned by reference to curses and judgements, pronounced sometimes in deadly earnest, sometimes by those who will themselves be victims as their words rebound upon them. Events are foreshadowed by these curses and we experience various sorts of satisfaction as we watch the forecasts working themselves out. *Macbeth* also prophecies its own development, most obviously by means of the witches, and our foreknowledge of the destiny that inexorably unrolls adds a further element of horror to Macbeth's career. In *Henry IV* part i, Prince Hal makes, in the second scene of the play, a famous statement of his intention to play with Falstaff and his company for a time but in the end to cast them off. Commentators have been puzzled about the implications of this speech for Hal's character. They have been less interested in its usefulness as a narrative device, but its advantages from this point of view are considerable. It sets out the ultimate arrival point of the action quite clearly: the audience, having heard it, need be in no confusion about the final outcome while the various intervening issues are being developed; and the playwright himself is free to exploit the possibilities of his material, at Court and Eastcheap and elsewhere, without being in danger of losing his way or fouling his lines. He has made the position quite plain at the start on the major story point and is then free to operate as he chooses. In *Hamlet* also there is a programme, that contained in the ghost's speeches on the battlements and Hamlet's replies; within that programme all kinds of complexity develop.

Shakespeare evidently liked these guide-lines. They helped him to keep the narrative clear and they left him free to attend to other matters than those required simply by the story-line. The story to some extent looks after itself when these aids are used and it is not at all surprising that Shakespeare, who was no born inventor of stories but liked to take over tales from somebody else, should have found them a congenial device.

Boccaccio's story of Gilette of Navarre offers, in the tasks set for Helena, exactly such a programme, capable of generating incident and, in fact, of providing quite adequate narrative interest. Having selected this narrative core, Shakespeare sets to work to provide an animated treatment of it and evolves a characteristically rich situation in which a number of characters are put in intricate motion. Tillyard found him to be particularly interested in characterisation in this play, and if so he is likely to have been doubly glad to have the story mechanism taken care of. But the programming device when he comes to use it, lets him down. Instead of assisting him, as Prince Hal's speech, for example, did, it frustrates him. Helena and Bertram are not made free, as Prince Hal and Falstaff are, but, on the contrary, enslaved. The failure of *All's Well that Ends Well* is a failure of story-telling technique. Shakespeare's hankering for a narrative prescription bespeaks a lack of interest in the values of story in itself and his use of Boccaccio's task motif betrays a misjudgement of its narrative character.

A different judgement of the play may be made from a different point of view, of course. The diminishment of Helena's character, for example, from the richness and particularity of the first two Acts may support a view that Shakespeare at this point in his career was developing a new manner and attempting to balance a naturalistic with a symbolic treatment of character. After Act III, sc. ii, there is certainly a strong temptation to regard the play as a parable and Bertram's humiliation in the last Act may be seen as the cleansing of a soul in preparation for redemption. A total view of the play (if there can be such a thing) requires that this and other perspectives be taken into account but the nature of the narrative situation remains itself unchanged. The conditions of Bertram's letter constitute a barrier which blocks development of the narrative interests in the manner which the early scenes have suggested and this being so the parabolic implications of the later part of the play may have been forced upon the playwright as the only means left him for giving any kind of depth to characters whose individual natures have been flattened out by the requirements of the story. In the circumstances, it is of particular interest to observe Shakespeare seizing an opportunity to develop a characteristically double-edged situation when he makes Parolles the central figure of the drum episode in Act IV, scs. i and iii.

In *Much Ado About Nothing*, Beatrice and Benedick, appearing originally merely as foils to Hero and Claudio, prove capable of a fullness of life which the 'main' figures cannot share. In particular, they bring to the play a blending of serious and comic, an awareness of both the subjective and objective views of a given situation, which gives to the whole play a special tone—amusement deepened by sympathy and sympathy enlivened by amusement. Parolles' role also develops and by its mingling of the contemptible with the endearing, the farcical with emotions genuinely if not deeply felt, he brings not only comedy to *All's Well* but also a view of the hopes, fears, weaknesses, resilience of human nature more subtly compounded than the later development of the Helena/Bertram story can provide.

The correction of Bertram's mis-estimates of Helena and Parolles is the major plot point made by the play. His recognition of Helena's worth is to depend on her production of a ring and a baby and Helena's character as an individual has to be submerged in order to achieve this. The exposure of Parolles involves no such disadvantages and, the main characters being imprisoned in the story, Shakespeare lavishes life, comedy and humanity where he still has freedom of action.

We have met Parolles often before the drum scenes. In the first scene, Helena describes him as 'a notorious liar, . . . a great way fool, solely a coward', but in spite of this he is evidently not totally objectionable and she is willing to jest with him. In Act II, sc. iii, while the marriage of Bertram and Helena takes place, Lafew arranges a demonstration (for the audience, since no one else is present) of Parolles's lies, folly and cowardice, but we see also his irrepressible and unshameable vivacity in the episode which follows, when Bertram enters in despair at his marriage and Parolles encourages him to defy the King and go to Italy. 'A very talented fellow and full of wickedness', the Countess calls him (III, ii, 85) but, though it is easy to see that he is a bad influence on Bertram, he is not by any means repellent.

The drum episode itself turns on a play-acting joke. Dramatic performances and the audience's comments upon them provide Shakespeare with congenial material in many plays but the play which the two lords and the soldiers put on has a new twist, for the stage 'audience' is blindfolded and some of the 'actors' step out of character to comment on the 'action'. The preliminary scene, Act IV, sc. i, and the main scene, Act IV, sc. iii, are full of fun and Parolles alternates to splendid comic effect between pedantic precision in his treachery: 'Five or six thousand horse, I said—I will say true—or thereabouts, set down, for I'll speak truth'—and excited fantasies of calumny ('He will steal, sir, an egg out of a cloister; for rapes and ravishments he parallels Nessus' etc.). There is nothing glorious about Parolles—even his letter to Diana warning her of Bertram's untrustworthiness is in the form of advice to make sure of his money before she grants him her favours; but his ignobility is transparent and finally acknowledged so completely—and cheerfully—by himself that he acquires a kind of innocence in comparison with the more devious Bertram whose lying in self-defence in the last scene is more dangerous than Parolles' extravagant slanders. When his eyes are unbound and 'the play' is over, the gravity and sang-froid of the Lords and Bertram make a finely effective touch as they greet him like men meeting outside a theatre, who have resumed their ordinary lives after the illusion of the performance:

BERTRAM: Good morrow, noble Captain.
SECOND LORD: God bless you, Captain Parolles
FIRST LORD: God save you, noble Captain
SECOND LORD: Captain, what greeting will you to my Lord
Lafew? I am for France.

(IV, iii, 291–5)

The soldier's blunter comment: 'You are undone, Captain, all but
your scarf; that has a knot on't yet', gives Parolles a chance to revive
for a moment: 'Who cannot be crushed with a plot?'; but he knows
his game is up and wastes no time in regret (or penitence). When we
see him again in Act V, sc. ii, he is at his lowest ebb and needs to be
humble to the clown but we know he is not of the sort to be flattened
for ever and when he gives his evidence in the last scene it takes
Lafew's reminder: 'He is a good drum, my Lord, but a naughty
orator', to restrain his irresistible impulse to swagger and show off.

Parolles lightens the atmosphere of the play for, although people
speak of him harshly, they do not treat him so and nothing he says or
does quite bears out his reputation for wickedness. In his role as
misleader of Bertram, he could have been a vicious character whisper-
ing evil suggestions to a deluded young man, but as it is he is good
humoured himself and a source of good humour in the play. It is
noticeable how the character of Lafew rises to the occasions with
which Parolles presents him. In his early scenes with the Countess
and the King, Lafew's speech suggests a pompous, fussy old man
and in his antiphonal dialogue with Parolles in Act II, sc. iii, he
speaks in language which Parolles is delighted to make his own:
'Just, you say well. So would I have said.' But later in the scene his
tone and manner change:

LAFEW: Your lord and master did well to make his recantation.
PAROLLES: Recantation! My Lord! My master!
LAFEW: Ay; is it not a language I speak?
PAROLLES: A most harsh one . . .

(II, iii, 185–8)

Lafew's language to and about Parolles is not, however, genuinely
harsh, only pithier and wittier than it is when he speaks to others.
The 'shrewd and unhappy' clown discomforts Lafew but 'good
Tom Drum' is another matter and at the end of the play there
promises to develop a mutually satisfactory and agreeable relation-

ship between Lafew and Parolles, like that of Dignity and Impudence in the famous picture. Contrast, in fact, is a clue to the role of Parolles who, like Barnardine in *Measure for Measure*, opposes an unshameable, unquenchable insistence on the ultimate importance of staying alive to the fine-drawn moral or other concerns of the principal characters. The contrast delights us in itself and endears Parolles and Barnardine to us. Taken by themselves and out of their dramatic context they and their ways of life might well appear mean and squalid but to take them out of context is obviously what we should not do. Shakespeare was adept in the uses of contrast and comparison, which he employed to many and diverse ends, and criticism which forces a division among his pairings and groupings does so at great risk of misrepresenting some of his most characteristic effects.

Dr Johnson thought Parolles comparable to Falstaff. Q (Quiller-Couch) thought him 'about the ineptest of all Shakespeare's inventions'. Modern criticism approaches him with characteristic refinement of analysis. Barbara Everett in the New Penguin edition writes of his function in establishing Helena's social position; Robert Hapgood relates his 'shame' to the situation of others in the play;[5] but the most significant aspect of him in the present context is the way in which he comes to escape out of the unyielding framework in which the other characters are bound. It embarrasses us to suspect that the Helena of the second part of the play may be not wholly unselfish and it equally embarrasses us to accept Bertram as her chosen partner. But Parolles allows us both to deplore him and to laugh at him. He functions 'ever to the world's pleasure and the increase of laughter' (II, iv, 34-5) and he calls, through Lafew, for our enjoyment and our charity. ('Wait on me home, I'll make sport with thee', V, iii, 315-16). What is paradigmatic elsewhere becomes human in Parolles:

> The web of our life is of a mingled yarn, good and ill together. Our virtues would be proud if our faults whipped them not, and our crimes would despair if they were not cherished by our virtues.
>
> (IV, iii, 67-70)

There are greater comic characters than Parolles in Shakespeare's

[5] 'The Life of Shame: Parolles and *All's Well*', *Essays in Criticism*, 15 (1965), pp. 269-78.

plays and the creative activity is not so rich here as it is elsewhere; but nevertheless its work is authentic and characteristic as, after the fading of Helena's promise, imagination flares into brilliance with, as Dr Johnson puts it, 'the character which Shakespeare delighted to draw, a fellow that had more wit than virtue'. The main plot inevitably becomes enigmatic with the change of mode after Act II but Parolles, braggart, coward, traitor as he is, ensures that it retains at least some of the warmth of life.

G. K. Hunter's introduction to the Arden edition of *All's Well that Ends Well* gives a scholarly, sensitive and sympathetic account of the play though he finds that its most distinguishing characteristic is 'A quality of *strain*' (p. xxix). His reading of the play is also marked by signs of strain. We are not to think of the Helena who fulfils Bertram's conditions as actively scheming to do so, he suggests, but 'Of course there are difficulties in the way of this view. In her conversations with the Widow Helena appears as a schemer, and the reader may well feel that no single view of her conduct is possible' (p. xxxii). Tracing the play's contrast between Helena's 'virtue' and Bertram's over-prizing of the 'honour' deriving from inheritance, he concludes (in a footnote) that there may be something to be said for Bertram's side of the affair when forced to accept Helena as his bride: 'But this point does not receive any clear emphasis in *All's Well*' (p. xl). Writing of Lavatch's role as a critical commentator on the good as well as on the wicked and foolish, he comments: 'no central, acceptable, and unified viewpoint is left defined in the midst of the follies and excesses of the rest of the play' (p. xxxv). In a footnote he describes 'the comic treatment of serious subjects' as a fruitful device but adds a note of caution: 'Where, as in *All's Well*, the play is searching for a central point of view, the addition of parallel perspectives can only have a critical and even disintegrating effect'. The whole play, he comments, is searching for a meaning which will interrelate the various levels of experience. It is not the heroine whose development is thwarted but the play itself, 'which seems intellectual because it is unfulfilled, and has failed to find human terms to express its vision, leaving the rough ends of its intellectual promptings still exposed' (p. lii).

The difficulty of coming to terms with the characters of Helena and Bertram has already been commented on as the price demanded by the crux of the story, the tasks imposed on Helena. Neither of

them develops the possibilities that are so excitingly offered in the
first two Acts and, like Helena, Bertram becomes a simplified figure,
in his case that of a young man rapidly becoming hard and bold in
sin. Professor Hunter's other point is somewhat elusive. It is difficult
to know that a play is 'searching for a central point of view' or for
'human terms to express its vision', especially if one also believes
that neither of these things has been found. The lack of *something*
is certainly felt in *All's Well* but to talk of 'a central point of view'
and 'a vision' is to make assumptions for which evidence can hardly,
in the nature of the case, be forthcoming. There are many aspects of
the play, as the Arden introduction brings out; but what is missing
at the most basic level is a story structure which will allow dominant
interests (however the critic may define them) to grow and prosper.
In the absence of these, tangles of various kinds occur: as Professor
Hunter notes, in discussing the state of the text, there is evidence of
'a difficult and uncertain course of composition'.

In *Measure for Measure* we again find Shakespeare dealing with
a story which causes him great difficulty. The tale of the apparently
uncorrupt and incorruptible magistrate who offers a brother's (or, in
some versions, husband's) life in exchange for the sister's (or wife's)
chastity is a strongly dramatic one and Shakespeare further intensifies
it by adding the circumstance that his Isabella is about to take the
veil. Her first interview with Angelo (Act II, sc. ii) is charged with
intellectual and emotional power as she pleads for mercy to Claudio
—since all men are sinners—and Angelo argues the magistrate's duty
to administer the law. When in the second interview (Act II, sc. iv)
he proposes the infamous bargain, the shock to her nature and her
sense of the appalling implications of what he asks of her (that she
should 'die for ever', l.108) create an immensely powerful situation.
When she visits her brother and finds him tempted to ask her to
accept Angelo's bargain, her belief that death—his or hers—is prefer-
able to a dishonour which would involve them both remains un-
shaken but the pressure exerted upon her by the two men, and her
isolation in face of the dreadful choice she is called upon to make,
drive her to repudiate Claudio violently. It is at this point that the
Duke steps in to arrange the substitution of Mariana for Isabella and
then to arrange the substitution of Barnardine's head for Claudio's
and then Ragazine's for Barnardine's . . . his machinations can easily
be made to sound absurd.

In the version of the story which Shakespeare drew upon for his play, the heroine accepts the magistrate's bargain, is later married to him and pleads for his life when his ill deeds are revealed and he is condemned to execution. Cinthio's Epitia, in the story from *Hecatommithi*, is concerned from the beginning only with the question of marriage. Unlike Isabella, who is outraged at Angelo's 'seeming, seeming!', she has no profound moral revulsion at the hypocrisy of Iuriste's position when, having condemned her brother for a similar sin, he proposes his infamous bargain to her. When Iuriste has Epitia's brother executed, in spite of her fulfilment of her side of the bargain, and also fails to marry her as she hoped he would, she accuses him of injustice and ingratitude—sins indeed, but the second of them indicates how far from Isabella's estimate of the situation Epitia's is. Cassandra also, in Whetstone's *Promos and Cassandra*, comforts herself with the hope that Promos will see that she 'deserves to be his wife'.[6] For both, marriage with the false magistrate at the end is a satisfactory conclusion, though Epitia has by that time some doubts about Iuriste's acceptability (in fact he reforms so that 'she lived with him in great happiness for the rest of her life'). Shakespeare, when he sharpened Isabella's dilemma in the choice which faces her by making her the novice of a convent, removed at the same time the possibility of marriage to Angelo from her calculations. As he develops her character, she is neither the kind of woman who would aspire to marry her seducer nor the kind who would prostitute her body, 'the unpolluted temple of the mind' in Milton's phrase, for any worldly consideration whatever.

The character of Isabella develops life and depth in Act II, sc. ii, a wonderful scene in which, under the pressure of the situation and urged on by Lucio, the girl who sought for even stricter restraints than those imposed on the nuns of Saint Clare (I, iv, 3–5), breaks through her inhibitions and speaks out with the courage and authority of one whose experience, though narrow, has been deep and ardent. Isabella begins her plea slowly and awkwardly, declaiming against sexual incontinence as the vice that she most abhors and ready to retire on Angelo's first refusal:

[6] All the sources are printed in Bullough, *Narrative and Dramatic Sources of Shakespeare*, vol. ii, and the most important of them in the Arden edition of *Measure for Measure*, ed. J. W. Lever.

> O just but severe law!
> I had a brother, then. Heaven keep your honour!
> (41–2)

In abstract intellectual terms she can go no further but Lucio will not let her leave and, in desperation, caught between love of her brother and distaste for her task, she at last finds eloquence as the theme of forgiveness engages both her intelligence and her emotion. She speaks with confidence and authority as she asserts that governors never show themselves more mighty than when they exercise mercy (57–63) and her words ring with passion as she reminds Angelo that in another perspective all men are beholding to the Divine Mercy:

> all the souls that were, were forfeit once;
> And He that might the vantage best have took
> Found out the remedy . . .
> (73–5)

Angelo retains control of the situation and makes strongly his case for unyielding justice but Isabella is now fully committed to her cause and not to be shaken off. She returns to the attack as she pours scorn on the 'antics' of 'man, proud man, Dress'd in a little brief authority' and the arts by which the great deceive themselves into believing that they are of different kind from other men.[7]

The force and energy of her words and the understanding she shows of the ways of men surprise Lucio and, moreover, they shake Angelo out of his pose of calm, judicial detachment.

The warming into life of Isabella in this scene is an exciting and moving revelation of a deeply thinking, deeply feeling nature, a young woman who has acutely observed the world she seeks to withdraw from, passed her judgement on it and sought to discipline human frailty in herself by the rule of the convent. As she says in Act II, sc. iv, acknowledging that women, like men, may fall— 'Women? Help, heaven!' (127). The pretty face that Lucio pays tribute to (IV, iii, 148) is unlikely by itself to have disturbed Angelo's long immunity to female charm but when the deep current of

[7]   We cannot weigh our brother with ourself (126)
is one of the 'sayings' that she 'puts upon' Angelo, as is quite clear when the Duke repeats the words in V, i, 111. The 'we' is the royal plural. The editor of the New Penguin edition misunderstands the line.

thought and feeling carries her so startlingly beyond what might be expected of her, the combination of effects sweeps him away too.

The intense interest generated by this scene spreads its influence over the following scenes, over Act II, sc. iv, when Angelo, a man divided against himself, tests and tempts Isabella until she obliges him to speak out plainly and to abandon all checks: '. . . I have begun,/And now I give my sensual race the rein'; and also over Act III, sc. i, with Claudio in prison.

This second scene picks up at its opening the thought of death, on which Isabella's speech at the end of Act II closes. The Duke's words to Claudio, intended to reconcile him to loss of life, form a bitterer chronicle of the course of human existence than Jaques' seven ages of man speech in *As You Like It* Act II, sc. vii, but it comes to rest on the same point, that all our yesterdays pave the way to 'palsied eld', 'Sans teeth, sans eyes, sans taste, sans everything'; or, as the Duke puts it:

> when thou art old and rich,
> Thou hast neither heat, affection, limb nor beauty,
> To make thy riches pleasant. What's yet in this
> That bears the name of life?
> (36–9)

Isabella, when she enters, adds the religious hope which is missing from the Duke's *contemptus mundi* and speaks of Claudio's imminent death as an embassy to heaven; but, to the young man, life and the world call strongly, in spite of all. Shakespeare's handling of the next move in his story, Isabella's meeting with her brother and report to him of Angelo's proposition, is astonishing. Cinthio's Epitia and Whetstone's Cassandra are both reluctant to yield their honour but make little resistance to their brothers' persuasion. In *Hecatommithi*: 'Vico wept as he spoke these words, and Epitia wept with him, embracing him and not leaving him before she was constrained—overcome as she was by her brother's laments—to promise that she would give herself to Iuriste, should he agree to save Vico's life and support her hope of marriage.' Shakespeare's Claudio pleads more strongly than his predecessors and opposes his vision of the dissolution and unknown terrors of death to the Duke's vision of the degeneracy of life:

> The weariest and most loathed worldly life
> That age, ache, penury and imprisonment,
> Can lay on nature is a paradise
> To what we fear of death.
>
> (130–3)

But the Isabella of the previous scenes is not a girl to be brought to connive at sin or to push aside her scruples for the hope of marriage. Shakespeare could have made her firm in her view of the situation, sad and grieving for Claudio because of the necessity, as she sees it, of her rejection, with the dignified purity befitting 'a thing enskied and sainted' as Lucio describes her when he sees her in the convent. But he does not. His Isabella is a girl whose nerves have been strung to an almost unbearable pitch by the scenes of Act II. She fears from the beginning of her interview with Claudio that he may impose further strain on her and doubts whether she can support it:

> I quake
> Lest thou a feverous life shouldst entertain,
> And six or seven winters more respect
> Than a perpetual honour . . .
>
> (75–8)

When he pleads for his life at any price, her self-control breaks and she turns on him with abuse, too distraught by all the emotional shocks of the last twenty-four hours or so to be capable of pity for Claudio. To sympathise with his weakness while maintaining her own sense of right and wrong would require an equanimity which the storm-tossed Isabella cannot at this moment muster.

It is astonishing how little sympathy and imagination critics have shown over this scene. 'Pretty Isabel' has every reason to be over-wrought at this point and that this accounts for her behaviour is a much more likely explanation than the frigid self-righteousness of which she is sometimes accused. We know from her scenes with Angelo that there are strong currents of feeling within her and we see them burst out again, in her reactions to the (false) news of Claudio's execution—'O, I will to him [Angelo] and pluck out his eyes!' (IV, iii, 116), and in her passionate tears, as the Duke tries to calm her.

To praise the subtlety and brilliance of Shakespeare's handling of the situation up to this point smacks of impertinence. A tremendous

degree of imaginative realisation, of Isabella's character in particular, has gone into tightening the mesh in which she, Angelo and
Claudio are all involved. Whether Isabella's chastity is 'really' worth
more than Claudio's life is, strictly, an irrelevant question (though
much asked by critics) since Isabella believes it is and the choice
presented to her enforces an inescapable but terrible answer. A point
which may need some elaboration, because it is not always noticed,
is that Shakespeare is careful to reinforce Isabella's attitude to
Angelo's bargain, so that it does not stand unsupported within the
play as an arbitrary individual judgement. 'More than our brother
is our chastity', she exclaims (II, iv, 185) and the use of the plural
pronoun here surely refers to her membership of the sisterhood of
white-clad nuns, dedicated Brides of Christ.[8] The play supports her
on another level too. 'I had rather my brother die by the law, than
my son should be unlawfully born', she tells the Duke (III, i, 187-9)
and the play makes a point of emphasising that partners in sexual
intercourse have a responsibility for the children who are born from
their embraces. The pregnant Juliet is brought on in II, iii for the
specific purpose of being rebuked by the Duke. Speaking of his plan
to substitute Mariana for Isabella, the Duke comments: 'If the
encounter acknowledge itself hereafter, it may compel him [Angelo]
to her recompense' (III, i, 240-2), and in the event he takes care to
marry them without delay in Act V. In the final meting out of
judgement, he cancels Lucio's punishment for offences against himself but insists that he marry the whore who is the mother of his
child.

Irresponsible tampering with life is an aspect of sexual licence
and in drawing attention to this the play both strengthens Isabella's
stand and also marks the act for which Claudio is condemned as a
seriously cupable one, in spite of the mitigating circumstances which
may be adduced. The cumulative effect of these touches is greatly to
strengthen the moral and personal drama of the first half of the play.

[8] There is a tension between the claims of this sisterhood and the
sisterly relation of Isabella to Claudio as there is between the Duke's
status as 'Friar' and the brotherhood he shares with the other, sinful,
men of the play. Both Isabella and the Duke finally abjure the religious
community for human relationships. Perhaps Shakespeare's natural
sympathies lay in this direction but this does not mean that he could not
respect and understand Isabella's other-worldly dedication at the beginning of the play.

But what is to happen next? As everyone knows, the Duke suddenly remembers Mariana and her ill-treatment at the hands of Angelo, of which he gave no hint earlier, the substitution is arranged, Claudio (and Barnardine) is saved and the mode of the play changes, from a close-knit drama of characters and emotions in conflict, to an affair of contrivances, manoeuvres and disguises. Amongst it all the splendidly conceived character of Isabella has little chance to show itself. We catch a glimpse of the far from passive nature beneath the surface in her reaction to the supposed death of Claudio and we see her capacity for strenuous moral effort in her plea for Angelo in V, i, 442–52; but, these moments apart, Shakespeare holds her from the intimate contact we had earlier and we can only guess at what is going on within.

The situation of Isabella, Angelo and Claudio has come alive in Shakespeare's hands but the life in it has then become too vibrant, too active, spreading its energies too far to be contained in the story. Shakespeare cuts the knot he has tied and releases the characters for the conventionally happy ending of marriages all round, but he can hardly be said to have completed the story that he tells so magnificently till half way through Act III, sc. i. In *All's Well that Ends Well* when the story ran into the ground, he found a channel for the vitality of his creative genius in Parolles; in *Measure for Measure*, he finds it also in the development of a kind of comedy but the result is less straightforward, either in kind or implications. How could the story of *Measure for Measure* be continued? One answer would be to allow Claudio to die (as he does in *Hecatommithi*) and to leave Isabella to bear the burden of the decision she has taken. Faced with the bitter reality of Claudio's death she might wonder if she was after all wrong, whether she had been deluded in her belief that there was a higher principle at stake than the safeguarding of a brother's life. And Angelo, who had woken to desire, would continue in his appearance of inflexible rectitude but would know now that it was a charade. He and Isabella, allied in their aspiration to discipline themselves out of human frailty at the beginning, would be allied also at the end in their experience of lost confidence and doubt, not only in themselves but also in the supports they had clung to. Such a conclusion is what modern taste hankers for and there is no reason to suppose that Shakespeare, who could see the temptations implicit in Brutus's idealism and the weakness latent in

Malvolio's Puritanism, should be blind to the possibility of a terrible reaction in Isabella, after the exertions which the crisis of the play force upon her.

But to continue the story in these terms would require a major rewriting of the source material of a kind which Shakespeare does not undertake. The changes he characteristically makes are in adjustment of episodes or situations and, above all, in deeper penetration into the essence of character or event. In *Measure for Measure* he retains the dénouement provided by the sources, which gives the exposure, marriage and pardon of Angelo, and he reuses the substitute bed-mate device, which the *All's Well that Ends Well* story provides, to save Isabella from pursuing to the end the course to which she is committed.

The result makes the second half of the play a very odd contrast with the beginning. Herbert Weil emphasises the comic aspects of the later acts.[9] The scenes following the Duke's intervention in III, i, he says, 'should be played as broad comedy of farcical insults, non-sequiturs, and fantasy'. The Duke, himself, in whom some have seen a figure of total, providential authority, he finds subject to comic exposure, as one who insufficiently knows himself. Mr Weil's argument is that Shakespeare 'carefully planned this change of mode', from potential tragedy to the comic, even farcical, and that he created 'an unusual formal coherence' by doing so. The 'anti-climactic rhythms and structure', he suggests, are designed to 'call the disparities between problem and solution to the attention of the spectator. Through Lucio and Pompey, the dramatist repeatedly draws our attention to the inadequacy of solutions that the perfectionists in the play—Angelo, Isabella, and the Duke—profess to find adequate'. Shakespeare 'finally makes us aware of the limitations of the very comic conventions and implausible devices he uses as he stretches them into new possibilities'.

As an antidote to the accounts of critics who use *Measure for Measure*, and especially the Duke's role in it, as a text on which to compose edifying sermons which nevertheless have little relation to literary or dramatic experience, Mr Weil's stress on comedy is welcome. But in the end he only replaces the fine-drawn moral-religious scheme which he rejects by another equally intellectualised

[9] 'Form and Contents in *Measure for Measure*', *Critical Quarterly*, 12 (Spring 1970), pp. 55–72.

formula. It seems unlikely that Shakespeare planned to generate 'a play of mind which is *not* completely reabsorbed by the action itself'. If that is a right description of what he does, the cause of this effect may well be that he is forced into a change of mode by the difficulties created by his imaginative engagement with Isabella and the impossibility of allowing her to accept any further the roles of Cinthio's Epitia or Whetstone's Cassandra.

When the main channel became blocked in *All's Well that Ends Well*, Shakespeare developed Parolles. His exposure, his humiliation, his acceptance of himself without camouflage—'even the very thing I am'—have their bearing on the main plot and comment on it with greater freedom and vitality than the affairs of Helena and Bertram in their later developments allow. In *Measure for Measure* Shakespeare again turned to the development of comic material when his main plot reached an impasse and made a virtue of his necessity which, characteristically, resists final analysis. Comic material has been present in the play from the second scene of Act I, in which Lucio and his two companions oppose their style of life and conversation to the opening trio of the Duke, Angelo and Escalus. It gathers further resources in Act II, sc. i when, after Angelo's and Escalus's high-minded discussion of temptation, crime and punishment, Elbow, Froth and Pompey come to 'lean upon justice' till it collapses in laughter. After the Duke's intervention in Act III, sc. i, it is the mood of the second of these early scenes which comes into prominence in the play offering, in the rest of the third act and Act IV, a strong challenge of irreverence to the concerns and attitudes of the main plot. Lucio is its only spokesman in Act V but he is equal to the occasion.

Act III, sc. i ends with a prose dialogue between the Duke and Isabella, in which he reveals for the first time the existence of Mariana and proposes that she be persuaded to take Isabella's place in Angelo's bed. Isabella's ready acceptance of the idea is astonishing, considering the strength of her feeling that wanton or careless indulgence in sexual intercourse is deeply abhorrent. The responses of the fully developed Isabella of earlier scenes seem suddenly to have been switched off as she answers quite characterlessly: 'The image of it gives me content already, and I trust it will grow to a most properous perfection' (249–51). The high drama of earlier episodes is reduced still further when, immediately following her exit, the law, in the person of Elbow, and the lawbreaker, Pompey the bawd, enter, with Elbow in the course of reproving Pompey:

> Nay, if there be no remedy for it, but that you will needs buy and sell men and women like beasts, we shall have all the world drink brown and white bastard.

'A bawd, a wicked bawd!' exclaims the Duke, who has remained on the scene after arranging that Isabella should, on behalf of Mariana, give Angelo 'promise of satisfaction'. He then proceeds to castigate Pompey for his exploitation of the sexual appetites of his customers. The scene parallels the earlier episode in Act II, sc. i, where Escalus took his turn at admonishing Pompey:

> How would you live Pompey? By being a bawd? What do you think of the trade, Pompey? Is it a lawful trade?
> (212–14)

Escalus fortifies his advice to reform with the threat of whipping if he does not; the Duke strives instead to rouse Pompey's conscience:

> Canst thou believe thy living is a life,
> So stinkingly depending? Go mend, go mend.
> (III, ii, 23–4)

but the result appears to be the same in both instances. As Pompey says to Escalus, 'I thank your worship for your good counsel', and as he adds to himself: 'But I shall follow it as the flesh and fortune shall better determine' (II, i, 240–1).

These two scenes echo each other but it is curious to notice how they echo preceding and intervening scenes too. From arranging with Isabella how to satisfy the sexual demands of Angelo, the Duke passes straight to his encounter with Pompey, the cheerful bawd, who acknowledges that his trade 'does stink in some sort' but thinks that he could find something to be said in defence of it. From exhorting Claudio to 'Be absolute for death' because life is not worth the cherishing, the Duke moves on to a depreciatory account of Pompey's existence. 'What's yet in this/That bears the name of life?' he asks Claudio (III, i, 38–9); 'Canst thou believe thy living is a life?' he challenges Pompey (III, ii, 23). Like Pompey, Claudio had given thanks for good counsel but followed it as flesh had determined when fortune seemed to offer an alternative to death. Not Pompey, nor Barnardine—nor yet Parolles—could be more absolute for life than Claudio becomes, when he tests the thought of death upon his pulses (III, ii, 130–3, quoted above).

In II, i, the case to be tried concerns the experiences of Elbow's wife in Mistress Overdone's house. Elbow wishes to indicate that the house and its occupants are all of ill-repute:

> First, an it like you, the house is a respected house; next, this is a respected fellow; and his mistress is a respected woman. (153–5)

To which Pompey replies: 'By the Lord, sir, his wife is a more respected person than any of us all', and he goes on to add that 'she was respected with him before he married her'. This goads Elbow to frenzy:

> O thou caitiff! O thou varlet! O thou wicked Hannibal! I respected with her before I was married to her! If ever I was respected with her, or she with me, let not your worship think me the poor Duke's officer. (166–71)

This is highly entertaining, but what is its relation to those tense preceding scenes in which we have heard how Claudio was 'respected' with Juliet before he married her? 'I have seen', says the Duke sternly in V, i, 'corruption boil and bubble/Till it o'errun the stew' (316–17) and the answer to the question could be that we are being shown this widespread corruption permeating all levels of society. The difficulty with any such proposition is that the invitation to rejoice in the dialogue of Pompey and Elbow is so palpable and irresistible. If we remember the extra-marital activities of Claudio (and Angelo) while we listen, the effect may be to persuade us to take them less, not more, seriously.

The effect of III, ii is similar. No doubt the Duke's arrangements for Mariana's bedding are quite different in intent from Pompey's practices and no doubt also Lucio's ebullience is both impertinent and irresponsible as he happily concocts fantastic slanders for the unwilling ear of the Duke;[10] but the Duke's status becomes distinctly

[10] When Lucio confides to the 'friar' that the Duke was a 'good woodman' he is adopting a Machiavellian explanation for the situation in Vienna: 'Princes ought not to complain of any fault committed by the peoples whom they govern because such faults are due either to their negligence or to their being themselves sullied by similar defects' (*Discorsi*, III. 29.1).

precarious under this barrage of irreverence. He needs to be shored up, both by his own moralising soliloquies (173–6, 243–64) and by Escalus's (solicited) testimonial to him (218–23).

In fact, the tensions in the composition of the play as it progresses are very considerable. Isabella's plight and her distress are eminently serious but when Pompey looks to Lucio to rescue him from the arms of the law, as Claudio looked to her, Lucio rejects him in a speech which is reminiscent of hers. 'Thy sin's not accidental, but a trade,' Isabella exclaims to her brother in bitterness of spirit: 'Mercy to thee would prove itself a bawd' (III, i, 150–1). 'Well, then, imprison him', Lucio encourages Elbow. 'If imprisonment be the due of a bawd, why, 'tis his right. Bawd is he doubtless and of antiquity too, bawd born' (III, ii, 64–5). 'Heaven shield my mother played my father fair', says Isabella (III, i, 142), casting the same aspersion on Claudio. Isabella and the Duke are well advanced in their plans for giving Mariana to Angelo's embraces when the Duke confesses (in what tone of voice?): 'I have not yet made known to Mariana/A word of this' (IV, i, 47–8). He plots similarly with a third party over the fate of Barnardine—'Call your executioner, and off with Barnardine's head' (IV, ii, 209–10)—but though he offers to perform for him the function he had fulfilled for Claudio ('Hearing how hastily you are to depart, I am come to advise you, comfort you and pray with you', IV, iii, 46–8), he finds Barnardine less tractable material than Mariana:

> BARNARDINE: I swear I will not die to-day for any man's persuasion.
>
> DUKE: But hear you—
>
> BARNARDINE: Not a word. If you have anything to say to me, come to my ward, for thence will I not to-day.
>
> (IV, iii, 56–9)

Counting up all the examples of echo and duplication that verge on parody, we may conclude that the comic underplot shadows the main one, as hard to be shaken off as Lucio is in his persistent attachment to the Duke: 'By my troth, I'll go with thee to the lane's end . . . Nay, friar, I am a kind of burr; I shall stick' (IV, iii, 171–4).

The echoes and duplicates cluster most thickly in the scenes following the introduction of Mariana as substitute bed-mate and they function at the most obvious level to assure us that a happy ending is coming. They reproduce in another key situations and interests of deep seriousness elsewhere and in doing so they exemplify Shakespeare's constant awareness that it needs only a slight change of angle to turn tragedy into comedy and comedy into tragedy. He knows too that the self-aware and morally sensitive may press themselves too hard and so damage both themselves and others, whereas commoner men may take a wholesomer view of natural processes. The most striking example of this occurs in *The Winter's Tale* when, after the poisoned passions of Leontes have produced tragedy or near-tragedy, the old shepherd finds the abandoned baby and comments:

> ... this has been some stair-work, some trunk-work, some behind-door-work. They were warmer that got this than the poor thing is here. I'll take it up for pity.

> (III, iii, 71-4)

Life and death meet in this scene and are accepted by the old man and his son as part of the nature of things, to be met by caring for the living and burying the dead. At the root of comedy lies a sense of perspective, a setting of the absorbing preoccupations of the individual consciousness against a scale in which their claims to be all-important dwindle away and the spectator sees through a wide lens instead of in close focus. The extraordinary quality of *The Winter's Tale* scene is that the focus alternates, from the roaring of Antigonus in pain and fear to the roaring of the bear in sport as he enjoys a good dinner, from the piteous cry of the poor shipwrecked souls to the sea swallowing the ship like a snapdragon. *The Winter's Tale* scene prepares for the restoration of healthy values in the second half of the play and the bringing to life of Hermione who was thought to be dead. In *Measure for Measure* too, life prevails and Claudio, Barnardine and Lucio are redeemed from the death with which all are threatened—even Angelo, who craved death more willingly than mercy, responds to the love of life and acquires a sparkle in his eye when he perceives he is safe from instant execution. A comic perspective is asserted, in which severe moral issues are left high and dry as matters for tragedy (close focus) and instead the characters accept that one living woman or one dead man can readily be substituted for another (the wide angle lens).

Critics have been glad to recognise in at least one Shakespearean title a pertinent reference to the subject matter of the play but perhaps, after all, they have been misled into making too much of the comment which 'measure for measure' seems to offer. The play's situations concern matters of law and judgement, it is true, but this does not mean that justice is a central issue, or that definitions are being attempted. For the man charged with administration of the law, Angelo's initial position is perfectly adequate. The Duke has imposed on him the office of curbing the laxity which the Duke himself has allowed to develop and, in order to carry out his instructions, he has revived an old act, one among those 'strict statutes and most biting laws' which the Duke regrets that he has allowed to lapse (I, iii, 19). In his capacity as dispenser of justice, Angelo claims, quite properly, that he is simply an instrument of the law: 'It is the law, not I, condemn your brother' (II, ii, 80), and he argues, again rightly, that justice is not the antithesis of mercy. 'Yet show some pity', pleads Isabella, and he answers:

> I show it most of all when I show justice;
> For then I pity those I do not know,
> Which a dismissed offense would after gall;
> And do him right that, answering one foul wrong,
> Lives not to act another . . .
>   (II, ii, 99–104)

As a defence of a governor's right to judge and condemn and an assertion of his duty to do so, Angelo's points seem to be unchallengeable. To go further than this would be for him to enter into discriminations based on an analysis of specific social, political, psychological situations and would belong to a different kind of play altogether. In Fulke Greville's drama *Mustapha*, the Emperor Soliman fears that his son means to dethrone him and he plans to remove the threat by having Mustapha murdered. His daughter, Camena, pleads for mercy for her brother and points out that, as men have different capacities, both in good and evil, punishment should take account of this:

> Martyrs few men can be even for the good;
> As few dare seal their mischief with their blood.
> The prince's wisdom and his office this,
> To see from whom, how far each one can move,
> To find what each man's God and devil is,

Judging and handling frailty with love.
For ignorance begetteth cruelty,
Misthinking each man everything can be.
The best may fall, the worst that is may mend.
You hedge in time, and do prescribe to God,
Where safety, not amendment you intend.
The last of all corrections is the rod,
And kings that circle in themselves with death
Poison the air wherein they draw their breath.[11]

There is an analysis, on both a political and a religious level, of the roles of justice and mercy in the government of men and, penetrating as it is, it has nothing whatever in common with the manner of thought in *Measure for Measure*.

Angelo, then, shows no lack of understanding about justice and mercy within the limits of the situation in which Shakespeare sets him. He has been called in specifically to counter the effects of non-execution of the law and at this juncture the need is for him to take a strong stand so that future mischief may be nipped in the bud. The weakness of Angelo's position does not lie in any misunderstanding of justice but in his over-confidence in himself, his faith that he is not as other men—a belief parodied by Lucio ('Some report a sea-maid spawned him; some that he was begot between two stock-fishes', III, ii, 101–2), as much else is, and belied, of course, when he falls into lust for Isabella and is led by this into deceit and treachery. If the play is to be said to be 'about' anything, then its unifying idea would seem to be the brotherhood of man. We are all brothers under the skin—the idea is expressed by Shakespeare in this play and elsewhere in a variety of tones. Lear voices his understanding of it in Act IV, sc. vi, first in relation to himself: 'Go to, they are not men of their words: they told me I was everything; 'tis a lie, I am not ague-proof' (102–5), and then more widely: 'Hark, in thine ear: change places, and, handy-dandy, which is the justice, which is the thief?' (153–5). In *Measure for Measure* it is enacted rather than articulated. The 'brotherhood' of Claudio, in relation to Isabella and others, is an essential feature of the play. Angelo has to recognise

[11] From the earlier version of *Mustapha*. See *Selected Writings of Fulke Greville*, ed. Joan Rees, Athlone Renaissance Library (London, 1973), pp. 168–9.

kinship with him and the Duke claims it at the end—'He is my brother too' (V, i, 491). Neither Angelo nor Isabella can maintain the isolation from human contact and involvement they aspire to at the start. As for the Duke, he and Lucio and Pompey and Elbow and Barnardine have, after all, common meeting ground, for comedy combines them. In the end, Isabella the novice and the Duke who thought himself too 'complete' to be pierced by 'the dribbling dart of love' (I, iii, 2) must condescend to marry, as do Claudio and Juliet, the incontinent lovers, and Angelo and Mariana, brought together against his will but by his sin, and Lucio and Kate Keep-down, the 'fantastic' and the whore whose child he must now accept as his responsibility. 'Judge not that ye be not judged' can hardly be a suitable text for a governor charged with responsibility for law and order but 'We are all members one of another' may be a salutary thought to have in mind, as may a line from yet another play: 'One touch of nature makes the whole world kin'.

Yet no reading of the play in terms of a theme or idea quite accounts for all its elements and we turn back to the handling of the story to take some further observations. The growth of the character of Isabella and the immediate effect which that has on the source materials has already been discussed. Mariana has to be provided as a substitute in order to satisfy Angelo, and the Duke, his role extended from that of the shadowy original in the sources, is drawn into service to deal with the emergency. But once the Duke has taken the burden off Isabella and Mariana and is acting on their behalf (the play is full of substitutes), he becomes involved in more and more business. While Isabella and Mariana have little to do but await the outcome of events, and are consequently little seen, the Duke is busy making things happen. He has important matters to arrange with the Provost, who treats the supposed friar with respect, but in between these interviews the low-life characters hold the stage much of the time and the Duke is frequently in their company, with results that are damaging to his dignity. What the effect of these scenes is has been suggested. Further consideration of the story situation may now throw more light on *why* they are as they are. The fact is that all the principal characters except the Duke are, in the second half of the play, to a large extent incapacitated. Claudio is in prison, Mariana, once she has accepted her role, must keep out of the way, Isabella is dependent on the Duke's machinations, Angelo needs only to express his guilty conscience, which he does in IV, iv, 18–32. Only the Duke has reason for coming and going and is free to do so. In between the phases of his plotting, vitality is sustained by the underworld characters and the Duke must, willy-nilly, be brought into their orbit. What Shakespeare can do to preserve his dignity he does by, for example, the soliloquies in Act III, sc. ii and Act IV, sc. i, but he allows Lucio to be still buzzing round him in Act V when, if ever, we might expect the Duke to rise to full stature and authority as the dispenser of final reward and punishment.

There is one other consequence of the replacement of Isabella by Mariana at the assignation with Angelo, namely that by this manoeuvre Isabella is left without a partner. As the play draws to its conclusion, the question presents itself, what is to become of her? Even supposing that Shakespeare's audience would have been content with an ending which showed the convent gates closing upon her, it would seem a very unlikely destiny for a girl who in the course of the action has been so much involved in worldly affairs and has even appeared in the open street to proclaim that she has forfeited her virginity on a bargain and not been paid for it. The comic elements of *Measure for Measure* culminate in a traditional ending, with marriage all round, and Isabella and the Duke make the only possible partners for each other. They have in common that both have worn religious garb and discarded it (Isabella surely cannot play Act V in her novice's habit) and they have been united in their endeavours since Act III, sc. i. True, they are not very convincing lovers but the grouping on stage at the end will be satisfactory and the best of it will be that the dramatist need not write any lines for Isabella to say—for whatever could she say to the Duke's proposal: 'The image of it gives me content already and I trust it will grow to a most prosperous perfection'? or 'Sir! Make me not your story'?

Whatever coherence we give to the role of the Duke, it seems likely that his origin lies in the need to meet situations in the development of the story. Some of the functions he is required to fulfil are not entirely compatible with each other, hence the wide possibility of contradiction inherent in every account of him. He should probably, in the acting, be allowed to respond to the needs of the moment without an attempt to synthesise all his aspects. If we trust Shakespeare with the moments, the play will pretty certainly look after itself. There is no one like Shakespeare for pulling chestnuts out of the fire with such verve and confidence that in the theatre, at any rate, we do not notice how near to being singed he is.

Act V of *Measure for Measure* is a fine example of this, beginning with the sensational entrance of Isabella (whom we first saw in a nunnery) making her clamour in the public street and setting the action afoot with the insistent rapid beat of repeated words: 'justice, justice, justice, justice', 'strange, strange', 'true, true'. Angelo's self-righteousness and exposure are repeated and Isabella also repeats her plea for mercy—on Angelo's behalf this time and on legal grounds only, for the wider point, that all men are frail and may fall, would not be relevant here. Lucio gets under the Duke's guard for the last time as we see that the 'slanders' strung too much to be quite forgiven, and a grand processional ending will get them all off stage. In his handling of Act V, Shakespeare would seem to be reassuring us about the story we have just witnessed. Here, he says, are the issues, run through quickly to remind us, and here are the solutions which meet the problems, and here, finally, is the Duke, like the Prince in *Romeo and Juliet,* to voice the appropriate re-actions to it all. We are not invited to speculate on the future lives of these characters but we are strongly encouraged to think that all ends have been tied up and that the last word has been said. The conclusion is firm, bland—and deceptive for, of course, the state-ment of the problems and their resolutions at the end does not match the situations as they were at the beginning.

Measure for Measure embodies in an acuter form the narrative situation of *All's Well that Ends Well.* An intensely imagined situation is denied the complete development that would take the play right away from the sources but whereas in *All's Well* creative freedom is won by the development of an individual comic role, the growth of comedy in *Measure for Measure* is more diffuse, its effects spread more widely, and they show themselves more surprisingly. The development of Isabella was the growth point of the play as we have it and the so-called 'open-ended' play might have been a suit-able form here as in *The Merchant of Venice,* when it could have accommodated the growth of Shylock in defiance of the main orientation of the play. But we can hardly regret what we have. Shakespeare tried many kinds of story and many ways of dealing with them. When, on analysis, we may reckon that the story and the play do not fit it is only, in the end, to admire even more warmly the wonderful manipulative and inventive facility which the plays exhibit. Beatrice and Benedick, Parolles and Lucio, Helena and Isabella—the names remind us of splendid individual inventions but they also bring whole plays along with them. Shakespeare may improvise, modify and adapt, but he never leaves a play with just one or two brilliant figures and desolation all around them. The creative spark may not burn evenly and in all parts of the play at once but in time it flickers at least into every corner and, when we remember the plays, we recall them as having life everywhere.

4

Doing without Events; or The Art of Conversation

The last two chapters have been concerned with adjustments of various kinds in the story-line of the plays in response to developments which take place in the course of writing. The present one will consider a different aspect of Shakespeare's handling of narrative, his use of scenes where the story, so to speak, stops. The examples will be drawn almost exclusively from comedy, though such scenes occur in other kinds of play too and some particularly striking examples will be encountered in later parts of this study. In comedy they may be described as 'conversation scenes' and one advantage of identifying them and looking closely at them is that this provides an approach to the art of Shakespeare's comedies which avoids treating them either as unsophisticated light-weight pieces or as 'statements' of Shakespeare's 'deep concern' over something or other. Both attitudes have existed and still do, though the latter has been much the more prevalent in recent years.

In a witty article some years ago, John Crow wrote about 'Deadly Sins of Criticism or Seven Ways to Get Shakespeare Wrong'.[1] One sin was Puritanism: 'No artist is respectable unless he is a preacher in disguise . . . We must seek and probe for a Message everywhere. We must have a dedicated determination to leave no stone without its sermon displayed.' John Crow was writing in 1958 but the Puritanical strain in Shakespeare criticism has continued to flourish in later years and displays its blooms abundantly in commentary on the comedies. It is unfortunate that the 'themes' which we are assured Shakespeare is 'exploring' or 'making a statement about' are not of startling profundity or originality and it is a relief to return to the plays themselves and discover that, as Lawrence said happened when people attempted to pin down the novel, they have walked away with the pin. This chapter, like the others in this book,

[1] *Shakespeare Quarterly*, 9 (1958), 301–6.

will concentrate on aspects of the creative inventiveness which gives life to the plays and joy to the readers or audience. The starting point will be some remarks by C. L. Barber in his book, *Shakespeare's Festive Comedy*. 'It is amazing', he writes:

> how little happens in *Twelfth Night*, how much of the time people are merely talking, especially in the first half, before the farcical complications are sprung. Shakespeare is so skilful by now in rendering attitudes by the gestures of easy conversation that when it suits him he can almost do without events. In the first two Acts of *Twelfth Night*, he holds our interest with a bare minimum of tension while unfolding a pattern of contrasting attitudes and tones in his several persons.[2]

'He can almost do without events. . .' The discussion so far of Shakespeare's handling of the patterns of events which make up stories has suggested some evidence that the stories were an embarrassment. Perhaps it was his ambition to 'do without events', to escape from the demands of story altogether. *Love's Labour's Lost* shows him substituting a pattern of parallels and contrasts for dynamically progressive action, and *The Tempest* at the end of his career shows a keen sense of the artificiality of tidy endings. 'How tired I am of stories', laments Bernard, the novelist character in Virginia Woolf's *The Waves*, 'how I distrust neat designs of life that are drawn up on half sheets of notepaper . . . But', he goes on, 'if there are no stories, what end can there be, or what beginning?' The same dilemma may well have been familiar to Shakespeare as his art matured and he progressively realised the limitations of narrative and at the same time its apparent indispensibility. Madeleine Doran writes of 'the Elizabethan fondness for a narrative technique in drama—that is, for presenting a story sequentially from beginning to end with as much action along the way as possible'. 'Elizabethan drama', she comments, 'was founded upon story. These fundamental characteristics of Elizabethan drama, multiplicity and sequentially presented action, are survivals of medieval narrative habits exemplified both in actual narrative and in drama.'[3] Shakespeare was to take many liberties with narrative demands, as the

---

[2] *Shakespeare's Festive Comedy* (Princeton, 1959), p. 242.
[3] *Endeavors of Art* (University of Wisconsin Press, 1954), pp. 252 and 261.

foregoing chapters have shown, and he was to evolve many variants on conventional narrative techniques, but he never broke down narrative structure altogether. He did, however, develop an extraordinary capacity for 'doing without events' while at the same time giving an audience a sense of continuous action and he combined this, with greater or lesser care, within a narrative framework bounded by a beginning and an end. This is a skill which he draws upon most fully and to brilliant effect in some of the comedies. Not all the examples to be considered in this chapter can be described as 'easy conversation' for some of the characters are under emotional pressure and some of the exchanges are more formal than others. But the atmosphere is the comparatively relaxed one of comedy and this being so, the scenes provide a special opportunity for observing one aspect of Shakespeare's creative genius—what he can do when he has neither event nor pressing dramatic situation to sustain him.

His genius in handling conversation did not emerge full grown and *The Merchant of Venice* offers some early attempts which are particularly interesting because of later effects to be developed from them. The action of the play pauses at the end of Act IV before the final *jeu d'esprit* of the ring plot, which brings the play to an end with a mock estrangement whose difficulties can be finally and fully resolved. The beginning of Act V marks the pause and something has already been said about Jessica's and Lorenzo's duet on music and moonlight (see Chapter 2). The mood of peace and harmony is prolonged by the entry of Portia and Nerissa who speak of night and silence and the moon and music. These conversations serve as bridge passages between the rapid and dramatic action of the parts of the story concerned with Shylock and Antonio's bond and the final pairings of the lovers in laughter and prosperity. A pause occurs earlier in the action also, in Act II, sc. vi, when Gratiano and Salarino wait for Lorenzo. Lorenzo is late and his friends comment on the fact. Gratiano, very uncharacteristically, takes advantage of the occasion to indulge in a little homily on the theme that: 'All things that are,/Are with more spirit chased than enjoy'd.' The evident purpose of this conversation-piece is to separate Jessica's last moments in her father's house from her elopement with Lorenzo. The talk between Gratiano and Salarino creates a time-gap during which Shylock may be presumed to have got well away from the premises and the interlude makes a convenient buffer between two blocks of action. The conversation in Act V serves more complex purposes for, in preparation for the happy ending, it slows down the pace and soothes feelings which have been disturbed by Shylock and the trial scene. Shakespeare may have found himself obliged to 'do without events' at this point because of the rapidity with which he has conducted the story so far (this also was discussed in Chapter 2) but characteristically he turns the needs of the moment to great advantage and the talk is exquisite.

None of it, however, can be described as 'easy' despite the intimacy of the relationships between the lovers and between Portia and her maid. The dialogue of Jessica and Lorenzo has the quality of an aria and Portia's language, though not so lyrical as theirs, is still not such as to allow an informal exchange with Nerissa. She moralises, in fact, rather as Gratiano does when he finds time on his hands in Act II and, if her language is less ostentatious than his, it still suggests that a set-piece, either lyrical or homiletic, was Shakespeare's first resource when he had to do (briefly at this stage of his career) without events. In Act V the lyrical beauty of the Jessica-Lorenzo dialogue carries the day and Portia has stature enough to give dignity and substance to her observations but the essential crudity of the technique in itself is exposed by the unsuitability of Gratiano's contribution to the waiting scene in Act II.

There is, however, an analogue to this latter, apparently very unpromising little conversation-piece, in a later play and one outside the range of comedy. Hamlet, when he waits on the battlements for the appearance of his father's ghost (Act I, sc. iv) turns to moralising, just as Gratiano and Portia had done. As in the Gratiano scene, there is an interval of time to be gone through and Hamlet, like Gratiano, fills it with some moral reflections arising from the circumstances of the moment. Hamlet's train of thought is set off by the noise accompanying Claudius's 'heavy-headed revel' down below and leads him to comment on the vitiating effect of one defect in an otherwise admirable nature. His sentence is complex and circuitous, suggesting a mind not fully fixed on what is being said but wandering away and being forced back by an act of will to complete the thought. Gratiano's adages sound trite and unconvincing in his mouth because they spring from nothing in his character or situation. Hamlet moralises equally conventionally but his speech is entirely dramatic, marking the tension he feels while he waits the appearance of the ghost and also the effort he is making to keep full control of himself. This is a remarkable example of Shakespeare retaining a technical device which he had initially used blatantly and unskilfully and using it again a few years later with an astonishing increase in subtlety and dramatic effectiveness. Shakespeare's imagination engages with what it must feel like to be Hamlet, waiting, and the sententious reflections which had served Gratiano (pompously) and Portia (gracefully) become a means to an intimate insight into a state of mind at a particular, highly-charged moment.

The Gratiano-Salarino scene and Hamlet's conversation with Horatio on the battlements might both be called dramatic in that they are embedded in a context of dynamic events and have distinct functions in relation to continuing action. The Act V conversations in *The Merchant of Venice*, however, mark a break in action and function to relax tension. For comparable scenes in other plays, we have to look to areas where characters are not keyed up to busy action but are at ease and freely talking. *As You Like It* is the obvious place to look first.

The area of ease and free talk is an extensive one in *As You Like It*. The play begins briskly with its quick summary of the existing situation between Oliver and Orlando and its rapid development of their hostility to crisis point. The antagonism between the other pair of brothers, Duke Senior and Duke Frederick, is also sketched in and the sudden flare-up which results in the banishment of Rosalind takes place in Act I, sc. iii. By Act II, all the principal characters are in the forest and then, as C. S. Lewis observed of both the play and Lodge's *Rosalynde*, which is its major source, 'no one has any further business than to make love and poetry and play at the pastoral life'.[4] The wheels of action turn rapidly again at the end of the play when Oliver enters the forest and at once falls in love with Celia, and Duke Frederick is converted on the instant by a chance encounter with an old religious man. All save Jaques and Frederick, who choose to stay in the forest, are thus released to take up their roles in the world again but the play ends with everyone still in Arden.

Though the initial situation is set up very rapidly and its problems resolved even more rapidly at the end, the play as a whole is remarkable for maintaining a prolonged stasis in which nothing very much happens and time virtually stands still—there are no

[4] *English Literature in the Sixteenth Century* (Oxford, 1954), p. 424.

clocks in the forest. Harold Jenkins, in a well-known essay, comments on the relative lack of action: 'It is in the defectiveness of its action that *As You Like It* differs from the rest of the major comedies—in its dearth not only of big theatrical scenes but of events linked together by the logical intricacies of cause and effect.'[5] This striking quality of the play has drawn commentators to give a good deal of attention to the interests which replace physical activity and there is no need to recapitulate here the list of topics on which comedy, satire, parody and sentiment are exercised. Held still as they are, within the frame of the forest and away from their usual environment, the characters stand before us with a vividness unblurred by distracting external circumstances or by conventional expectations attaching to their social roles. Thus we see Duke Senior without the trappings of his dukedom and know that he is essentially a good man. And we know that Orlando, whatever abuses and deprivations he has suffered at the hands of society (represented by his brother and the usurping Duke), is incapable of bitterness or rancour and is open-hearted and good-feeling, an affirmer of positive values. Jaques is apparently an exception to this rule for he brings his social role of melancholic man into Arden with him and does not, and evidently does not wish to, shake it off. Yet this fact of itself reveals him and the limitations of his nature and outlook more clearly than perhaps anything else could.

Most important of all we see the heroine as she could never be shown out of Arden. Shakespeare does not trouble to give any explanation of why Rosalind should retain her masculine disguise after she has met Orlando and her father in the forest, but he makes full use of the paradox that in this disguise she may be uninhibitedly herself. 'The lady shall say her mind freely, or the blank verse shall halt for it', Hamlet promises the actors (Act II, sc. ii) but, as his words suggest, the role of 'the lady', in literature and in life, has not commonly allowed for freedom of speech. Poor Ophelia has to go mad before she can speak what is in her mind. Among the young women dressed as boys Rosalind is particularly privileged, as she exercises her wit and her liveliness of spirit on her beloved and woos him ardently and unashamedly.

The characters, then, for most of four Acts, talk and do little. Once in the forest, as Harold Jenkins puts it, 'the manner of the

[5] *Shakespeare Survey*, 8 (1955), pp. 40–52.

play . . . is to let two people drift together, talk a little, and part, to be followed by two more'. The play, as he notes, is comparable with *Love's Labour's Lost* where also there is much talking and little action: '*Love's Labour's Lost* is the most formally constructed of all the comedies' but, in *As You Like It*, the 'formal parallelisms of *Love's Labour's Lost* are replaced by a more complex design, one loose enough to hold all sorts of asymmetries within it'.

Comparisons and contrasts between the two plays are reflected in the kind and quality of the talk that goes on in them. In kind, there is a considerable degree of similarity. The formal wit-combats of *Love's Labour's Lost* have their counterparts in 'sets of wit' played in *As You Like It*. When Touchstone meets Corin or Jaques Orlando or Rosalind almost anybody, the encounters provide so many opportunities for display of verbal skill and speed of response. Nearly everyone in the play can bear a part in these set-piece dialogues. To this extent the conversations of the play share the formality of *Love's Labour's Lost*, but some of the effects are more complex than any in the earlier play. The heart of the difference is Rosalind, for she is at once the quickest-witted and most various player of the game of wits and also the character least bounded by it. She can, for example, deliver what is virtually a comic monologue on the theme that 'men have died from time to time, and worms have eaten them, but not for love' (IV, i, 93–4) but the quasi-monologue is embedded in a dialogue with Orlando and Shakespeare constantly reminds us of the tender and susceptible feelings of both lovers. The true voice of feeling cuts into the high-spirited displays and we have something quite different from a series of self-confident and self-conscious acts put on for applause. The delightful suspense in which we watch Rosalind's brilliant and precarious performances replaces excitement of the what-happens-next variety. The repartee may at any moment fail, we feel, the brilliant juggler with words and ideas may drop one of the spinning discs and the whole delicately poised act will collapse. 'I would not have my right Rosalind of this mind, for I protest her frown might kill me', says Orlando with some seriousness after Rosalind's disquisition on the non-fatality of love, and when he tells her that he will leave her for two hours, it is a girl deep in love who cries: 'Alas dear love, I cannot lack thee these two hours!'

Her faint when she hears of Orlando's wounding by the bear is the moment when her assumed role as Ganymede and her 'real' situation most strikingly intersect but the presence of a sub-text is a constant effect in the Rosalind scenes. If we should be in danger of forgetting it, there is Celia to remind us, when the girls are alone together. The little scenes with Celia allow of a genuinely relaxed conversational style between equals who may confide, sympathise and tease but have no reason for disguise or display. The scenes are functional in that they allow Rosalind to express her specifically feminine feelings and so, since her disguise gives her masculine freedom of speech, enable us to have the completest possible picture of her. Celia is also the only person able to poke fun at Rosalind and this is a useful service in a play where the heroine acts as a critic of many others and needs to be shown vulnerable herself, lest she seem to become over-bearing. We remember that shrewishness, which in Shakespearean comedy is itself a kind of disguise, can be an alternative route to free speech but Shakespeare does not want another Katherine or Beatrice in this play. The skill with which he distinguishes Rosalind from Beatrice, another quick-witted and sharp-minded girl, is especially worth notice. It is to be seen in the conversations with Orlando, where the under-currents always make themselves felt, and in the free and open conversations with Celia where the other face of Rosalind shows free of all veils, that of the love-struck girl who is touching and absurd at the same time.

The talk in *As You Like It*, though witty, exuberant and wide-ranging, is on different planes, not merely because of social differences between characters but more importantly because of Shakespeare's decision to make Rosalind the centre of the play. So her conversations with Orlando have an extra piquancy because the girl in love is never lost inside the guise of the pert boy and her conversations with Celia are marked off from all the others by the trust and mutual sympathy which allow for complete unreserve. Rosalind's play-acting as Ganymede is a play-within-a-play and in the Celia scenes she comes off-stage. It is Celia who scores the witty points at these times but there is no question of a wit-contest for Rosalind's guard is down and Celia's wit never outstrips her sympathy and affection.

In *Much Ado About Nothing* we learn to recognise that the verbal displays of Beatrice and Benedick disguise or disclaim their real capacity for feeling but we (and they) are helped to this realisation

by the intervention of others. Rosalind's deliberately assumed disguise is another matter and Lodge had shown what kinds of opportunity it could provide. Shakespeare reduces the amount of action
which *Rosalynde* contained, tightens the wit of the conversations and
increases the naturalness. He throws all the weight of the play,
indeed, on to the talk and he gives it heart as well as sparkle by
putting at the centre a character whose role for most of the time is to
be a double talker. In *Love's Labour's Lost* he sustained a play with
as few events as *As You Like It* but the creative imagination makes
a subtler and more varied work of art of the conversations in the
later play.

'Shakespeare is so skilful by now in rendering attitudes by the
gestures of easy conversation that when it suits him he can almost do
without events': Professor Barber's comment provides a lead into a
discussion of several plays but the whole passage, already quoted,
refers in particular to *Twelfth Night*: 'It is amazing how little
happens in *Twelfth Night*', Professor Barber writes, 'how much of
the time people are merely talking, especially in the first half . . . In
the first two Acts of *Twelfth Night* [Shakespeare] holds our interest
with a bare minimum of tension while unfolding a pattern of contrasting attitudes and tones in his several persons.' *Twelfth Night*
and *As You Like It* appear to have been written within a short time
of each other but though 'doing without events' is a notable characteristic of *As You Like It* and Professor Barber finds *Twelfth Night*
also to be a play in which for a considerable part of its length, 'little
happens', yet the conversational kinds and effects in the two plays
are not duplicated.

As You Like It begins with a rapid building up of situations in
order to convey all the important characters to Arden as quickly as
possible. *Twelfth Night* begins with a more leisurely assembly of its
various story elements. The first three scenes introduce us to the
pivotal situations, Orsino's love for Olivia, Viola's shipwreck, loss
of her brother and determination to disguise herself and to serve
Orsino, Sir Toby's position and behaviour in Olivia's household and
Sir Andrew's pretensions to her hand. As yet these remain three
separate worlds though the 'contrasting attitudes and tones' give
edge and interest to them. Orsino meditates on love and music in
lyric speech whose rhythms and images reproduce the 'dying fall' of
the melody he calls for, and he makes punning allusion to the

favourite Renaissance fable of Actaeon. The report we hear of Olivia intensifies the mood of exquisite indulgence in feeling as she vows to mourn her dead brother for seven years with daily tears. Orsino's response touches the pastoral note:

> How will she love when the rich golden shaft
> Hath kill'd the flock of all affections else
> That live in her . . .

thus making up the opening chord of literary motifs and rarefied sentiment. Next we encounter Viola, the sea-captain and the sailors and the mood is altogether brisker and more business-like. Orsino may liken love to the sea and Olivia may plan to 'Water once a day her chamber round With eye-offending brine' but to Viola, newly saved herself from shipwreck and fearing for the life of her brother, the sea and death by drowning are matters of grievous experience, not indulgent metaphor. Stranded on a strange shore, she takes stock of her situation and makes competent arrangements for dealing with it. Scene iii presents Sir Toby Belch, Maria and Sir Andrew Aguecheek. Sir Toby gives short shrift to laments for brothers and Sir Andrew is a parody of a courtly lover: 'I would I had bestowed that time in the tongues that I have in fencing, dancing, and bear-baiting. O, had I but followed the arts!'

After these separate introductions, the interlacing of characters and situations begins in scene iv with Viola already installed in Orsino's service and in love with him. It continues in scene v, with Viola's first meeting with Olivia and the introduction of Malvolio whose story, as it develops, will make further links between the various plot elements already assembled. Act I having prepared the ground, Act II proceeds in leisurely fashion to build upon it and it is not till well on in Act III that the various entanglements and mistakes begin to move towards their crises. In these circumstances, it is evidently appropriate to look closely at scenes in which 'people are merely talking' and to consider how they rouse and retain our interest. Two scenes in particular, in each of the first two Acts, claim attention as 'conversation scenes', Act I, scs. iii and v, and Act II, scs. iii and iv. Act I, sc. iii and Act II, sc. iii feature Sir Toby and Sir Andrew and friends; in Act I, sc. v and Act II, sc. iv, Viola is a principal figure. It will be convenient to treat them in pairs, beginning with the Toby–Andrew group.

Sir Andrew is the gull, Sir Toby is his randy and unscrupulous exploiter, Maria is the sharp-witted waiting woman. Basically they are the characters of eternal farce. Much of the weight of the revelling scenes is to fall on Sir Andrew and, so that the audience will be prepared with laughter ready for him, Sir Toby and Maria provide a lengthy introduction in their opening dialogue in Act I, sc. iii, before his first entrance. Sir Andrew has money and a feeble intellect, is physically maladroit and weakly endowed. By the end of this first scene we have had all this demonstrated and at his exit he is being flattered by Sir Toby into cutting capers, a grotesque and farcical sight, no doubt, on any stage. The basis of such comedy is old, coarse and even brutal. Some modern producers have played it like that but to do so is to disregard the qualities of the talk in the scene which create subtler effects out of the basic materials. Sir Toby is boozy, though he keeps an open eye for Sir Andrew's ducats, but he is also an educated man of some wit who makes a good speech. Sir Andrew is a fool but by no means a featureless one. Our hearts warm to his mixture of ridiculous self-reproach—'O, had I but followed the arts!'—and equally ridiculous self-congratulation on the merits of his leg—'it does indifferent well in a flame-coloured stock'. He even has moments of sense, as when he recognises that Olivia will never marry him, but he is easily persuaded that these are an illusion. As for Maria, she is forthright and quick-witted and on terms of considerable familiarity with her lady's uncle. From the way she speaks to him and the nature of her reproofs, it is clear enough that outside the room where Olivia proposes to weep seven years for her brother's death, domestic management could easily get out of hand.

Herein lies, on one level, the importance of Malvolio. 'I would not have him miscarry for the half of my dowry', Olivia says (III, iv, 60–2) and we can see for ourselves that with a kinsman like Sir Toby in the house to draw spirits of misrule to him and with a lady retired, and cherishing an indulgent grief, the steward has an onerous and responsible job. We meet Malvolio first in Act I, sc. v and see him as the embodiment of outraged propriety in Act II, sc. iii when he comes to interrupt the midnight revelry.

This is the second Sir Toby–Sir Andrew scene and like the first it builds on well-worn and rugged ground, this time a drunken party which traditionally provides ample scope for tumbling and hic-

cupping. We know the participants from our previous meeting with
them and they at once reassert their characteristics. Sir Toby dredges
up scraps of his squandered education, Sir Andrew produces some of
his naïve truths. As he is willing to take a lead from Sir Toby, so he
is lavish with his admiration of Feste also, for he is a generous
innocent, eminently exploitable but having a very enjoyable time for
his money. Feste's presence adds a new ingredient to the scene. He
sings his song of love and the transience of youth, a surprisingly
delicate and plangent version of the *carpe diem* theme to be heard
in this atmosphere of drink and tobacco. It is followed at once by a
raucous catch. This is a splendidly entertaining scene, with intelligence enough present (mainly in the person of Feste) to add a spice
of mockery to the revels. There is one to act the fool 'more natural'
and one 'with a better grace' and before we have quite lost our
sense of the demands of normal social life, without which the flout-
ing of decorum lacks zest, there is Maria to enter and call the rowdy
good-fellowship the 'caterwauling' it must seem to sober citizens
who are trying to sleep in their beds.

With the entry of Malvolio all the effects are heightened. Malvolio
is genuinely amazed that anyone could so cast aside all that common
convention and prudence dictate. Sir Toby, egged on by Feste,
becomes more outrageous and in the general excitement Sir Andrew
makes an implausible show of belligerence. Out of it all Maria's
plan is hatched to make of the strait-laced Malvolio a fool in his turn,
a butt of those whose clowning he so despises.

Very little, it may be said, has happened in either of these scenes
though a plot has been laid for the future; but it would be equally
true to say that a great deal has been going on, especially in the scene
from Act II which brings the seeds sown in Act I to an advanced
stage of development. Sir Toby, Sir Andrew and Feste are all in
good revelling form and their personalities make the most of the
occasion but the intervention of Malvolio brings into prominence
what was only hinted in the earlier scene, the potentially subversive
nature of Sir Toby's way of life. Malvolio defends the values of the
sober citizenry who know what is owing to place, persons and time.
Olivia, as the lady of the house, is responsible for its good order and
the message she hands down through Malvolio is a model of
measured judgement:

> My lady bade me tell you that though she harbours you as her
> kinsman, she's nothing allied to your disorders. If you can separate
> yourself and your misdemeanours, you are welcome to the house.
> If not, and it would please you to take leave of her, she is very
> willing to bid you farewell.

But at this the rebellion boils over. Sir Toby rejects the message and
insults Malvolio. Cakes and ale take precedence over law and order.
Misrule is king.

This is a situation which, at different levels of seriousness and
intensity, recurs in Shakespeare's plays. The cakes and ale (or sherris-
sack) of Eastcheap challenge authority and responsibility in
Henry IV, the revelry of Egypt challenges the efficient order of
Rome in *Antony and Cleopatra*: Sir Toby challenges the whole
world of social regulation and observance in *Twelfth Night*. But
this is a comedy. Shakespeare has no wish to make the confrontation
a major issue pursued to the annihilation of one party. Though it is
in fact Olivia's authority, delegated to Malvolio, which is being
challenged, the attack is deflected on to Malvolio himself who becomes her scape-goat. And since we know already of Malvolio that
he is 'sick of self-love' and tastes 'with a distempered appetite'
(I, v, 85–6), we cannot think that it will do him much harm to be
made absurd for once nor pain ourselves over his wounded dignity.
The rebel company, which by this time includes Maria, constitute
themselves a kind of alternative society alongside the one that other
people know, in which values are inverted, meanings are changed,
neither events nor people are what they seem. Malvolio, the guardian
of law and order, becomes a huge joke from their point of view,
Viola and Sir Andrew are represented to each other as fire-eating
monsters—whatever is taken seriously by the world at large becomes
matter of game for them. It is great fun for everyone in the know,
which includes the audience, but it cannot last. The social norm is
too strong for the jesters and Sir Toby receives a bloody pate in
token of the fact. His marriage to Maria will ensure that he does not
break bounds too flagrantly in future. Feste and Fabian are glad to
claim Olivia's protection once more. Only Malvolio, who can never
find time for laughter, is unaccommodated. 'I'll be revenged on
the whole pack of you', he vows, and, if life is real and life is earnest,
he will of course. Even within the play it is acknowledged that

insouciance cannot win in the end. Sir Toby, threatened with eviction from Olivia's house and favour, may defiantly call for a stoup of wine but 'the rain it raineth every day', as Feste sings, and for Sir Andrew there is going to be a costly day of reckoning for all this merry-making.

Out of a meeting between a waiting woman and a fool, and a drunken evening interrupted by the representative of outraged respectability, Shakespeare creates scenes full of laughter but also big with suggestion and possibility. We recognise that Sir Toby, taken anything but comically, could be a brute, that the challenge to authority might be a serious matter and that Malvolio's position might be genuinely distressing. Shakespeare widens the interest of his scenes and deepens the vitality by evoking our awareness of all this and increasing our delight by ensuring that the worst does *not* happen. We may be dancing on a tight-rope, but we dance with glee. Thus does conversation, during which nothing very much 'happens', become a source of dramatic interest and the liveliest enjoyment. The surface is easy, informal conversation—much of it tipsy—but the texture is made up of many fine threads, so skilfully woven as to support a considerable part of the weight of the play.

When we turn to the other two scenes, Act I, sc. v and Act II, sc. iv, we find similar food for meditation on the subtlety of Shakespearean 'conversation'. The first of these is a long scene and gives us our first sight of Olivia, of whose mourning for her dead brother we have heard in the first scene of the play where it was matched with Orsino's romantic love-melancholy. Her first words are an order to 'Take the fool away' but this is a mood, easily overcome, not a settled antipathy, for she takes delight in Feste and rebukes Malvolio for his inability to do so. The little collision that takes place here between Feste and Malvolio prefigures the bigger one in Act II, sc. iii. Olivia acts as arbiter in this first encounter, reproving both parties for their excesses, but she is aware of the value of both, sending Malvolio to deal with the count's messenger and Feste to look after Sir Toby, who has made a brief, unsteady, appearance. The arrival of Viola as Caesario and the sudden growth of Olivia's misplaced passion will introduce the element which upsets the equilibrium, for Olivia, 'much out of quiet' after her interview with him, will send Malvolio to clamp down on Sir Toby and his associates, thus producing the sub-plot. The romantic complications, of course, follow naturally from her reactions to Orsino's 'boy'.

The meeting of Olivia and Caesario is the main 'event' then of this scene and it has a lengthy introduction, involving, as well as Olivia herself, Feste, Malvolio, Maria and Sir Toby. These smaller scenes within the large one each have their separate points and unobtrusively but most ingeniously they are tying together the separate elements of the play, preparing the entanglements in which all will later be caught.

Viola in her boy's attire is in Rosalind's position, but she does not play the same boy. 'I will speak to him like a saucy lacquey, and under that habit play the knave with him', Rosalind promises herself when she first sees Orlando in Arden (III, ii) and she at once takes the initiative and begins a brilliant display of wit and vivacity. Viola presents herself to Olivia in a much more diffident manner, as an inexperienced and gauche boy. He is one, however, who, in spite of his immaturity, can make an occasional pointed remark and can hold his own in a verbal exchange. The mixture of boldness and timidity perfectly bears out Malvolio's description of him: 'tis with him e'en standing water, between boy and man' and since the supposed youth is also 'very well-favoured' it is hardly surprising that Olivia finds the blend of qualities piquant. When at his request Olivia removes her veil, Caesario takes advantage of the concession to increase the pressure in his proxy wooing. Olivia parries with mockery but yields to the pressure in her next speech so far as to move into verse, like Viola. The tongue-tied youth has now become an eloquent exponent of passionate devotion and Olivia says little, but enough to show that she has been impressed. The pattern of the scene is remarkably similar to that which shapes the first interview between Angelo and Isabella in *Measure for Measure*, Act II, sc. ii. Isabella begins hesitantly and with few words at her command. As the scene develops, Angelo counters her arguments confidently but then she has the great outbursts on the subject of the presumptions of men in authority and Angelo falls silent save for a few brief words. Like Olivia when Caesario leaves her, Angelo breaks into soliloquy when Isabella departs and exclaims in amazement at the feelings which have been aroused in him. The scene in *Measure for Measure* is highly-charged, powerful, and intensely dramatic. Its dialogue is not at all 'easy conversation'. All the more striking is the evidence it offers that the *Twelfth Night* scene, despite its softer colours and its relaxed atmosphere, has a dramatic structure which is strong enough to be used successfully for much tauter, tougher purposes.

Viola plays a very ambiguous part in Act I, sc. v, for not only is she a girl dressed as a boy, wooing another woman on behalf of the man whom she herself loves, but she is playing a boy at the point of emerging from callow adolescence into manhood and subject to contradictory impulses of timidity and independence. A boy's voice when it is breaking may change pitch unexpectedly from treble to baritone and Caesario's behaviour in this scene has something of the same effect. In her scene with Orsino, Act II, sc. iv, the situation is to some degree simpler in that, although she is still disguised, her real feelings lie only just beneath the surface and she expresses them, though he does not know it, to the man she loves.

Orsino begins by calling for music, 'the food of love', as he did at the very beginning of the play, and this is indeed to be a love-scene, full of love, love concealed, love unrequited and love growing, unaware, to be recognised, fully developed, much later. Feste, who is to sing an 'old and antique song' which pleased Orsino the previous night, has to be sought for and we remember that when we last heard Feste he was performing in riotous antiphony with Sir Toby in the small hours of the morning. He seems to move between the two houses as he moves between two worlds of music, quite freely. While they wait for him to be found, Orsino talks idly and indulgently to his 'boy'. He talks, of course, of love and what he says rehearses conventional attitudes. Yet, absorbed as he is in the luxury of his own sentiments, he is alert to the words and the tone of voice of his companion. He hears at once the true voice of feeling in Caesario's reply to his query about the music:

> It gives a very echo to the seat
> Where Love is throned. . .

and he fires some direct questions at him. His eye soon turns inward again, however, and he goes back to his repertoire of stereotypes, offering an idealised view of women's constancy, and a time-worn comment on the fragility of female beauty:

> women are as roses whose fair flower
> Being once displayed, doth fall that very hour.

Viola's responses to all this are very brief and in strong contrast. What she says comes from the heart and to the audience's ears her words must convey the pain she feels. Once Orsino hears the note too and is roused to attention but after a few sharp glances at his 'boy' his eyes cloud over once more.

With the entry of Feste, Orsino's mood of romantic nostalgia and sensibility reaches its lyric climax. His introduction of Feste's song is most beautiful and the song itself makes the ultimate gesture in the courtly lover's repertoire: 'I am slain by a fair cruel maid.' Feste, however, is fully aware of the distinction between the role and the actor. 'There's for thy pains', Orsino says, giving him money and choosing a word which sorts well with the griefs of love which Feste has sung. But Feste knows that in acting love-melancholy one may be enjoying oneself very much: 'No pains sir. I take pleasure in singing, sir.'

Orsino is courteous throughout these exchanges but Feste has a sharp eye as well as a quick tongue. He is not impressed by Orsino's image of himself as devoted lover: 'thy mind is a very opal', he tells him; but it will take more than this to shake Orsino out of his role. When Feste has gone he returns with renewed vigour to thoughts of his courtship of Olivia, instructing Viola to urge his disinterested devotion. 'But if she cannot love you, sir?', asks Viola quietly:

ORSINO: I cannot be so answered.
VIOLA: 'Sooth, but you must.

This little exchange is a telling one for Viola is attacking the root of Orsino's position. Love for him is not a reciprocal relationship— we have never seen him in Olivia's company nor heard of their meetings—but it is something nourished and cherished in the imagination, demanding satisfaction but concerning itself little with the needs and feelings of the other party. Orsino's is a selfish passion and Viola is trying to disturb his self-involvement and stir him into an awareness of a less egocentric world. His response is bluster:

> There is no woman's sides
> Can bide the beating of so strong a passion
> As love doth give my heart: no woman's heart
> So big to hold so much; they lack retention.

No matter that this contradicts entirely what he said earlier of woman's love compared with man's. He adopts the position which suits his conception of himself at the moment: the experienced man giving advice to the fledgeling boy, or the outraged heroic lover defying anyone to share or emulate the grandeur of his passion. Viola receives his rant at face value, simply opposing to it a sad and poignant picture of a woman's love. It quietens Orsino and it impresses him. He looks, listens and takes notice, as he did earlier when Caesario confessed to being in love. But the time has not come yet for complete revelation and the scene ends with Viola despatched once more to importune Olivia.

There is no event at all in this scene. Two people talk together and a third sings. The texture of the scene is rich. It contains comedy in Feste's retorts to Orsino and it contains the mournful luxury of 'Come away, come away death', Viola's famous speech about her sister who pined away for love, and Orsino's marvellous evocation of 'The spinsters and the knitters in the sun'. It contains, moreover, the contrast in awareness and depth of feeling between Viola and Orsino and it records Viola's capacity to penetrate, momentarily but effectively, Orsino's self-absorption. The unreality of Orsino's love for Olivia is plain to the audience. We know that Viola will win him in the end and this scene does the work of psychological preparation which enables us to accept that he will recognise and welcome the real state of affairs in Act V. When we next see him, in Act V, sc. ii, he is not only on his feet but in motion and actually going in person to see Olivia. He has another encounter with Feste and gives him money again but this time he is rather more in touch with the situation and in control of the run of the Fool's wit than he was previously. Before Olivia enters, he is seen enquiring officially as Duke into the affairs of Antonio—this is the first time we have seen Orsino in any public capacity or known him concerned about anything but his emotional states. When Olivia appears, he defers completion of this business but his speech with Olivia is itself very short and he accepts without argument his rejection. In his reactions now, his anger, his turning on Caesario for vengeance, his contempt and hurt when he is told that his 'boy' has secretly married Olivia while Orsino believed him faithful and devoted to his interests, in all this he is behaving naturally and instinctively; there is no longer any question of role-playing. By the end of the scene and of the play, Orsino has emerged into full daylight, a man capable of bearing a sensible and responsible part in the final arrangements, to whom can fittingly be left the last spoken words. Unless the values of the 'conversation' in Act II, sc. iv are given their full weight, this development of Orsino's character can seem altogether too abrupt and be dismissed as unaccountable or unsatisfactory. The earlier scene has, in reality, laid the foundation of it all by its delicate suggestion of the shifts, readjustments and recognitions which are taking place in Orsino, just out of the reach of full consciousness. In a 'conversation scene', a scene in which Shakespeare 'does without events', the talk at once conceals and reveals a network of responses and reactions whose vibrations decisively affect the development of the play.

The artistry of such a scene is extraordinary. The imagination which plays so powerfully on its materials that it is able to give depth and life by such 'easy' means deserves celebration in scenes like these as well as in its more spectacular and sensational manifestations.

Underpinning these conversation scenes is a sense of relationships. The individuals are realised as separate persons and given their characteristic styles of speech but Shakespeare goes beyond that to give us a vivid awareness of the links that bind one to another. Thus we have a sense of Olivia's household and the tensions and affinities at different social levels. In the Caesario scenes, as in the Ganymede scenes in *As You Like It*, we are constantly aware of the real relationships between the girls and the people they talk to, even while they establish and maintain assumed ones. That Shakespeare was remarkably sensitive to relationships, and to how they modify, complicate or deepen situations, may be illustrated by examples from other plays in which he makes a point of drawing attention to them in contexts where they might well be overlooked. Romeo begs forgiveness of the dead Paris and calls him 'cousin' at the moment when, having killed Paris and discovered the apparently dead body of Juliet, he is about to kill himself. 'Forgive me, cousin', he says and the claim to kinship heightens our awareness of the tragic waste which takes place in *Romeo and Juliet*, as young lives which should enjoy natural companionship and sympathy are forced into unnatural enmity and kill each other. At the end of *Much Ado About Nothing*, on the other hand, the cousinship emphasised by Claudio and Benedick is a token of the integrating effects of comedy, a sign of mutual friendship, common interests and common sympathies. Family bonds, for

Shakespeare, involve the closest of relationships and the most intimate and far-reaching interactions. They are always powerful considerations in his plays but his sense of interrelationships extends also over groups brought together by more casual circumstances. So it is that when he 'does without events' in conversation scenes he can set our interest alight and reveal to us through the 'gestures of easy conversation' little dramas of advance and retreat, small shifts in position and adjustments in perception–minutiae which, in fact, are immensely important in determining our attitudes to persons and events in the framework of the individual plays.

There is no more brilliant example of this than in *The Tempest*, a play which makes striking innovations in its handling of events but contains one 'conversation scene' of consummate artistry.

Act II, sc. i, is a long scene. It introduces us to Alonso and his courtiers and it includes Antonio's temptation of Sebastian and their attempted murder of the king. We are given here the most extensive view we ever have of the people whom Prospero has taken in hand and we see how they react to the first impact of their experience. When the scene opens, they are not engaging in or planning any action but merely talking together, assessing in their own ways the significance of their present situation. Gonzalo begins with the homely exhortation to count one's blessings, an excellent piece of advice though one difficult to accept when a new grief presses hard, as it does on Alonso. Gonzalo perseveres in his efforts to comfort and encourage and in this he is abetted by Adrian, a man of good heart evidently, but one without sufficient imagination to know that a fact may sometimes be well sacrificed for the sake of a greater object. He and Gonzalo part company over Gonzalo's rash assertion that Tunis and Carthage are the same place. Adrian does not persist in his protest and leaves the old man the last word but thereafter he drops out of the dialogue.

This passage, with the talk of 'widow Dido' and Carthage/Tunis has drawn some unfavourable comments. The Arden edition, in a note to line 74, quotes Lytton Strachey's attribution of 'the dreary puns and interminable conspiracies' of this scene to Shakespeare's fatigue and comments that if the 'apparently trivial allusions to the theme of Dido and Aeneas' are to be taken at face value, then Strachey's strictures are perfectly justified. Professor Kermode adds, however: 'But we must not take them at their face value' and in the introduction to the volume he works Gonzalo's mistakes and solecisms into the total pattern of significance which he finds in the play. The tiredness which Lytton Strachey finds and the profundity which Professor Kermode seeks seem equally to miss the life of this encounter. Gonzalo is talking for the sake of talking as Hamlet talked on the battlements before the ghost's appearance, and, as with Hamlet, his full attention is not on what he is saying because he is preoccupied with something else. Gonzalo wishes above all to rouse Alonso from his despair and, in his concern that he is not getting a response, his words become a little wild. He puts down Adrian firmly, and perhaps with some asperity, because to him the urgent need to keep conversation going is more important than the literal truth of what is said: Adrian should have kept the ball in play rather than arrested the movement as he did. Antonio and Sebastian seize on the old man's mistake and worry away at their jests, for they have no interest in helping Alonso through his dark hour. Gonzalo refuses to be defeated and tries again, addressing Alonso directly and harping on his daughter, 'who is now Queen', as if to turn the King's thoughts into a cheerful direction rather than to the loss of his son. He is rewarded with a response, not in itself an encouraging one, but at least Alonso has been roused for the moment and Francisco is given an opportunity to offer some hope of Ferdinand's survival of the shipwreck. Antonio and Sebastian, according to their natures, instantly turn their attention to thwarting Gonzalo's kindly ruse, by souring the King's recollection of his daughter and rubbing in the loss of his son. Gonzalo exerts himself once more and begins his quite gratuitous fantasy of his island plantation. To apply a sharp critical scrutiny to this utopia, as if it were a statement of ideas standing by itself, is to mistreat it in context for, like almost everything else in Gonzalo's role in this part of the scene, it is directed to arousing, by any means he can compass, Alonso's interest. In sober judgement on another day, he might choose his words more carefully, a probability which, however, does not preclude our deducing from the evidence that the warmth of his heart is greater than the coolness of his brain.

In this scene, while the strangers are alone together and before Ariel's first entry, Shakespeare brings them to life, simply by what they say and without the aid of action. What he achieves is a wonderful piece of character creation, carried out with extraordinary brevity and yet giving us a complete sense of what manner of man each is. The dialogue is so sensitive to the situation and to the interrelationships within the group that every speech sets up vibrations in an atmosphere fraught with animosities, anxieties and perplexities. The rarely broken silence of Alonso itself speaks eloquently of a despair sunk below the reach of comfort and stimulus. Rhythm and movement are given to the scene by the successive moves which Gonzalo makes to touch the King to life and by the thwarting of his efforts. While he is concentrated on his purpose, Antonio and Sebastian try to break his concentration by quibbles about what he says but not until the last seconds before Ariel's entry does he allow himself to notice and reply to their goadings. The direct exchanges between him and them suitably bring this movement of the scene to an end.

To show these aspects of the conversational art in this scene is not by any means to deny that there is more in it. Commentators have noted the different responses of the 'good' and 'bad' characters to the qualities of the island and the apparent disagreement about the condition of their clothes. No doubt these touches add to our sense of the magic qualities of the island. The echo of Montaigne's essay 'Of Cannibals' in Gonzalo's description of his Utopia has also been a fruitful topic and the lines have been taken as integral to the development of certain ideas in the play. As J. P. Brockbank puts it: 'The secret dialogue that, metaphorically speaking, Shakespeare conducts with Florio's Montaigne, is an intricate one. Gonzalo's Utopian vision is at its centre.'[6] Scholarship may perhaps discover other layers of material in the scene and our knowledge of all that feeds into it may ramify; but however many interconnections of ideas there may be, the quality which makes the scene worth attention is the vitality of imagination which informs every word of it.

Shakespeare's creative imagination may be seen as well in such scenes as these as in bigger set-pieces, though the humanity, the delicate and yet comprehensive perceptions which they contain are easily overlooked when critics are concerned to elicit grand moral or philosophic lessons from the plays. To create Prospero, Ariel and Caliban was the work of genius but to write the dialogue between

[6] 'Conventions of Art and Empire' in *Later Shakespeare* (Stratford upon Avon Studies, 8, 1966), ed. J. R. Brown and Bernard Harris. Reprinted in *Shakespeare's Later Comedies* (Penguin Shakespeare Library, 1971), ed. D. J. Palmer.

the courtiers in Act II, sc. i, was also unmistakably so. There is no one hall-mark of Shakespeare's creative imagination, for he excelled in so much, but one could point to this dialogue of some two hundred lines and say that the creative power which operates there with so much subtlety and assurance is distinctively his.

The 'art of conversation' has been illustrated in this chapter almost exclusively from comedies, but it is an art which Shakespeare seems first to have learnt in writing *Henry IV*, part i and he used it again in *Hamlet* where, amongst all the tension and pressure of events, we are occasionally given the relaxed gestures of 'easy conversation' and our sense of the human tragedy involved is thereby heightened. This wonderful resource which Shakespeare develops is capable of revealing many levels of a situation at once. Its subtleties seem not always to be fully appreciated in comedy, where subtlety is more often sought in ethical statements, but they are among the glories of these plays and a prime reason why we can return to them time and again and find in them renewed interest and undiminished delight.

Earlier John Crow's ironic statement of contemporary critical doctrine was quoted, that 'We must seek and probe for a Message everywhere'. More recently Richard Levin has delivered what ought to be crippling blows at literary Puritans and thematists of the 'This-play-makes-a-statement-about' school. The chapter can well conclude with a sentence from his 'Third Thoughts on Thematics': 'The task of criticism, I believe, is to lead us back into the play, to enrich the experience which it was designed to produce, and the greatest disadvantage of thematism is that it leads us away'.[7] Let us indeed go back to the plays and read with imagination what was written with imagination: Shakespeare's art is greater than critical moralising.

[7] *Modern Language Review*, 70 (July 1975), pp. 81–96.

5

Good Husbandry

The intention of this study is to lay particular emphasis on Shakespeare's creative energy and in previous chapters examples have been grouped together to illustrate how, in some plays, a sudden surge of creative power has pushed stories out of line and in others creative vitality has sought new channels when its initial flow has been obstructed. The imaginative vigour and comprehensiveness which transform scenes of 'conversation' into great works of creation has also been noted. The plays to be considered in this chapter are grouped together because they are all, to a greater or lesser extent, affected by a situation in which resourcefulness and invention and the free play of imagination are of necessity restricted. The treatment of history, ancient or modern, imposes an inevitable discipline and the dramatist can no longer claim the free hand which fiction allows him. Nevertheless, he needs to shape and point his material dramatically and early treatments of English history show Shakespeare to be much impressed by the need to give distinct patterns to the rambling sequences of historical event. Both *Richard III* and *Richard II* are controlled by strikingly formal patterns, the workings of Divine Justice in *Richard III*, the turn of Fortune's Wheel in *Richard II* with, set against this, the counter-movement of audience sympathy as Richard and Bolingbroke change places from high to low. Within the design of *Richard II* the character of the king takes shape and enriches the tragic design. In *Richard III* the character of the king has a vitality and zest which tend to strain against the simple scheme of crime and punishment and he has to be pushed back into place somewhat roughly at the end. The development of Richard in this play provides an early example of the creative surge which will disturb the even run of *The Merchant of Venice* and *Measure for Measure*, but Richard is kept on a tighter rein than Shylock and there can be no question of modifying the story to accommodate him as with Isabella.

Some feeling of restraint, or of problems not quite satisfactorily

solved, influences critical judgement of these plays.[1] But however it
may be elsewhere, when he writes the two parts of *Henry IV*,
Shakespeare manages to make history his own. In these plays he
combines a masterly arrangement of source material with a special
kind of imaginative responsiveness and the result gives to both parts
a unique radiance among his treatments of English history.

The nature of Shakespeare's materials in the *Henry IV* plays and
his treatment of them have been often and amply commented on.
The point to be focused here is the way in which Shakespeare finds
an entry into the historical matter through which he can add a new
element of imaginative life. *Richard III* and *Richard II* are very
clever plays and the genius of a great poet and dramatist is clearly to
be seen in them but the contrasts and the interweaving of material
in the two parts of *Henry IV* are even cleverer while the plays also
contain elements which require a different kind of commentary
altogether. Act II of part i is a case in point. This is a wonderfully
rich Act establishing very firmly the play's contrasts and correspond-
ences between affairs of state and Eastcheap, between Hotspur and
Hal, between Falstaff and Henry IV, between Hal's time of irresponsibility and his forthcoming kingship, and doing so—here lies the
immediate point—with a vitality and inventiveness that draws freely
on intimate knowledge of a wide variety of kinds and conditions of
English characters. The special imaginative quality of the *Henry IV*
plays depends very largely upon this, the dramatist's exploitation of
his own relationship to the history he is reconstructing. These men
of the past are his countrymen, he knows by right of birth their
ways of speech, their social gradations, how they talk and behave.
He makes them contemporaries, fusing the life of his own time with
the inert stuff of the past and creating out of their encounters dialogues which, like the conversation pieces discussed in the last chapter, are alive in every syllable with a vibrant sense of 'felt life'. The
richness of texture of these exchanges is a source of immense delight
as Shakespeare performs, within the compass of an historical drama,
that distinctive act of creation which characterises his handling of the
more malleable material of fiction.

In Act II of part i we climb the social ladder, beginning in the
inn yard at Rochester with talk of the bots and the fleas and poor

[1] See for example, the essay on *Richard II* in A. P. Rossiter's *Angel
with Horns* (London, 1961).

Robin Ostler who died of the high price of oats and left disorder behind him. Gadshill and the Chamberlain take over the dialogue and are rather more sophisticated in their badinage, each anxious to keep his end up, Gadshill hinting mysteriously at his powerful associates, the Chamberlain trying by his smart rejoinders to keep on equal terms, and presenting himself as a wit. We then move much higher up the social scale to the Prince and Falstaff and their company. Falstaff's assumption of righteous indignation at the dishonourable conduct of the thieves he robs with lifts the humour of the Act on to a different level and his execration upon Hal: 'Hang thy self in thine own heir-apparent garters!' gives a new zest to the hanging joke which Gadshill and the Chamberlain laboured for rather lengthily. The scene of the double robbery is followed by the entry of Hotspur reading a letter of excuse from a lord whose support in rebellion he has solicited. While Hal is playing the fool on Gadshill, Hotspur is plotting war. The scene reminds us of this and also, by introducing Percy's wife, it fills out the picture of him, preparing us to find matter for tears in his death. The language of this scene is characterised by its intimate informality as the language of the carriers, and of Gadshill and the Chamberlain, and Falstaff and Hal has been. It seems, as we read or listen, that we are catching exactly the tone and the level of familiar conversation that all the speakers would adopt according to rank and relationship. The scenes draw fullness of life out of the rich particularity of the language. What the characters say creates a three-dimensional world full of properties and circumstances. Its business fills the speakers' thoughts and so lively is the treatment that we may be more than half-inclined to believe that its affairs continue when the actors have passed out of our sight.

Racy vivacity of language is not, of course, a novel introduction into the *Henry IV* plays. *Love's Labour's Lost*, one of the very earliest of the plays, is full of linguistic exuberance and Moth fantasticates adroitly on a basis of contemporary allusion—see Act III, sc. i, 9–24 and the notes to the Arden edition which provide the underpinning of topical reference. But in *Henry IV* such passages serve a more sophisticated purpose than to provide solo performances for individuals (though they may do that as well). They extend and deepen the lives of the characters and they bridge the gulf that separates the past from Shakespeare's present. For us his present is now also the past but the vitality of the world he creates for his people gives a ring to their voices even yet and continues to sustain their undiminished and unfading life.

The next transition is to the Boar's Head, with the Prince rejoicing that he has learnt the language of drawers. The whole Act, as Shakespeare ranges up and down the social scale, embodies a demonstration of the social discriminations implicit in language and it is appropriate that Prince Hal, who is to represent the whole nation in his own person, should master its tongues.

> The Prince but studies his companions
> Like a strange tongue. . .   ,

Warwick will tell the King in part ii (Act IV, sc. iv, 68–9) but Hal is studying language itself in part i, whether it be that of the sadly limited Francis or that of 'the Hotspur of the north, he that kills me six or seven dozen of Scots at a breakfast, washes his hands and says to his wife, 'Fie upon this quiet life, I want work'. With the entry of Falstaff in this scene, we come to the radiating centre of this area of the play's imaginative vitality. The verbal energy of previous scenes is intensified in him and the wide scope of social and topical reference already covered is further extended and animated. His preposterous account of Gad's Hill is prefaced by his equally preposterous lamentations over the degeneration of the species: 'if manhood, good manhood, be not forgot upon the face of the earth, then I am a shotten herring; there lives not three good men unhanged in England, and one of them is fat and grows old, God help the while, a bad world I say'. Falstaff makes of his fiction a splendid game in which the denotative quality of language is cast to the winds in favour of its use as extravagant gesture. Two men, four men, seven men, nine men, eleven men, some of them seen to be dressed in Kendal Green on a pitch black night: he goes on inflating his lies to bursting point and caps them with a shameless appeal to rectitude and probity: 'Is not the truth the truth?' Then with great dignity, and remembering the English lanes in late summer, he refuses to be bullied into explaining himself: 'If reasons were as plentiful as blackberries, I would give no man a reason upon compulsion'. The whole scene is full of exuberant references—Falstaff's claim that 'When I was about thy years, Hal, I was not an eagle's talon in the waist. I could have crept into any alderman's thumb-ring'; his description of Glendower: 'he of Wales that gave Amamon the bastinado and made Lucifer cuckold, and swore the devil his true liegeman upon the cross of a Welsh hook . . .'; his measure of the effects of rebellion: 'you may buy land now as cheap as stinking mackerel'. The whole wonderful sequence culminates with the play-acting, Falstaff as king parodying Lyly, and perhaps others, in mockery of regal grandeur, and descending bathetically to: 'Tell me, thou naughty varlet, tell me where hast thou been this month?'

The jokes, the parodies, the references, all the linguistic bravura of this act, derive from observation of shades of speech and social nuances and an awareness and enjoyment of the lives, habits, interests, reading and attitudes of Shakespeare's countrymen. Shakespeare employs for the first time, in this history play, the technique in dialogue which he will use to such splendid effect in comedies which follow. It will enable him to use a minimal story, to sustain interest, and even to intensify it, in scenes where the story stops altogether, to grip our attention by the interplay of personalities simply being themselves and by the penetrative insight which endows their speech with individual life. This insight extends not only to individuals but to the relations between them also, so that a web of multiple significances is woven round their conversations, its threads composed of every shade of meaning: though the story may appear to be stationary in such scenes our understanding of the action grows immeasurably by these means. We should notice that Shakespeare found his way to this manifestation of his creative genius in seeking to give himself room for free composition within the restrictions of historical drama. Growth takes place because Shakespeare submits himself to pressure. Some such observation might almost sum up his whole career, for he continually ventured on new undertakings and, as often, found responses which astonish us to the demands he was called upon to meet.

Pressure is evidently responsible also for some of the finest effects of part ii. In this play Shakespeare is to some extent engaged in an exercise of variation and amplification. Its major interests, the relations between Prince Hal and his father and between Hal and Falstaff, the consequences of the murder of Richard II working themselves out in rebellion throughout the reign of Henry IV, and the progress of Prince Hal towards kingship, have all been richly developed in part i. The material has ranged widely and has also

been drawn skilfully together. Hal's early statement, that he intends
when the time is ripe to win golden opinions by his unlooked-for
reformation, provides a clear, firm, major story-line which the
audience can hold on to while Shakespeare exploits the opportunities
which he finds both at court and at Eastcheap. The multiple interests
and contrasts all draw to a common point in the Battle of Shrews-
bury where Hal saves his father's life and says his farewell to Falstaff,
who is apparently dead on the field:

> O, I should have a heavy miss of thee,
> If I were much in love with vanity.
>   (V, iv, 105–6)

His reputation is restored, Falstaff is put aside, and the story line has
been fully worked out.

Part ii goes back over the same areas, varying the treatment and
drawing out some implications of the situations for more extended
treatment. Hal appears to be back in a pre-Shrewsbury situation,
suspected of disloyalty to his father and neglecting his responsibilities
in the kingdom. This theme, first broached in Act II, sc. ii, is then
reintroduced and given a splendid culmination in Act IV, sc. iv,
where the clearing of misunderstandings and final reconciliation
between father and son is more extensively developed and more
fully orchestrated than in the comparable scene in part i (Act III,
sc. ii). If this is amplification, the treatment of rebellion is an example
of variation. The rebellion of the Archbishop of York does not come
to resolution through conflict as Hotspur's did. Instead, the King on
the one side and the Archbishop on the other discuss a philosophy
of history and the ethics of rebellion (Act III, sc. i and Act IV, sc. i)
but the only movement which takes place is Prince John's arrest of
the Archbishop and his associates after a peace has been concluded.
The material connected with Falstaff also undergoes variation.
Falstaff is given some fresh companions but he is allowed less time
with Prince Hal than in part i. The Lord Chief Justice is introduced
as a new foil to him and his sense of public duty serves to highlight
the irresponsibility of Eastcheap. As for Prince Hal, his earlier high
spirits are shadowed in part ii. He finally comes to the throne and
repudiates Falstaff in fact, as he had done in the play-acting of
part i, Act II, sc. iv. He had dismissed him from his life also in
Act V, sc. iv, when he thought Falstaff had been killed at Shrews-

bury, but the new king who has adopted the Lord Chief Justice as a father-figure (V, ii, 118) cannot afford the expression of private feeling that the Prince of Wales, alone as he thinks, on the battle-field can indulge:

> Poor Jack farewell!
> I could have better spar'd a better man.
> (pt i, V, iv, 103-4).

The language of the great men in part ii develops themes and tropes in moods of reflection and lacks the sharpness of men engaged in action, which characterises part i. Henry IV takes the favourite and much-handled topic of sleep and raises it to a new power in Act III, sc. i. Prince Hal treats the old theme of the pains of greatness in Act IV, sc. v. Falstaff also has his reflections—on sherris-sack and the wonderful ways of Justice Shallow. Splendid or entertaining or simply interesting as the meditations, arguments and set-pieces of the play are, and clever though the variation and amplification of already worked material is, there is also some risk of loss of animation in part ii. Mistress Quickly, Doll Tearsheet and other new Boar's Head characters partly insure against this but the play is moving inexorably towards Hal's kingship and the shadow of approaching doom hangs over Eastcheap. 'I am old, I am old', says Falstaff (II, iv, 261), and Doll 'comes blubbered' to say good-bye (377). In the light of things to come, it is evident that not very much more can be made of Eastcheap as a source of vitality in the play.

Into all this Shakespeare injects a totally different element. After two Acts of the tight-drawn and unrefreshing world of high politics and London humours, Henry IV comforts himself with the thought of entering a cleaner, fresher moral climate one day:

> were these inward wars once out of hand,
> We would, dear Lords, unto the Holy Land.
> (III, i, 107-8)

With no interlude and no warning, and with Henry's voice still in our ears, we pass at once to Gloucestershire and the very different accents of Justice Shallow, the king of his little community, with his chief courtier, Justice Silence, his band of henchmen and even (as it will turn out in Act V, sc. i) his miniature Hotspur in Davy, who stands up for William Visor of Woncot, as Harry Percy did for

Mortimer, and claims, as the Percys did, that services rendered should suffice to buy his friend's freedom. But the acerbities and jealousies of court are missing in Gloucestershire. Benignity and complacency fill their place, together with a very slow and ponderous intellectual machinery:

> SHALLOW: Come on, come on, come on: give me your hand, sir; give me your hand, sir; an early stirrer, by the rood! And how doth my good cousin Silence?
>
> SILENCE: Good morrow, good cousin Shallow.
>
> SHALLOW: And how doth my cousin, your bed-fellow? and your fairest daughter and mine, my god-daughter Ellen?
>
> SILENCE: Alas, a black woosel, cousin Shallow!
>
> SHALLOW: By yea and no, sir. I dare say my cousin William is become a good scholar; he is at Oxford still, is he not?
>
> SILENCE: Indeed, sir, to my cost.
>
> SHALLOW: A must then to the Inns o' Court shortly...
>
> (III, ii, 1–12)

In a moment we are in a world thoroughly known, intimately understood, all its perspectives familiar. There is no pace in Justice Shallow's thinking. One idea has to be thoroughly masticated before he can start on the next one. But within his little round of notions he has the confidence of great familiarity and before long we are confidently familiar with them too. We know what he is like and what he was like, what the circumstances and activities which made up his life are, and what the sum of experience which composes his small stock of ideas. The Gloucestershire scenes, with all that goes into them, constitute a great enrichment of *Henry IV* part ii. They fill out the picture of England by adding the countryside, its way of life and its social levels, to the more sophisticated life and characters depicted elsewhere. They show Falstaff at his most unscrupulous. They also show him old. His rebuke to the Lord Chief Justice in Act I, 'You that are old consider not the capacities of us that are young' (I, ii, 166–8), is comic impudence there, but he cannot swagger out of his years in Gloucestershire where the two old men claim him as a crony. The contrast with this slow-witted but firmly rooted pair also brings to our conscious attention how many of the normal accompaniments of old age he lacks, wife, family, home, friends of his own age and station:

> my way of life
> Is fall'n into the sear, the yellow leaf;
> And that which should accompany old age,
> As honour, love, obedience, troops of friends,
> I must not look to have. . .

The words are Macbeth's and Falstaff makes no such acknowledgement. He notes what Shallow has, in order to assess what he can get out of him, but the point that Shallow is a solid man in a solid background and that he himself is not does not escape him.

The scenes deepen the play in many ways. They remove Falstaff from London just at the crucial time when the old king dies and the Prince succeeds, and it is in Gloucestershire that he receives the news that his 'tender lambkin now is King'. His arrival in the streets 'stained with travel, and sweating with desire to see him'—and all ignorant of the great change that has taken place in Hal during his absence—sets up the special drama of the rejection scene. Master Shallow is with him, come, like the country mouse, to see the wonders of the town, and producing a countryman's shrewd comment on what passes before him. 'This that you have heard was but a colour', says Falstaff, with an attempt at his usual bravado, to which Shallow replies: 'A colour that I fear you will die in, Sir John' (V, v, 88–9).

All the effects of the Shallow scenes become possible because of the infusion of particular detail in the way they are treated: the rhythms of speech, the references, the manners. Taking Falstaff to Gloucestershire is a great tonic in a play where the London air threatens to become suffocating and where the devices of amplification and variation of material are being pressed hard. Gloucestershire provides Shakespeare with an unworked vein and gives fresh stimulus to his imagination. The vitality and richness of the result denote a great creative act, as a fount of fresh life springs up in the play and, as Shakespeare sees the possibilities of it, this surge of fresh life serves the whole drama.

In *Henry IV*, parts i and ii the free creative imagination finds room for itself within the framework of a history play. Some of the experience which has been gained will be put to use in the comedies which follow but if we look to see comparable effects in a history play, we have to look further ahead.

'Shakespeare does seem to be amazingly at his ease'. These are Granville-Barker's words and the play he is discussing is *Antony and Cleopatra*.[2] Granville-Barker goes on: 'He brings in characters lavishly, flings Plutarch into dialogue; his verse is at its supplest, we are hardly conscious of the convention, and he shifts to prose and back again without a jar . . . though endowed with but a line or two, the characters never fail to come to life'. 'Amazingly at his ease', with creative vitality powerfully flowing: all the more amazing when we consider that the conditions which gave their special quality to Act II of *Henry IV* part i and the Gloucester scenes in part ii do not obtain here. The scene is ancient Rome or ancient Egypt, the material is not the recent history of the dramatist's native land but derived from Plutarch with no possible point of intimate contact in Shakespeare's own experience. The technique which Shakespeare brings to bear, however, is in some respects strikingly like that which he employed in the *Henry IV* plays.

In the first place, he employs contrast, as he has done in the English plays. Antony is pulled between the worlds of Rome and Alexandria as Prince Hal was between court and Eastcheap and, as with Hal in the earlier plays, part of him responds to both. *Henry IV* part i opens with a court scene followed by a Falstaff scene and marks its opposites in the first lines of each: 'So shaken as we are, so wan with care', the King begins, while Falstaff lazily enquires the time of day: 'Now, Hal, what time of day is it, lad?' Time pressess upon the King and his company but, as the Prince points out, in Falstaff's world the clock is superfluous, for Falstaff has no calls on his time and no responsibilities to discharge. *Antony and Cleopatra* is even more economical in establishing the poles between which it will move. Rome, in the persons of Demetrius and Philo, has the first word, introducing Antony:

> The triple pillar of the world transform'd
> Into a strumpet's fool. . .

Antony then speaks for himself, claiming a boundless love of infinite riches. A few lines later, the opposing values are brought together in sharp conflict:

> Let Rome in Tiber melt, and the wide arch
> Of the rang'd empire fall! Here is my space.

[2] *Prefaces to Shakespeare* (Batsford edn., 1963), iii, p. 4.

In this pull of worlds, Cleopatra seeks to draw Antony away from what moral law calls 'duty' and she deploys the extensive range of her skills to keep him under her influence, sparring with him, teasing him, as in the past she has laughed with and at him, revelling with him, and just occasionally allowing warmth of feeling to express itself in speech. Though she is herself a ruler, the role she plays is akin to that of the Lord of Misrule whose part is an element in Falstaff's make-up. What she does in holding Antony from his Roman self, he does in relation to Hal and both exercise their wit to keep their partners amused: 'I will devise matter enough out of this Shallow', Falstaff says, 'to keep Prince Harry in continual laughter the wearing out of six fashions' (*Henry IV* part ii, V, i, 72–8). Falstaff and Cleopatra have in fact, much in common. The quick shifts and turns of her wit which, for example, dazzle Antony in Act I, sc. iii, are comparable to the adroitness with which Falstaff shifts his ground in encounter after encounter. 'Sirrah, what humour's the Prince of?' Doll asks him in part ii, Act II, sc. iv, and Falstaff replies: 'A good shallow young fellow; a would have made a good pantler, a would ha' chipped bread well' (226–8). When the Prince throws his words back at him and threatens vengeance, Falstaff turns the situation quite round by his reply: 'I dispraised him before the wicked that the wicked might not fall in love with him; in which doing I have done the part of a careful friend and a true subject'. Compare with that Cleopatra's capacity, in a more extreme situation, to make a rapid change of front. In Act V, sc. ii, she prostrates herself before Caesar, positively grovels at his feet, flattering him with a sense of his power and even the illusion of magnanimity; and when he goes, she calmly speaks the assessment of the situation that her cool brain has been making during the emotional display of the preceding interview:

> He words me, girls, he words me, that I should not
> Be noble to myself. . .

The quick wits of Falstaff and Cleopatra incessantly devise roles for themselves and for others, shifting from one guise to another dexterously and audaciously. This makes a large part of their attractiveness, constituting that 'infinite variety' which custom does not, and cannot, stale.

Cleopatra's physical vitality and her sexual magnetism seem

inexhaustible but age does wither Falstaff. He had once bitterly
resented Hal's joke about the apple-johns (part ii, II, iv, 1–9) but age
grows on him willy-nilly in *Henry IV* part ii and when Hal strips
him of his hopes and pretensions in Act V, a 'dry, round, old,
withered knight' is what he becomes. *Antony and Cleopatra* gives
us the other ending, the alternative resolution of the conflict between
the worlds of duty and irresponsibility that both plays set up. Where
Hal repudiated Falstaff, Antony chooses Cleopatra and, though both
Antony and Cleopatra die for it, in their deaths they find a glory
which leaves Caesar, who has won all the battles, looking curiously
like a loser. The tone of the Egyptian world is as 'low' as the world
of Eastcheap and the count against Antony and Cleopatra personally,
on moral grounds, is at least as heavy as that against Falstaff, but the
sense that there are values other than those of power and public life
is allowed its full development in the later play. Nothing is ex-
tenuated, nothing left out in this account of two middle-aged,
much-experienced and much-tarnished lovers but they are given
magnificence at their endings. 'The end crowns all', and for the
Elizabethans the manner of death stamped the quality of the life.
In *Antony and Cleopatra* Shakespeare gives Falstaff's case that
full statement which would not be in place in *Henry IV* and which
can there be only hinted at. The plays, in fact, offer reversed images
of a similar situation: in the *Henry IV* plays the values of the great
world have pre-eminence and Falstaff must go down, 'true piece of
gold' though in some ways he is; in *Antony and Cleopatra* it is the
world of discipline and order whose claims can make themselves
felt only obliquely—as when we see the grief and shame which
Antony's 'strong Egyptian fetters' impose upon Octavia, for
instance. Otherwise, 'great Caesar' stands as 'ass unpolicied' in
contrast to the 'lass unparalleled' and her lover, whose death leaves
the world 'no better than a sty'.

The connections between the plays, represented by the system of
contrasts which both plays employ and the common opposition
which activates both of them, seem to have stimulated Shakespeare,
consciously or unconsciously, to a similarity of manner. The relaxed
conversations of *Henry IV* parts i and ii have their counterparts in
Antony and Cleopatra, in Egyptian scenes, in scenes where Romans
discuss Egypt, and in that most 'Egyptian' of Roman scenes, Act II,
sc. vii, on Pompey's galley, when Antony and Enobarbus teach

Egyptian revelry to Lepidus and Octavius. Neither is an apt pupil, though Lepidus shows plentiful goodwill.

The effects in such scenes in *Antony and Cleopatra* are secured, inevitably, by different means from those in *Henry IV*. The particularity of local reference and the authenticity of accent which help Shakespeare to create a sense of three-dimensional life in the English plays are out of the question here. Instead he depends on topics which are ageless and placeless, equally up-to-date whether in ancient Egypt or modern London (of his day or ours)—sex, drink, and the joviality induced by even temporary camaraderie. The sex, the revelry, the comradeship, are here in a context which enlivens them far beyond the commonplace and gives them special edge, for the focus of the sex interest is the woman whom Enobarbus describes in Act II, sc. ii, the comradeship is a reminder of campaigns fought by Antony, a Mars among men, and the revelry associates the two of them in 'That time-O times!' when they 'did sleep day out of countenance and made the night light with drinking' (II, ii, 180–2). To find room for creative freedom of the kind so splendidly exemplified in the scenes of the *Henry IV* plays which have been discussed, Shakespeare did not need in the later play to make openings in his material, for Plutarch provides abundant episode and detail and touches of character. In his handling of it all, however, the assurance derived from his successes in *Henry IV* seems to have played a considerable part. The creative activity, which produced the scenes between Falstaff and Hal and the Gloucestershire scenes, imbues wide areas of *Antony and Cleopatra* as he sets about giving us a sense of the different colourings life may take when seen through different eyes. There is no psychological struggle in Act II, sc. iii, when Antony abruptly decides to return to Egypt, despite his promises to Octavia: Shakespeare's interest does not lie in the choice itself but in the character of the two worlds he must choose between and, especially, in the quality of amoral Egypt. The 'amazing ease' with which he presents it all, the confident familiarity with which he treats character and conversation, harks back to those other historical plays of ten years before, *Henry IV*, parts i and ii.

In Act I, sc. ii of *Antony and Cleopatra*, Enobarbus acts the role of witty and bawdy fool to the sombre Antony. His commentaries on Fulvia's death and Cleopatra's anticipated grief if Antony leaves Egypt show vivacity and ingenuity enough to have commended him to Falstaff and Hal. His comment that 'the tears live in an onion that should water this sorrow' could even be one of Falstaff's own sayings for it has the same racy use of common experience to enliven his point. But Antony stops him: 'No more light answers'. The exchange in its small way embodies a characteristic of this play, where transitions from 'light' to serious, from high to 'low' are continually being made. The easy familiarity of some scenes or passages sets the uneasy formality of others in sharp contrast; the indignities of language and behaviour at times mean that, when the tone rises, the heights to which we are swept may be dizzying. What Shakespeare discovered in *Henry IV* about ways of developing contrast, in tone as well as situation, he used again in *Antony and Cleopatra* for effects so original that critics baffle themselves in their attempts to categorise the play; but one of the means by which the effects are achieved may be traced to that extension which took place when Shakespeare grappled with the problems of historical drama years before.

To bring out what *Antony and Cleopatra* and the *Henry IV* plays have in common seems to be illuminating and the comparison reinforces the point made earlier that Shakespeare felt the need to move with particular care when working on historical material Having found a valuable method of working in *Henry IV*, he makes use of a similar pattern and technique again. Another pair of history plays, both Roman, show him once more finding a pattern and re-using it. The similarities and divergencies in the handling of material in *Julius Caesar* and *Coriolanus* will enable us to take a further look at Shakespeare's good husbandry when his treatment of material is restrained by the fact that he is working with what is, or purports to be, history.

Both *Julius Caesar* and *Coriolanus* are more severely Roman than *Antony and Cleopatra*. Egypt and Cleopatra made it possible for Shakespeare to develop the 'Falstaff vein' and to employ the technique of informal conversation which he mastered in the *Henry IV* plays. But *Julius Caesar* and *Coriolanus* allow of no Falstaffs and, as for easy conversation, two scenes pinpoint the change of tone. In *Henry IV* part i, Act II, sc. iii, Lady Percy reproaches Hotspur with keeping from her the secret which troubles his sleep and absorbs all his attention. These are great persons but the scene takes us into their intimate personal lives. Between themselves they are Kate and

Harry, he teasing, she wheedling, making love to each other with mock insults and mock threats. If we put alongside it the scene in *Julius Caesar* where Portia similarly protests that Brutus is keeping from her some knowledge which is evidently of great importance to him (Act II, sc. i), the contrast is at once apparent. The *Julius Caesar* scene may be moving in its context but these are not approachable figures who speak as any of us may speak. In this closest domestic moment, they retain a high and stately dignity. 'Upon my knees', says Portia:

> I charm you, by my once commended beauty,
> By all your vows of love, and that great vow
> Which did incorporate and make us one,
> That you unfold to me, your self, your half,
> Why you are heavy. . .
> $$(270-5)$$

What worlds away this is from Lady Percy! 'Out, you mad-headed ape!' she exclaims:

> A weasel hath not such a deal of spleen
> As you are toss'd with. In faith,
> I'll know your business, Harry, that I will.
> $$(75-7)$$

Coriolanus is in some ways a more personal play than *Julius Caesar* and it has one scene of agreeable informality when the ladies sit together with Virgilia sewing and Valeria chattering like a good neighbour (Act I, sc. iii). The scene has considerable effectiveness in a context dominated by male aggression in war and politics but, like the Brutus-Portia episode in *Julius Caesar*, it lacks the rich vitality, the intimate familiarity of language and manners that the Hotspur/ Kate scene has. In both *Julius Caesar* and *Coriolanus* Shakespeare is working within a situation which offers neither the opportunities of his native English scene nor the outlet for uninhibited creativity of a similar kind which Egypt provided. It is of the greatest interest to see how he sets about dealing with the situation.

In effect, he identifies among the events and people provided for him by his sources four areas of interest: a political confrontation, the situation of a noble figure surrounded by less noble characters, a particular personal opposition—one man opposed to and contrasted with another—and a tension between the personal life and the public figure. These interests are common to both plays and underlie the surface characteristics.

The basic political confrontation in *Julius Caesar* between Caesarism and Republicanism is clear enough. The questions are raised whether the natural tendency of the state is towards government by one man and, if such government develops, whether it should be resisted—if so, by what means. But the political issues, sharply focussed though they are at moments, do not dominate the other interests. The particular personal situation of Brutus is in the limelight throughout and his superior moral nature is emphasised, from the beginning when Cassius seeks his support for the plot against Caesar to the end when Antony speaks of him as 'the noblest Roman of them all'. Cassius, working on Brutus to induce him to give his name and prestige to the conspiracy, sees very well the difference in stature between them. '. . . it is meet', he remarks sardonically to himself:

> That noble minds keep ever with their likes;
> For who so firm that cannot be seduced?

> (I, ii, 309–11)

But there is no 'like' for Brutus to keep with. He is essentially a lonely figure, surrounded by political calculators who disappoint, disillusion and almost embitter him. Cassius, in particular, functions as his foil and, in the early part of the play, Cassius's unscrupulousness is stressed in contradistinction to Brutus's fine moral sense. Later, when the relative standing of the two men has been firmly established, Shakespeare allows some shading into the picture. Cassius's pragmatism is supported by shrewd judgement and he is not without warmth of heart. Brutus's idealism, on the other hand, is dangerously remote from practical realities and his conscious rectitude comes at times perilously close to self-righteousness. Cassius has begun as a manipulator figure, one of an important company among Shakespeare's *dramatis personae*, but he loses the role to Mark Antony who takes over from him as manager of events. Both Cassius and Antony contrast sharply with Brutus and both pay tribute to a purer nature than their own, Cassius by his anxiety to enlist Brutus's support at the beginning and his continued respect for him, Mark Antony by his words over his dead body: but Antony does not pay his tribute till he has destroyed Brutus.

The tension between the claims of private life and the obligations, real or fancied, of a public figure, is a feature of the treatment of both Caesar and Brutus. Caesar acts and speaks as a man become a legend in his own life-time, who has come himself to believe that he is immune to the weaknesses of other men:

> I rather tell thee what is to be feared,
> Than what I fear; for always I am Caesar.
>
> (I, ii, 211–12)

But the claim to more than human strength is immediately countered by an exposure of his vulnerability to human failings: 'Come on my right hand, for this ear is deaf' (213). As he is a private man, Caesar is susceptible to the influence of others, Calphurnia for example, and capable of affection for Brutus and Mark Antony and of good-fellowship towards the conspirators when they call to escort him to the Capitol. As he sees himself in his public role, he disowns his common kinship with the rest of men and claims a distinction which sets him apart from humanity:

> I am constant as the Northern Star
> Of whose true-fixed and resting quality
> There is no fellow in the firmament.
> The skies are painted with unnumbered sparks,
> They are all fire and every one doth shine;
> But there's but one in all doth hold his place.
> So in the world; 'tis furnished well with men,
> And men are flesh and blood, and apprehensive;
> Yet in the number I do know but one
> That unassailable holds on his rank,
> Unshaked of motion; and that I am he ...
>
> (III, i, 60–70)

In this speech Caesar reaches the peak of *hubris* and claims most completely to be impervious to the shifts and changings of mortality. Metellus Cimber has pleaded for his brother and been spurned with scorn. As Caesar rejects the promptings of common feeling, Brutus and Cassius join their appeals to those of Metellus, but Caesar glories in disowning humanity—'Hence! Wilt thou lift up Olympus?' His mortality is immediately brought home to him by the daggers of the conspirators and Caesar, now no more but e'en a man, falls, with words for Brutus, whom he loved, on his lips.

As for Brutus himself, his hesitation over joining the conspiracy balances between his experience of Caesar the man: 'I know no personal cause to spurn at him' (II, i, 11)—and a speculative fear that, once crowned, he will 'Change his nature'. Before he can join the conspiracy to kill, Brutus must see Caesar not as an individual but as an abstraction of self-centred power:

> lowliness is young ambition's ladder,
> Whereto the climber-upward turns his face;
> But when he once attains the upmost round,
> He then unto the ladder turns his back,
> Looks in the clouds, scorning the base degrees
> By which he did ascend. So Caesar may.
>
> (II, i, 22–7)

As he says to the conspirators a little later in the same scene:

> O, that we then could come by Caesar's spirit,
> And not dismember Caesar!
>
> (169–70)

but since that cannot be done, he dehumanises Caesar in his own mind as far as he can:

> think him as a serpent's egg,
> Which, hatch'd, would as his kind grow mischievous,
> And kill him in the shell.
>
> (32–4)

That Brutus is not naturally an inhumane man is made plain to us by his relations with Portia his wife, with Lucius his boy and, in the last scene just before his death, with his companions. Yet he deliberately makes himself into an instrument of execution, rejecting the claims of friendship and compassion for the sake of enforcing a philosophy of government. Both Brutus and Caesar put the claims of common humanity lower than those of the ideas which possess them.

The play raises questions of political morality but issues of individual morals lie perhaps closer to its heart. We are not finally told whether Brutus is a greater or a lesser man for his sacrifice of private feelings to a concept of public duty, any more than we are offered a decisive verdict on Caesar or Caesarism or arrive at a black and white judgement on Cassius or the ambivalent Mark Antony. The four areas of interest which Shakespeare has identified have provided the ground on which he can set out character and situation with his usual extraordinary imaginative insight. The result is that we in turn are stimulated to greater comprehensiveness of understanding though, less myriad-minded than he, we feel the compulsion to narrow to a conclusion, to arrive at 'right answers' somewhere embedded in the play. Much critical comment seeks such answers by reckoning up points for or against Brutus or Caesar, but it would seem more useful, instead, to concentrate on the nature of the imaginative activity. It is not of the same kind as in *Henry IV* or *Antony and Cleopatra* for, although conflict between personal and public roles is a major element in *Julius Caesar*, we are given only a few inconclusive glimpses into the private recesses of personality. Yet, though the characters are somewhat stiffly posed, Shakespeare has given them great scenes, the murder of Caesar and Antony's speech in the market-place most strikingly amongst them, but other smaller episodes are also vividly dramatised. It is into this dramatic rendering of the sequence of events that imaginative energy seems principally to have gone, so that it can be said of *Julius Caesar* that the characters derive their vitality and interest from the actions they are involved in. In other plays, action matters less, for the characters have within themselves a life which spreads all round and beyond the record of what occurs; so that we can believe that Falstaff, for example, lives in scenes that we are not shown. An attempt has been made in earlier pages of this chapter to identify some of the means by which this effect is achieved.

Yet if Brutus's Rome does not have the depth of perspective of Eastcheap or of Justice Shallow's Gloucestershire, this is not to say that Shakespeare gives no solidity to his scene. There is a good deal of reference to the past and tribunes and plebs help to people the city. A perhaps even more effective touch in persuading us that continuing life is lived in these streets is the scene (Act I, sc. ii) in which Casca reports on Mark Antony's offer of the crown to Caesar, Cassius invites him to supper 'to-morrow', and Brutus remembers what the 'blunt fellow' was like when he went to school. There is little scope for this kind of thing in *Julius Caesar* but to eke out what there is, Shakespeare draws on another resource.

He cannot freely create a background for his story out of intimate

first-hand knowledge of habit and idiom but he can and does read
Plutarch alertly and responsively. How imagination operates on
these materials to add further dimensions to action immediately in
hand can be illustrated by two small but telling examples.

When, in Act III, sc. i, Antony enters to the conspirators after the
murder of Caesar, he first tests their intentions concerning himself
and then he shakes hands with them, naming them one by one as he
does so:

> First, Marcus Brutus, will I shake with you;
> Next Caius Cassius, do I take your hand;
> Now Decius Brutus, yours; now yours, Metullus;
> Yours Cinna;—and my valiant Casca, yours;
> Though last, not least in love, yours, good Trebonius.
>
> (185-90)

Why does he bestow the epithets on Casca and Trebonius, but
simply name the others? The answers are in the play but they are
more obvious in Plutarch. 'Valiant' Casca was the first to strike at
Caesar—from behind his back; Trebonius did not strike at all but
led Antony out of the way so that he might not defend Caesar
against his murderers. 'Though last not least in love': the words
become a threat when all the circumstances, as Plutarch describes
them, enact themselves in the reader's or audience's mind as clearly
they did in Shakespeare's.

In the same scene occurs a second speech which reference to
Plutarch fills in, to remarkable effect. 'Friends am I with you all,
and love you all', says Antony:

> Upon this hope, that you shall give me reasons
> Why and wherein Caesar was dangerous,

to which Brutus replies:

> BRUTUS: Or else were this a savage spectacle.
> Our reasons are so full of good regard
> That were you, Antony, the son of Caesar,
> You should be satisfied.
>
> ANTONY: That's all I seek.
>
> (221-7)

We should register a pregnant pause before Antony's reply and we
should see, on stage or in our mind's eye, the conspirators exchang-
ing startled glances behind Brutus's back. At the beginning of his

Life of Marcus Brutus, Plutarch explains at some length the circumstances of the love affair between Caesar and Servilia, Brutus's
mother, and refers to the story, well-known in Rome he suggests,
that Brutus was born 'while their love was at the hottest' and that
Caesar believed him to be his own son. Shakespeare suppresses this
story[3] as he suppresses or emphasises a number of matters relating to
Brutus in order to build him up as 'the noblest Roman of them all',
sans peur et sans reproche. Only at this point in the play does he
allow reference to the possibility that Brutus may have conspired
against and murdered, not simply his friend and leader, but his
father. The reference must certainly be made in innocence by Brutus,
but for those in the know (and the actors playing the conspirators
should be among them) his words will give an extra twist to the
personal/political conflict and connect present events with a remem-
bered past. In the immediate situation on stage, if the others show
by their reactions that they are aware that sensitive ground has just
been touched on, Brutus's patent innocence will make a point about
his remoteness, for good or ill, from common knowledge and common gossip.

Shakespeare responded to all the implications of the events he
dramatised as far as his information, enlivened by his imagination,
allowed him but *Julius Caesar* remains nevertheless an unexpansive
play. Between its writing and that of *Coriolanus* he made another
excursion into ancient history, or pseudo-history, in *Troilus and
Cressida*. There he sought to give himself scope within which to
work by bringing together a variety of materials; but *Coriolanus*
returns to Plutarch and the methods of *Julius Caesar*. In the later
play Shakespeare takes the same areas of interest as in the earlier
and there are signs that the previous experience gives him greater
confidence this time. He has a clearer view from the start of what
the four areas involve and what they can be made to yield and he
sets to work by announcing them firmly in the first Act.

The political issue here concerns the relative rights and interests
of plebs and patricians in the state and the very first scene presents
the alternative attitudes: the rebellion of the plebs against the over-
riding of their claims on one hand; the autocratic disdain of the
common people voiced by Caius Martius on the other; and

[3] In *Henry VI* part ii, Act IV, sc. i, there is an explicit statement that
Brutus's 'bastard hand' stabbed Caesar.

Menenius's fable of the interdependence of parts in the body politic
by which he seeks to reconcile opposites. The second scene introduces
Aufidius and presents him as Coriolanus's rival. The third scene
introduces Volumnia and Virgilia, and with them the conflict which,
in this play, will centre on Coriolanus, between public and private
lives. As this scene defines it, it is a conflict between an ethos of
blood or *virtù* on the one hand and private affections and loyalties
on the other. Scenes iv–ix show Coriolanus earning his title at
Corioli and receiving deserved commendation for his surpassing
valour and skill. Scene x shows Aufidius, his greatest enemy,
acknowledging in his way Coriolanus's superiority:

> Five times, Martius,
> I have fought with thee; so often hast thou beat me,
> And would'st do so, I think, should we encounter
> As often as we eat.—By the elements
> If e'er again I meet him beard to beard,
> He's mine or I am his. Mine emulation
> Hath not that honour in't it had, for where
> I thought to crush him, in an equal force,
> True sword to sword, I'll potch at him some way
> Or wrath or craft may get him . . .

Here again are the same four areas which Shakespeare developed
for the Roman material in *Julius Caesar*: political confrontation, the
situation of a noble figure surrounded by less noble characters, a
particular personal opposition, tension between the personal life and
the public figure.

The element of political debate is given fuller treatment here than
in *Julius Caesar* but, as in the earlier play, the opposition which
fires the action of the play is not resolved in political terms during
the course of it. Again, as in *Julius Caesar*, the political interest as
such becomes overshadowed in the later acts of the play by the
development of the other interests.

Though Coriolanus is not a figure who has endeared himself to
many, he is undoubtedly noble. He is immensely brave and puts
himself at the service of the community in war without at all counting the personal cost; and he is faithful to the highest standards of
conduct which he can conceive. Menenius, the other patricians and
his mother, Volumnia, urge him to practice hypocrisy in order to

gain the consulship and Volumnia justifies her advice by some specious analogies with conduct in war (III, ii, 58–9). Coriolanus allows himself to be persuaded but he cannot, when it comes to the point, subdue his nature to the deception. For all his faults, no-one in the play reaches his stature.

The central contrast of characters is that between Coriolanus and Aufidius. Both are great soldiers but Coriolanus is the abler and he has also the finer nature. As early as the end of Act I, as has already been noted, Aufidius confesses that honourable competition with Coriolanus has now become on his part ignoble jealousy and that he will not scruple to destroy him by any means within his power. These are the words of a mean-souled man and Coriolanus's behaviour when he goes to Aufidius in Act IV stands in clear contrast. He offers himself either as victim of Aufidius's jealousy or as co-adjutor in the destruction of Rome, and though he acts, as he says, 'in mere spite', there is a grandeur in his whole deportment and in his announcement of himself:

> My name is Caius Martius, who hath done
> To thee particularly and to all the Volsces
> Great hurt and mischief

(IV, v, 65–7)

which compels, temporarily, an admiring response from Aufidius himself. Though the contrast between Coriolanus and Aufidius is not so strongly marked as that between Brutus and Cassius, or Brutus and Antony, it is a real contrast nevertheless, and has an important influence in establishing Coriolanus's claim to our respect.

The fourth area of interest, the relation, or lack of relation, between the private man and the public figure is both more fully and more subtly developed in *Coriolanus* than in *Julius Caesar*. In the latter the distinction between the human and the political aspects of Brutus and Caesar is a central point but scenes in which the claims of humanity are contrasted with those of political necessity or expediency give the impression of being 'planted' for obvious effect. Thus in Act II, sc. ii, Caesar greets the conspirators who have come to escort him to his death in the Capitol with a kindness and good-fellowship which is very different from his usual tone. In Brutus's behaviour to Lucius and Varro and Claudius in Act IV, sc. iii, our sense of him as a kindly and considerate man is sharpened just at the point when the ghost of Caesar appears to augur his downfall. Even in Brutus's soliloquy in his orchard at the beginning of Act II, there is very little development of the conflict between personal and public claims. The mutual affection of Brutus and Portia draws attention to the human sympathy which is left out of account in the political struggle, but the issues are to some extent confused. Though Portia is full of anxiety for Brutus on the day of Caesar's assassination, she does not question his justification for what he does. 'O Brutus!', she exclaims, 'The heavens speed thee in thine enterprise!' (II, iv, 39–40). She does not represent a gentle, life-sustaining spirit in contrast to the harsh antipathies of the male political world but instead will bring herself as nearly as she can into line with masculine codes:

> I grant I am a woman; but withal
> A woman that Lord Brutus took to wife.
> I grant I am a woman; but withal
> A woman well reputed, Cato's daughter.
> Think you I am no stronger than my sex,
> Being so fathered and so husbanded?
>   (II, i, 292–7)

As proof of her worthiness to share Brutus's secrets, she gives herself a wound in the thigh and she dies violently by her own hand. In what she does and says she aligns herself with an ethic in which unflinching resolution, regardless of the appeals of nature, represents a summit of virtue.

Portia, in spirit, is Volumnia's daughter, but Volumnia's daughter-in-law brings a different point of view altogether to *Coriolanus*. Shakespeare took advantage of the lack of definition of Coriolanus's wife in the sources to make Virgilia a quiet but effective contributor to that questioning of the public ethic, here one of martial prowess and authority, which is woven more intricately into this play as a whole than it is into *Julius Caesar*. The conversation between mother and wife, in *Coriolanus*, Act I, sc. iii, first sets side by side the antithetic principles of blood and humanity. Volumnia exults in anticipation of Coriolanus's feats as scourge and destroyer of the Volsces:

> Methinks I see him stamp thus
>   . . .   his bloody brow

With his mailed hand then wiping, forth he goes,
Like to a harvest man that's task'd to mow
Or all or lose his hire . . .

And Virgilia exclaims: 'His bloody brow! O Jupiter, no blood!'

Volumnia has brought him up to be a man of war and to believe that valour is virtue enough, but the play develops various ironies in the situation. One, most obviously, is that the man who bases his claim to Rome's respect on his being her fearless champion becomes, through his sense of his own deserts, in intention her ruthless destroyer. This is the irony of his public life but, underlying that there is another level, for Coriolanus's acceptance of his mother's doctrine of blood is itself an aspect of his private self, his heart-felt devotion to her. Because this is so she is able to play upon his feelings at the end and persuade him, whatever the cost, to act as man, husband and father rather than as the 'thing of blood, whose every motion/Was timed with dying cries', whom Cominius, seconded by Menenius, had praised in Act II, sc. ii (107–8). The public role, with all its aggression and blood-letting, is founded on a private relationship and it is the mother who in the end destroys the figure she has created. A final irony is that Menenius is wrong in the account of Coriolanus which he gives to the Romans: 'He sits in his state as a thing made for Alexander. . . There is no more mercy in him than there is milk in a male tiger' (V, iv). Coriolanus has rejected him, as Henry V in assuming the supra-personal role of King rejected Falstaff, another father-figure, but behind the dehumanised exterior of Coriolanus we are allowed to see a warmer response to a pitiful situation than we are shown in Henry:

This last old man,
Whom with a cracked heart I have sent to Rome,
Loved me above the measure of a father,
Nay, godded me indeed. . .
. . . for whose old love I have—
Though I showed sourly to him—once more offered
The first conditions, which they did refuse
And cannot now accept, to grace him only
That thought he could do more. . .
(V, iii, 8–16)

Though it needs his mother, with the powerful emotional claims she makes on him, to break down the public image which has been moulded to her design, the humane, even sensitive aspects of Coriolanus's nature are never for long lost to sight.

Two views of life exist side by side in Coriolanus himself but the play draws attention to the public/private antithesis not in his character alone but in many other ways too. A good example showing how it is made an integral part of the treatment of the action is provided by one scene in particular, Act II, sc. i. When the scene opens, Menenius is amusing himself in routing the tribunes in verbal encounter—they are far too slow and clumsy to be a match for him. Volumnia, Virgilia and Valeria enter, eagerly hastening forward. They have news that Coriolanus is approaching, laden with fresh honours, and Volumnia is at the same time maternal and martial: 'my boy Martius approaches', 'He hath in this action outdone his former deeds doubly'. Coriolanus has sent letters ahead of him, one of which Volumnia excitedly shows. When Menenius learns that there is another 'at home' for him, his joy matches that of the ladies. From delight at this sign of the young man's affection for him, his thoughts turn to the public honours which will accrue to Coriolanus. The exchange which follows includes characteristic comments from Virgilia and Volumnia:

> MENENIUS: Is he not wounded? He was wont to come home wounded.
>
> VIRGILIA: O, no, no, no.
>
> VOLUMNIA: O, he is wounded, I thank the gods for't.
>
> MENENIUS: So do I too—if it be not too much. Brings 'a victory in his pocket, the wounds become him.
>
> (110–16)

The triumphal procession draws nearer and Volumnia again announces the approach of 'her boy Martius' but in strikingly different terms this time:

> Before him he carries noise, and behind him he leaves tears.
> Death, that dark spirit, in's nervy arm doth lie,
> Which, being advanced, declines, and then men die.
>
> (150–2)

The oscillation in the scene so far between the values of family love and friendship on the one hand and Roman *virtù* on the other presents Coriolanus with something like the technique of an anamorphic picture. Cleopatra has such a painting in mind when she describes Antony:

> Though he be painted one way like a Gorgon
> T'other way he's a Mars. . .
>
> (II, v, 116–17)

but Mars and the Gorgon are identified in Coriolanus and *his* other face is that of a young man who, in the hour of victory, remembers not only Menenius but also the kindness of a humble man who once befriended him, who loves the wife whom he addresses as 'My gracious silence' and whom we shall not be surprised to find framing images of delicate purity to describe Valeria:

> chaste as the icicle
> That's curdied by the frost from purest snow
> And hangs on Dian's temple. . .
>
> (V, iii, 65–7)

When Coriolanus enters, the contrasts continue. Cominius will describe him, in the next scene, as he was in the battle:

> He was a thing of blood, whose every motion
> Was timed with dying cries. . . (107–8)

and, hearing of Coriolanus's activities, we may remember another bloody man:

> head to foot
> Now is he total gules; horridly trick'd
> With blood of fathers, mothers, daughters, sons. . .
>
> (*Hamlet*, II, ii, 450–2)

But in *Coriolanus* the man who is a 'thing of blood' is addressed as 'gentle Martius' by his mother, greeted with fond joy by the elderly man who stands as a father to him, and himself responds with warmth to the friends and family who clearly not only admire but love him. At two moments, however, we are reminded sharply of Coriolanus's other face and other role: 'Ah, my dear,' he says, to Virgilia, who is crying for happiness at seeing him again:

> Such eyes the widows in Corioles wear,
> And mothers that lack sons. . . (II, i, 168–70)

and Volumnia cannot resist a first preparatory move towards the achievement of her next ambition for her son, the consulship.

The interweaving of public and personal in the character of Coriolanus himself is a subtle matter and the treatment of this area of interest in the play is more complicated and, despite the absence of soliloquy, more inward than in *Julius Caesar*. In the earlier play, Mark Antony and Portia, as well as Brutus and Caesar, felt some pull between private feelings and public roles but what *Coriolanus* loses in variety, it gains immensely in depth by the manner of presentation of its central figure.

When Coriolanus rejects Menenius in Act V, sc. ii, it seems temporarily that he has simplified his situation by destroying the world of personal relationships. That the scene recalls the rejection of Falstaff has already been suggested and when we consider other qualities of *Coriolanus* another, perhaps surprising, similarity comes to mind; for *Coriolanus*, like *Antony and Cleopatra*, regains something of the freedom of treatment of the *Henry IV* plays. The play is less formal than *Julius Caesar* and the accents of Shakespeare's own world from time to time vivify Rome and Antium. The serving men of Aufidius's house in Act IV, sc. v, for example, would be quite at home in company of a latter age and the point of their remarks would be readily taken: 'they will out of their burrows like conies after rain', 'This peace is nothing but to rust iron, increase tailors, and breed ballad-makers'. Volumnia too can deal in homely images, as when she instructs Coriolanus how to win the citizens' votes:

> Now humble as the ripest mulberry
> That will not hold the handling, say to them
> Thou art their soldier. . .
>   (III, ii, 79–80).

Scenes have a lively immediacy, as in Act IV, sc. ii when the Junoesque wrath of Volumnia and an unexpected show of spirit by Virgilia are bordered by the comic dismay of Sicinius and Brutus who wilt under the encounter. Act II, sc. i begins with Menenius baiting the tribunes as two of those inefficient officers of the law who appear in many periods of history and many countries in Shakespeare's plays. Of these two Menenius says:

You are ambitious for poor knaves' caps and legs. You wear out a good wholesome forenoon in hearing a cause between an orange-wife and a faucet-seller, and then rejourn the controversy of threepence to a second day of audience. (II, i, 64–9)

He speaks in verse to Coriolanus but his comments are equally homely:

> We have some old crab-trees here at home that will not
> Be grafted to your relish. . .
>
> (II, i, 179–80)

and, when the tribunes step forward after the exit of the patricians, Brutus's account of the popular acclaim for their returning warrior localises the scene in contemporary London:

> The kitchen malkin pins
> Her richest lockram 'bout her reechy neck,
> Clambering the walls to eye him. Stalls, bulks, windows
> Are smothered up, leads filled, and ridges horsed
> With variable complexions, all agreeing
> In earnestness to see him. . .
>
> (198–203)

For this play Shakespeare took a remoter and far less familiar period of history than in *Julius Caesar* and he could not, as for the earlier play he could, expect his audience to be in varying degrees prepared to take up hints and to bring some of their own resources of information and imagination to contribute to the scenes and characters he set before them. He worked very carefully to shape the material, using his experience of the method he employed in *Julius Caesar*, and *Coriolanus* has been described as 'the most unified and symmetrical of all Shakespeare's tragedies'.[4] He let his imagination play acutely upon the Roman history, as T. J. B. Spencer has demonstrated,[5] and he also found a way into the life of the ancient past which released the free creative process and enabled him to bring the people and events sharply into immediate life. The outbreak of rioting in the midland counties in 1607, which was provoked by a

---

[4] *Coriolanus*, ed. G. R. Hibbard (New Penguin Shakespeare), p. 8.
[5] 'Shakespeare and the Elizabethan Romans', *Shakespeare Survey* 10 (1957), pp. 27–38.

prolonged dearth, may perhaps have encouraged him to draw attention to the common humanity shared by his ancient Romans and the men and women of later societies, but the coincidence of the riot was perhaps an incidental matter. The opening out of possibilities in the personal/public tension, adumbrated but not fully developed in *Julius Caesar*, would by itself account for the greater informality of treatment in *Coriolanus*. In the *Henry IV* plays he had strikingly extended his range of approach to historical material but he was on home ground there. Not long before *Coriolanus*, however, he had written *Antony and Cleopatra* and there had applied to a famous antique story and legendary figures something of the same techniques which had vivified the presentation of the recent English past. All this experience feeds into the confident and brilliant *Coriolanus*, a play whose sympathetic humanity seems commonly to be much underestimated.

Two other plays of Shakespeare's maturity draw on ancient history, *Troilus and Cressida* and *Timon of Athens*. Though neither of them is primarily a 'history play', both may be called in evidence, briefly, to add to this examination of Shakespeare's handling of a kind of story material which claims greater authority than that of fiction.

For *Troilus and Cressida* Shakespeare had a great diversity of source material to work on and the medieval precedents gave him greater freedom in the treatment of it than with the Roman plays. Nevertheless, Brian Morris draws attention to 'the paucity of stage-action' in Shakespeare's selection of material concerning the war: 'The combat between Ajax and Hector supplies the only vigorous movement before the tumult of the battle scenes which ends Act Five'.[6] He describes the stories on which the play is based as 'rather static'. Alongside these comments may be put some observations of Ernst Honigmann in another *Shakespeare Quarterly* article[7] in which, discussing *Timon of Athens*, he writes of what he calls the 'plotlessness' of the play and adds 'it is possible that the author foresaw and resigned himself to this'.

Such comments provoke the question: why did Shakespeare choose 'static' or 'plotless' material for these plays? In his other

[6] 'The Tragic Structure of *Troilus and Cressida*', *Shakespeare Quarterly*, 10 (1959), p. 483.
[7] 12 (1961), pp. 3–20.

excursions into ancient history, stage action and plot are by no means lacking and *Julius Caesar*, the first of the Roman plays, is particularly notable for its great theatrical moments, the enactment of Caesar's murder and Antony's performance to the crowd. *Antony and Cleopatra*, a few years later, was to be rich with both character and action.

The relation of *Julius Caesar* to *Coriolanus* has been suggested in this chapter—also the links between *Antony and Cleopatra* and the *Henry IV* plays. *Troilus and Cressida* and *Timon of Athens* seem to compose a third pairing, another kind of approach to the dramatic handling of remote history. In *Julius Caesar* and *Coriolanus* Shakespeare carefully identified the four areas of interest in the material which promised profitable working. In *Antony and Cleopatra* he made use of what he had learnt in *Henry IV* about vivifying the past and adapted it with astonishing results to antique and semi-legendary figures. He does neither of these things in *Troilus and Cressida* and *Timon of Athens* but in the forefront of their composition stands what occurs only incidentally in the other plays—satire.

It is easy to see that satire provides a view-point on history. It can be an organising principle and it can, even in the absence of the sort of familiar circumstantial detail which brings a story home to an audience's or reader's imagination across many centuries—even without that it can strike at men's business and bosoms with its pointed barbs. After *Julius Caesar* and before *Antony and Cleopatra* Shakespeare tried out this method and its possibilities. Later, whether before or after writing *Antony and Cleopatra*, is not known, he returned to it. As when in writing *Coriolanus* he returned to the methods of *Julius Caesar*, with an enhanced understanding of their potentialities, so, when he began on *Timon of Athens*, he focussed more sharply on the nature of the method he was using than in the earlier play and his material is more overtly structured as satirical drama. The *dramatis personae*, for example, include clearly representative figures—a poet, a painter, a jeweller, a merchant— sycophants in a society based on rapacious greed. Lucius, Lucullus and Sempronius have names but are less individuals than types of hypocrisy, meanness and ingratitude. A comparison with Ben Jonson is inevitable. Lucius, Lucullus and Sempronius are dominated by one 'humour', just as Corvino, Corbaccio and Voltore are exemplars of greed in *Volpone* and Face, Subtle, Doll, and the various gulls are dominated by lust for gold in *The Alchemist*. The brilliance of Jonson's handling of his figures is high-lighted by the near-tragic treatment of one play and the lightness of touch of the other; but Shakespeare is subtler still for, whereas Jonson's 'humour' characters are distinguished from each other by age or attributes (Corvino's wife, Corbaccio's son, Voltore's profession), or by rank and station (like the gulls in *The Alchemist*), there are no external aids of this kind to distinguish Shakespeare's blood-suckers, yet distinguished they are, and utterly convincing.

Like so many of Shakespeare's plays, *Timon of Athens* builds much on contrasts: Timon in prosperity and Timon in bankruptcy, Timon at enmity with Athens and Alcibiades at war with the city, Apemantus the professional misanthrope and Timon a bitter convert to hatred of mankind who can make no terms with society. The contrasted pairs of characters and situations comment satirically on each other. Timon in his cave calls into question the validity of the liberality and trustfulness of Timon in his palace, but equally, the ideal of brotherhood which dominates Timon's former life and the influence it exerts on Flavius and the other servants is a criticism of his savagery in the desert. The association of Apemantus and Timon is perhaps the most interesting of these pairings and it leads to a debate between them in Act IV, sc. iii. Distinctions in misanthropy are here discriminated, as types of manners and hypocrisy are discriminated in Lucius, Lucullus and Sempronius, but the analysis is deeper here for the issue is a judgement upon humanity and the value of life. Apemantus is content to live without ideals or expectations, accepting life on those terms, but Timon violently repudiates this attitude. If there is nothing noble in humanity, then he is 'sick of this false world' and will give his body to be washed clean of contact with men by 'the light foam of the sea'.

Debate figures importantly in three plays of this period, *Timon* itself, *Troilus and Cressida*, and *Measure for Measure*. In *Measure for Measure*, Angelo's case for law and Isabella's for mercy are set against each other and the balance is tilted by the eruption of passion. In *Troilus and Cressida*, Act II, sc. ii, Hector and Troilus are the principal spokesmen for opposing estimates of the grounds of human conduct and again the deadlock is broken by the introduction of something from outside the debate—in this case, Hector's previous decision to send a challenge to the Greeks. Both these debates constitute crises in the story—the life of Claudio depends on one, the continuation of the Trojan war on the other. No narrative point is involved in the Timon-Apemantus debate, though it may be said to underscore Timon's alienation from society by the distinction it makes between the quality of his disillusion and that of Apemantus. What follows after is a coda, composed from an extreme satiric view-point, when all hope for humanity has been abandoned and all attachment to it severed. Even his recognition of 'one honest man' in the faithful steward fails to mitigate Timon's loathing of the world. His valediction to Flavius is terrible:

> Go, live rich and happy,
> But thus condition'd: thou shalt build from men;
> Hate all, curse all, show charity to none,
> But let the famish'd flesh slide from the bone
> Ere thou relieve the beggar; give to dogs
> What thou deniest to men; let prisons swallow 'em,
> Debts wither 'em to nothing; be men like blasted woods;
> And may diseases lick up their false bloods!
> And so farewell, and thrive.
>
> (IV, iii, 525–33)

Timon of Athens is a powerful play but a very spare one. As a second working of an approach to ancient history, it reverses the situation observed in *Julius Caesar* and *Coriolanus*. Whereas *Coriolanus* is fuller of human reference and authenticating detail than *Julius Caesar*, *Timon of Athens* is more rigorous in its satirical mode than *Troilus and Cressida* which is, nevertheless, the earlier play.

Troilus and Cressida, in fact, as the multiformity of critical comment testifies, is a play of several dimensions, but among them the satirical is very prominent. Shakespeare has bound together three strands, the situation in the Greek camp, with Achilles sulking in his tent: this culminates in Achilles' slaying of Hector; the situation in the Trojan camp with the leaders at first divided over the merits of keeping Helen but then united by Hector's challenge to the Greeks: this culminates, like the Greek story, in the murder of Hector, but though the threads meet, there is no sense of inevitable convergence; and thirdly, the love-story of Troilus and Cressida: this culminates in Cressida's infidelity of which the war situation is the immediate cause, and it is Troilus who, deserted by Cressida, speaks the fullest response to his brother Hector's murder and who in the end goes bitterly to inevitable death in the Trojan wars.

The Greek material is treated with a good deal of satire. The council meeting in Act I, sc. iii is marked by preposterously inflated rhetoric. The ponderousness and scope of Agamemnon's illustrations of the point that big enterprises are not easily accomplished would befit a much more abstruse idea. Nestor's echo of Agamemnon's pedantically elaborated proposition is similarly disproportionate and full of immensely vigorous imagery:

> The strong-ribb'd bark through liquid mountains cut,
> Bounding between the two moist elements

and the extraordinary:

> when the splitting wind
> Makes flexible the knees of knotted oaks,
> And flies fled under shade. . .

The over-energetic verbal activity of Nestor, the very old man, topples over into the ludicrous and Ulysses' speech which follows, in which he apostrophises the other two, constitutes a parody of their own high flown and unsuitable rhetoric.

To accentuate the satiric tone of the scene, Ulysses sets out to view the portraits which Patroclus paints of Agamemnon and Nestor:

> Sometime, great Agamemnon,
> Thy topless deputation he puts on;
> And, like a strutting player, whose conceit
> Lies in his hamstring, and doth think it rich
> To hear the wooden dialogue and sound
> 'Twixt his stretch'd footing and the scaffoldage,
> Such to-be-pitied and o'erwrested seeming
> He acts thy greatness in; and when he speaks
> 'Tis like a chime a-mending; with terms unsquar'd,
> Which, from the tongue of roaring Typhon dropp'd
> Would seem hyperboles. At this fusty stuff
> The large Achilles, on his press'd bed lolling,
> From his deep chest laughs out a loud applause;
> Cries, 'Excellent! 'tis Agamemnon just.

Now play me Nestor; hem, and stroke thy beard,
As he being drest to some oration'.
                    (I, iii, 151–66)

Patroclus's performance, faithfully (and tactlessly, or maliciously)
reproduced by Ulysses, draws attention to an element of play-acting
in the whole scene where Agamemnon and Nestor talk to the height
of their sense of what their position demands and make themselves
ridiculous by straining the tone too far. Ulysses responds to them in
their own key, himself an ironist before he begins to re-enact
Patroclus's parodies (see lines 54–69). Aeneas, when he enters, picks
up the same tone of mocking adulation and rouses the suspicion of
even Agamemnon. The play draws attention on many occasions to
the false façade which language puts up, behind which all kinds of
folly, weakness, vanity, and ugliness may lurk. Act III, sc. iii, 274–
280 are one example, the greetings of Aeneas and Diomedes in
Act IV, sc. i are another. In the end we see how the deceit of
language invades the love-story also, as Troilus tears up Cressida's
letter: 'Words, words, mere words, no matter from the heart' (V,
iii, 108).

The Trojans in their council scene (Act II, sc. ii) make at first
sight a very good showing in comparison with the Greeks. Hector
speaks like a man of serious and subtle habits of thought and Troilus
is intelligent, and fertile and vigorous in argument. When Thersites
walks on to begin his monologue as the Trojans go out, the contrast
is a jolting one; but if we have by this time forgotten, or discounted,
the tone of the conversation between Cressida and Pandarus in
Act I, sc. ii, the beginning of Act III reminds us that there is a low
and trivial side of Trojan life too. Act III, sc. i begins with play on
words between Pandarus and a servant and a bandying of words
with Helen. Grandiose words betrayed the hollowness of the Greeks,
trivial words expose Helen, false words deepen Cressida's perfidy:
this motif is one means by which the three elements of *Troilus and
Cressida* are held in the same frame.

Another is Shakespeare's favourite device of contrast. To be
assailed by Thersites while the voices of Hector and Troilus still
sound in our ears is one example of that. Another, a particularly
shocking one, is formed by the juxtaposition of the scene of Cressida's
parting from Troy and Troilus's deep grief at her going, with that

of her reception in the Greek camp. The men pay her little respect and Cressida responds with a pertness that shows their freedom is by no means offensive to her and that Troilus is already out of mind. The contrasts work to expose illusions about one's own or other people's worth and, by extension, about the epic subjects of love and war. Men allow themselves to be deceived even when their judgement teaches them better, as does Hector when he rejects 'truth' for a concept of honour:

> a cause that hath no means dependence
> Upon our joint and several dignities.
> (II, ii, 192–3)

He does here what he does again at the end of the play, pursues a fair appearance which conceals a 'putrified core'.

The episode of the killing of the Greek for his 'goodly armour' (Act V, scs. vi and vii) is an emblematic one which sums up the play's comments on fine—and false—shows (of words or other things) and on misvaluations. *Timon of Athens* also employs visual emblems to drive home its satiric points, beginning with the Poet's description of Fortune's hill and including the very effective presentation of the two feasts:—the first, the great banquet of Act I, sc. ii with its lavish distribution of gifts, and the second, in Act III, sc. vi, prepared in anger and hatred and served, such as it is, with insults and blows. The emblematic mode suits quite naturally the general tone and temper of *Timon of Athens*, for the characters compose themselves readily into tableaux where they have representative or otherwise significant roles. The situation in *Troilus and Cressida* is nothing like so clear-cut. Hector's encounter with the emblematic Greek is disconcerting because Hector himself has been presented as an individualised figure, shown in a number of relationships. He does not belong to an emblematic world. Troilus and Cressida may have significant and even proverbial roles in a well-known story: 'As true as Troilus', 'As false as Cressid'—but they are also a young man and young woman who feel the sharpness of the early morning air and who mix love with practicality. 'Night hath been too brief', says Cressida and Troilus responds with a touching mixture of poetic ardour and down-to-earth solicitude:

> Beshrew the witch! With venomous wights she stays
> As tediously as hell, but flies the grasps of love

With wings more momentary-swift than thought.
You will catch cold and curse me.
(IV, ii, 12–15)

Though satire on the illusions and self-deceptions of mankind is a
guiding impulse of *Troilus and Cressida*, the satiric points are
swathed in other things, largely because some of the characters have
too many aspects for straight satiric roles. *Timon of Athens* pares
the *dramatis personae* down and the result is a starker satirical treatment than elsewhere in Shakespeare. The period is remote, the
country alien, and the source material provides nothing of the sort of
detail which in other history plays enabled Shakespeare to make an
imaginative entry into the life of other times and peoples, and
achieve an intimate relationship with them. The play stands as
evidence of his continual experimentation, his refusal to remain
within already charted territory, his apparently inexhaustible interest
in exploring the possibilities of new approaches to material and
different kinds of dramatic effect.

In *Troilus and Cressida* the satiric commentator within the play
is Thersites, a character who properly attaches to himself all the
odium which such a persona may attract.[8] We must acknowledge
that he often speaks truth, even though we despise him. In *Timon of
Athens*, the role is at first taken by Apemantus. He is less abhorrent
than Thersites but he too makes few if any claims on the audience's
sympathy. In the second half of the play, however, Timon himself
steps into the part of satiric commentator and some severe tensions
are then set up. The satirist is by definition unbalanced in his view,
uncharitable in his judgement, directing his eyes to one side of
experience only. This is his function and his strength as satirist and
in this role we are likely to concede his palpable hits. But if he goes
beyond this, to stake a claim to a hero's part, if he calls for our
sympathy or admiration, the situation becomes disturbing. It is felt
impossible to absorb Vindice into the reconstructed world at the end
of *The Revenger's Tragedy* and he is summarily despatched. Timon
also dies, by his own will, and leaves us with mixed feelings. As his
misanthropic passion grows in the last Acts and demands from us

---

[8] See Alvin Kernan, *The Cankered Muse* (New Haven, 1959) for an
interesting discussion of the ambivalence of the satiric commentator in
contemporary literature.

more and more involvement with his experience, we are inclined to draw back and resist his wholesale condemnation of humanity, ascribing it to the diseased view of one who has ever but imperfectly known himself: 'The middle of humanity thou never knewest, but the extremity of both ends', as Apemantus tells him. Yet at the same time an alternative view presses itself upon us and we begin to see Timon in the woods as a tragic figure, desperately wounded by his experience, betrayed there where he has garnered up his heart, knowing the agony of chaos come again, and pushing out, alone and suffering, into dark regions of the soul.

To discuss Timon in such terms as these is to move the play into a different area of Shakespeare's work altogether. Timon's translation from principal figure in a satirical drama to something like tragic hero has led to the play's being often discussed in relation to *King Lear*, but it has seemed useful here to consider it alongside other plays which draw on historical or quasi-historical sources. Shakespeare's free inventiveness is curbed by such material but the various approaches he makes to the problems involved show, as this study of them has demonstrated, that imaginative vitality operates with an energy, a creative range and brilliance as superlative in these plays as elsewhere. He works carefully with his sources, to get the most he can out of his material, especially in the Greek and Roman plays but, even in *Timon of Athens*, where the material supplied is exiguous and the dominant mode of treatment is spare, the creative fire kindles and casts new lights and shadows on the story so that the play stirs responses at a level beyond anything achieved by Jonson, supreme satirist as he was.

As for the other histories, the word wrongs them, for they live with the life of an everlasting present.

6

More Patterns and Variants: Crimes and Consequences

Similarities of pattern in pairs of history plays were discussed in the last chapter. The similarity of the pattern in the plays to be considered now lies nearer the surface and has often been scrutinised. In *Cymbeline*, *The Winter's Tale* and *The Tempest* Shakespeare is dealing with fictional material so that the exigencies of historical narrative do not impose restrictions on him. What we have in the late romances is, rather, three different attempts to shape and manage a new kind of narrative structure and the first requirement in reviewing them is to separate out the various narrative strands of which they are composed.

An event and its consequences is the basic formula of all stories, even if the sequence is held together by no stronger thread than the '... and so ... and so ... and so ...' of Mopsa's story to Pamela. If the initial event is a crime, or other wilfully performed evil act, there appear to be three broad types of narrative development possible. One is the revenge plot, one hinges on retribution, and the third moves towards reconciliation of the estranged parties. *Cymbeline*, *The Winter's Tale* and *The Tempest* all move towards reconciliation but they include, to a greater or lesser degree, the other possibilities as well. They also make a fresh distribution of comic and tragic potentialities. The plays take as their point of departure dire situations which might be productive of tragedy and they force a rift between characters who ought properly to be in close sympathy. The severity of the original situations is too great for comedy, the movement towards harmony at the end deflects the impulse towards tragedy. They represent a new amalgam of elements in Shakespeare's work, although Shakespearean comedy has always moved towards reconciliation and revenge and retribution have been the motive force of earlier tragedies. *Hamlet*, as the prime example of the revenge plot, will be reserved for fuller discussion in the next chapter but it will be convenient here to look briefly at two earlier treatments of the retribution development of the crime and consequences story. *Richard III* and *Macbeth* provide another example of a double working of a basically similar story pattern and to consider them at this point will contribute to the background against which Shakespeare's re-handling of familiar material and development of new in the romances needs to be seen.

Retribution offers dramatic material comparable to, though not identical with, revenge. Personal revenge may make a part of it but the retribution plot has as its core the assumption that the sheer momentum of evil will in time create its own punishment, that the career of the wrong-doer is a violation of some ultimately inexorable law and cannot, in the nature of things, triumph. *Richard III* and *Macbeth* are both founded on the retribution plot.

Shakespeare wrote *Richard III* early in his career and was evidently working to achieve a tighter patterning of the historical material than the episodic structure of the *Henry VI* plays. The working out of curses provides an appropriate programme and prophetic dreams also help to dramatise the material. The basic plot is simple. Richard in an opening soliloquy informs the audience that he is determined to prove a villain, we then see the course of his villainies, culminating in the murder of the little princes in the Tower, and finally he is killed by a 'good' man who inherits the throne and will restore the kingdom to health. On this simple level the material offers plenty of opportunity as Richard is seen picking off his victims one by one.

A number of variations can be developed from the basic situation and Shakespeare responds to the opportunities with zest. Thus we have the magnificent poetry with which Clarence pleads with his murderers for his life, a spectacular demonstration of gullibility as Ann falls into Richard's trap, copious dramatic irony as Hastings boasts his confidence in his position even while Richard plans to dispose of him; then finally, bad dreams, defeat and death, at the hands of 'ministers of chastisement'. It is not an essential part of this material that Richard should be a lively, intelligent, self-aware, humorous character. That he is so in the play constitutes the Shakespearean bonus, the element which makes the play so much more than a paradigmatic handling of crime and retribution.

This element enters the play as early as the very first speech when what begins as choric exposition modulates into an individual voice with its own distinctive character and intonation. This speech is of very great interest in the history of Shakespeare's development as a dramatist. Barbara Everett has claimed that the Nurse's speech, in *Romeo and Juliet*, Act I, sc. iii, marks the first time that a genuinely individual speaking voice sounds in Shakespeare's plays,[1] but Richard III comes before the Nurse and the breaking in of a personal voice among some of the less assured devices in the play constitutes a remarkable feature of this early drama. Richard's opening speech in Act I begins with a passage giving information to the audience about the point reached in the historical sequence: the Yorkists are in the ascendancy and peace now reigns. This passage is written very elaborately and the audience's attention is engaged for the opening of the play by rhetorical flourishes. The end of the speech is a brisk summing up of immediately antecedent events and the following entry of Clarence and Brakenbury signals the opening of the play proper. In between these two pieces of choric writing comes a passage of quite a different kind:

> But I, that am not shaped for sportive tricks,
> Nor made to court an amorous looking-glass;
> I, that am rudely stamped, and want love's majesty
> To strut before a wanton ambling nymph;
> I, that am curtailed of this fair proportion,
> Cheated of feature by dissembling nature,
> Deformed, unfinished, sent before my time
> Into this breathing world scarce half made up,
> And that so lamely and unfashionable
> That dogs bark at me as I halt by them—
> Why, I, in this weak piping time of peace,
> Have no delight to pass away the time,
> Unless to spy my shadow in the sun,
> And descant on mine own deformity.

The compound expressed here, of bitterness at his own deformity and scorn for the others whose physique entitles them, as he puts it,

---

[1] 'The Nurse's speech . . . is perhaps Shakespeare's first greatly human verse speech.' *Critical Quarterly*, 14 (1972), p. 130.

to 'strut before a wanton ambling nymph', is very striking and so is the ruthless wit with which Richard speaks of his deformity in the last lines. The passage, with its placing of the emphatic 'I', its rhythm, and the collocation of sounds, brings us into immediate contact with a living man, one who is activated by the tension which exists between his sense of physical inferiority on the one hand, and, on the other, his need to dominate, a need sustained by keen intelligence and 'alacrity of spirit'.

The achievement is not consistent throughout *Richard III* and Richard's speeches are more than once used for other functions than to express himself. Even so, the creative impulse animating Richard has so much force that it kindles the whole play. It is not surprising that *Richard III* should be as popular as it is in the Shakespearean repertory for it provides plenty of action developing naturally from the initial premises, plus a character whose capacity to delight is in excess of what could be expected from the situations of the plot.

The same could be said of *Macbeth*. Again we have a central character determined on evil doing, we assist at his villainies, and we see him finally destroyed by a good prince who comes to save the stricken kingdom. Though the basic material is similar, a difference in the treatment of the retributive agency becomes crucial. In *Richard III*, there is imperfect cohesion between Richard's crimes and the retribution which they earn. The murder of the little princes is a pivotal point in the play, an act by which Richard reveals the depth of his cold-blooded cruelty. He slaughters innocents and even the hired murderers are overcome by conscience and remorse. From that time onwards the forces of retribution gather momentum, but the murder of the children does not of itself produce this result. On the night before the battle of Bosworth Field, Richard feels some stabbings of conscience but this situation is not developed very far and he dies, not only defiant, but full of the old vigour and unscrupulous intelligence. His speech of exhortation to his soldiers in Act V, sc. v appeals to prejudice against the foreigner, fear of loss of property and of ravishment of wives and daughters with the same sort of gusto as characterised his sanctimonious performance before the mayor and citizens of London in Act III, sc. vii.

In *Macbeth* the key episode and the hero-villain's reactions to the crimes he commits are both handled differently. Shakespeare shows us the murderers attacking Lady Macduff and her son, instead of relying on a report as in *Richard III*. In the earlier play he sought to evoke a sense of the direness of the deed by painting an emblematic picture of innocence:

'O thus', quoth Dighton, 'lay the gentle babes'—
'Thus, thus', quoth Forrest, 'girdling one another,
Within their alabaster innocent arms.
Their lips were four red roses on a stalk,
And in their summer beauty kiss'd each other.
A book of prayers on their pillow lay . . .

(IV, iii, 9–14)

In *Macbeth* he gives us a real woman, smarting with grievance at her husband's desertion of the family, and a pert, question-asking child. He shows Macduff himself receiving the news of the loss of all his family:

I cannot but remember such things were
That were most precious to me

and it is Macduff who, fulfilling part of the conditions of the prophecy, will strike down Macbeth.

As for the effect on the inner man of the career of blood which he pursues, this is an aspect of the material which Shakespeare develops in *Macbeth* to a degree and with a subtlety quite unknown in *Richard III*. Richard is a play-actor, staging a series of successive scenes in which he leads his victims by the nose to their ruin, only to be overtaken at the end and cut off in his career. Shakespeare's account of Richard's career constitutes one very effective way of using retribution as dramatic material, but *Macbeth*, so similar in general outline, is turned to very different effect. At the beginning and at the end of the play, Macbeth is a deeply introspective man, reflecting at first on his ambition and the price he is prepared to pay to achieve it, and at the end wearily recognising the futility of his attempt to dominate 'this bank and shoal of time'. In the middle scenes he is absorbed in a frenzy of bloody action but still a man who sees ghosts and who seeks desperately for assurances that he is buying for himself some kind of real success. As Shakespeare develops the role of Lady Macbeth, it brings out more fully the strain and cost of the course on which the pair have set themselves. At the beginning of the play she is a powerful agent of the circumstances

which foster Macbeth's leaning to murder, allying herself with the
witches when she invokes evil spirits to unsex her, and projecting
the worst of Macbeth's nature when she reminds him of his ambition
and how much he wants the throne. After the murder of Duncan,
her hold on Macbeth weakens and the two of them, cut off from
the rest of humanity, are also isolated from each other in their
separate hells. The collapse of her mind and her suicide indicate the
torment which Macbeth endures and underline the fact that retribution in this play is not simply a dramatic finale imposed on the
action, when we have all had a good time watching the hero-villain
manipulate events for the greater part of the play, but that here it
springs from and accompanies the action at every stage, from beginning to end. The inwardness of the handling of the retribution plot
in *Macbeth* is comparable with the inwardness of the handling of
the revenge plot in *Hamlet*.

In that it provides strong situations and strong resolutions, the
retribution plot offers similar advantages as dramatic material to
those provided by the revenge plot. The story material is basically
the same for each, but whereas, when revenge is the motive, attention is focussed on the avenger, when the story hinges on retribution,
attention is focussed on the evil-doer. The retribution story is not
subject, consequently, to the implicit disadvantage of the revenge
story, that an interval has to be filled between the occasion of
vengeance and the execution of it. In the retribution story the evil
doer has the initiative and may be allowed to retain it until the last
moment, wading further and further in sin until the last scene or
two. The comparison of *Richard III* and *Macbeth* demonstrates how
in the earlier play Shakespeare uses the more obvious elements in the
material (but adds to them, by an independent act of creation, the
magnificent character of Richard) and in the later play eschews
the easier method and gives us a view, not merely of external events,
but of the consciousness of the man directing them. Richard, always
playing for an audience, even if it is only his own sardonic self, has
considerable variety of styles of speech. Macbeth is not given this
range but Shakespeare endows him with an utterance full of images
that bespeaks a complex and highly developed nature. In narrative
terms, *Macbeth* is the simplest of Shakespeare's versions of the crime
and punishment story. Marco Mintoff writes that it is 'the only
one of Shakespeare's plays in which the action follows a clear, simple

line without deviations and complications'.[2] It is (therefore?) short. In these two plays, Shakespeare draws out the possibilities of the retribution plot, one of the developments of the basic crime-and its-consequences story. There remains the third form which this story may take: reconciliation. Instead of the focus of interest being the act of vengeance or the inexorable bringing of a malefactor to his just deserts, this third variant of the story moves towards harmonisation of the original oppositions. It produces an ending of concord, instead of a fiercely affirmed act of justice. Its dominant impulses are penitence and forgiveness. It opens out, in fact, a whole territory of the crime and consequences story still left to be explored when revenge and retribution have had their day. The approach, however, has its problems.

While retribution has elements in common with revenge, reconciliation as a state of mind disavows revenge and the reconciliation plot would seem to have no connection with the revenge plot except by opposition. Like revenge it is likely to provide strong dramatic material at the start but its principal difficulty lies in the ending. Deprived of the naturally dramatic finales of revenge and retribution, it risks anticlimax as it brings its characters out of pain and passion into peace. Interest must be sustained in the central episodes which mediate between initial crisis and resolution and also in the last act's clearing away of the clouds. Shakespeare's three versions of this narrative pattern afford views into the problems of invention and organisation which are involved and of the various measures which he took to meet them.

The characteristics of *Cymbeline* have drawn diverse comments from its critics. Dr Johnson's views are well known: 'To remark the folly of the fiction, the absurdity of the conduct, the confusion of the names and manners of different times, the impossibility of the events in any system of life, were to waste criticism upon unresisting imbecility, upon faults too evident for detection, and too gross for aggravation'. F. R. Leavis speaks of the 'odd and distinctive music' which is created by the 'interplay of contrasting themes and modes',[3] which is another way of reacting to similar characteristics. The

[2] 'The Structural Pattern of Shakespeare's Tragedies', *Shakespeare Survey*, 3 (1950), p. 63.
[3] 'The Criticism of Shakespeare's Late Plays: a Caveat' in *The Common Pursuit* (London, 1952), p. 174.

difference in approach between Johnson and Leavis is the vital difference between pre- and post-Romantic criticism of Shakespeare, failure to recognise the consummate artistry of Shakespeare on the one hand and, on the other, unwillingness to admit that the artistry ever fails. The second attitude is the sounder one, proved so time and again when it leads to ever fuller illumination of the work; but over-interpretation is a real danger arising from it.

A play which brings together so many kinds of material as *Cymbeline* does offers even more avenues of exploration than usual. There is not far to go along the path of historical enquiry, for example, before the play is seen to focus on a great historical water-shed, a point where the might of Rome and ancient Britain come into alliance, while in a far Roman province the Christ child is born giving another dimension to the peace which is established in Britain at the end of the play. Perhaps, as Emrys Jones has suggested,[4] historical implications and topical allusions were readily present to the first audiences; but *Cymbeline* does not read or act like a serious historical or political piece. Accepting the work of the commentators, therefore, with gratitude but with reservations, we turn to the story elements in themselves for the light which their disposition may throw on Shakespeare at work on the play.

Cymbeline opens with the separation of Imogen and Posthumus by order of the king and the early episodes are rapidly and powerfully executed. The sorrowful parting of husband and wife, the young men in Paris irritating each other till the wager on Imogen's chastity is provoked and accepted, Iachimo's interview with Imogen and his night in her room, his taunting of Posthumus with the 'evidence' that Imogen has succumbed to him, Posthumus's violent repudiation of his wife—the initial situation is developed with great speed and economy in the early Acts. When Act III opens, the business of the plot, from then on, will be to repair, as far as may be, the harm done.

The estrangement of Posthumus and Imogen stems from a deliberate lie and the undoing of the damage need not, therefore, be a very difficult matter but Shakespeare assembles a remarkable collection of narrative lines to keep his story going and to produce a scene of revelation and reunion by extremely complicated means. Imogen is given a crude lover, Cloten, to contrast with the noble

---

[4] In 'Stuart *Cymbeline*', reprinted in *Shakespeare's Later Comedies*, ed. D. J. Palmer (Penguin Shakespeare Library), 1971, pp. 248–63.

one, Posthumus, and his idiocy provides some comic interludes; she is given, besides, a wicked stepmother who is also the mother of Cloten and who is prepared to go to any lengths, including murder, to put her son on the throne. As Plutarch's Cleopatra uses prisoners for experiments in various modes of dying (a detail which Shakespeare did not use in *Antony and Cleopatra*), so Cymbeline's queen is willing to try out poisons 'on such creatures as,/We count not worth the hanging'. She adds, 'but none human', though the doctor, wisely, does not trust her.

In addition to the family complications, *Cymbeline* includes a national crisis: the Romans send to demand tribute and Cymbeline denies it, thereby making inevitable a Roman invasion. Meanwhile Posthumus, made madly jealous by Iachimo, orders his servant to kill Imogen. Imogen, wandering the countryside disguised as a boy, comes upon an old man and his supposed sons who live as outlaws in a cave. The 'sons' are, in fact, her long-lost brothers who were abducted as babies. In the end, Posthumus, Imogen, Romans, Iachimo, Cymbeline's sons, and Cymbeline himself all come together. Cloten is missing, having been decapitated in an unexpectedly violent scene, and the queen is missing, having died (off-stage) confessing her whole perfidy.

Considering this hodge-podge or gallimaufry of action, we may well be surprised that Shakespeare should adopt a narrative style of this kind at this stage of his career. Popular romances gave him the model but the man who chose and followed them was, after all, the same who had mined beneath the surface of action in *Hamlet* and found there material to engage his greatest creative energies. Yet the situation is not without precedent in Shakespeare's work and we can recognise in *Cymbeline* the first stage of a procedure which he has followed before. Shakespeare's first approach to the revenge plot was *Titus Andronicus*, a play in which the brutalities of physical action were very prominent. *Hamlet*, with its different method, came after. The first handling of the retribution plot was *Richard III* in which, as has been noted, there is little of the inner exploration of *Macbeth*. Shakespeare is following the course thus set when, in *Cymbeline*, he makes what is probably his first independent approach to the reconciliation story through the medium of abundant exterior action. The episodic vivacity and variety of *Titus* and *Richard III* suggest that in his first handling of revenge and retribution, and before he is certain of how much implicit interest the basic situation will yield, Shakespeare takes care to provide a great deal of episodic activity. In *Cymbeline*, aware perhaps of the danger of anti-climax threatening the ending, he, in fact, over-provided. Here is one of the signs of that insecurity in the pace and distribution of narrative material which, as this study is suggesting, provides the occasion, time after time, for some of the most soaring flights of Shakespeare's imagination. Over provision, however, is rather an impediment than an incentive and the creative imagination is much confined in *Cymbeline*.

Over-provision affects the queen whose character, interestingly hinted at at the beginning of the play, is later squandered. Belarius and the boys, among the press of events in which they are involved, have little chance to become anything but talking puppets. To keep pace with the exigencies of the action Cloten at various times must play the roles of comic buffoon, a Falconbridge figure aiding an Elinor to bolster a weak king against a foreign power, and a dull-brained monster with a diseased imagination, pursuing Posthumus and Imogen to execute murder and rape. Apart from providing cramped conditions for a number of the characters, the proliferation of story-lines in *Cymbeline* produces another consequence in that when moments of strong passion emerge from the mêlée, they astound us with their sudden force. The hysterical virulence of Posthumus's outburst in Act II, sc. v is astonishing and Imogen's speech in Act IV, sc. ii over the dead body of Cloten is even more remarkable. Only the complete sympathy of the audience with Imogen's emotion can prevent the speech appearing ludicrous, yet the concentration and preparation which would seem required to achieve this are not given. An actress has a formidable task, though, experience shows, not an impossible one. The intensity of expression in these and other speeches of the play makes its mark, but the variety of the surrounding material distracts from, rather than supports, this aspect of the play. There are, of course, moments which stand by their own power, regardless of all else, like that one which Tennyson said never failed to move him: 'when Imogen in tender rebuke says to her husband,

> Why did you throw your wedded lady from you?
> Think that you are upon a rock; and now
> Throw me again!

and Posthumus does not ask forgiveness, but answers, kissing her,

> Hang there like fruit, my soul,
> Till the tree die.'

Much is brought within the web of episodes in this play but some things which might have been there are excluded, involving the discarding of aspects of narrative material which have been central to other plays. It is Cloten and the queen, for instance, 'bad' characters, who carry the patriotic motif, and Cymbeline at the end renounces it, promising, in spite of the British victory, still to pay tribute to Rome. Revenge also is repudiated, most strikingly when, in Act V, sc. i, Posthumus repents his order to Pisanio to kill Imogen, although he still believes her guilty. He forgives Iachimo also in the last scene. The fact is that, while the accumulation of supplementary material round the central story of estrangement and reunion overcrowds the play, it also has the effect of producing a purer treatment of the reconciliation plot than in either *The Winter's Tale* or *The Tempest*. In his exploration of this ground, Shakespeare reduces to a minimum the rival attractions of revenge and retribution which lie contiguous to it. At the end of Act II, Posthumus is in the grip of a mad and violent jealousy but, though he orders the murder of Imogen, the audience is at once assured that Pisanio will not carry it out. When Posthumus appears again at the beginning of Act V he has already repented of his anger, and abjured his vengeful thoughts. We are not told how and when the change occurred in him for Posthumus's bloody intentions are only one among many narrative issues and the interval between his appearances has been full of other things. As revenge is acknowledged only to be rejected, so retribution also is recognised as a possibility of the material but is allowed only a token place in the play. The queen, frustrated in all her plots, takes her own life and dies in despair but Cymbeline, on behalf of the author, dismisses her and her fate with consummate briskness: 'O she was naught'.

The handling of the last two Acts of the play is of particular interest for, as has been noted, the need to avoid an anti-climactic ending must be an important consideration. We may notice, in the first place, how Shakespeare seeks to deepen the tone of his play by introducing the idea of death. This again is not a new departure, since he had used a similar tactic in *Love's Labour's Lost* when, in the last Act, he dropped the false bottom out of the apparently shallow world of that play and allowed the announcement of a death to open the depths beneath. Here the romance improbabilities of *Cymbeline* draw to a serious point. Cloten, the clown, meets a violent death and the queen dies 'shameless-desperate', but these two are not the only ones touched by death nor is death-as-punishment the only point made. Thoughts of death are especially concentrated in Act IV, sc. ii.

Man and man should be brothers, Imogen remarks in the first few lines:

> But clay and clay differs in dignity,
> Whose dust is both alike . . .

The two ideas contained in these lines echo throughout the scene. 'He was a queen's son, boys', Belarius says of the dead Cloten:

> And though he came our enemy, remember,
> He was paid for that: though mean and mighty, rotting
> Together have one dust, yet reverence
> (That angel of the world) doth make distinction
> Of place 'tween high and low. Our foe was princely,
> And though you took his life, as being our foe,
> Yet bury him as a Prince . . .
> (244–51)

To which Guiderius replies:

> Pray you fetch him hither,
> Thersites' body is as good as Ajax',
> When neither are alive.

The decapitated body of Cloten, which Imogen mourns as Posthumus's, underlines the point. The man noble by nature and the ignoble prince are indistinguishable in death, 'Whose dust is both alike'.

Posthumus makes his own comment on the theme when he addresses the gods in Act V, sc. iv:

> For Imogen's dear life, take mine and though
> 'Tis not so dear, yet 'tis a life; you coin'd it:
> 'Tween man and man they weigh not every stamp.

The supposed death of Imogen has served to focus Posthumus's mind on essentials, to make him confess that his wife, though guilty (as he still believes) of a 'little fault' with Iachimo, was yet far better than himself. He welcomes his own death as an expiation. The death of the queen provokes confession from her, too, and in receiving the news Cymbeline voices one of the play's resonant comments. The lines repeat once more that death is no respecter of persons:

> Who worse than a physician
> Would this report become? But I consider
> By med'cine life may be prolong'd, yet death
> Will seize the doctor too. . .
>
> (V, v, 27–30)

How to accommodate the fact of death is also a concern of the characters. Belarius and the boys speak a chorus of elegies over the apparently dead body of Imogen/Fidele:

> . . . The bird is dead
> That we have made so much on . . .
>
> . . . O sweetest, fairest lily
>
> . . . O melancholy!
> Whoever yet could sound thy bottom? find
> The ooze to show what coast thy sluggish crare
> Might'st easiliest harbour in? . . .
>
> With female fairies will his tomb be haunted
> And worms will not come to thee.

Arviragus speaks the most extended passage, a beautiful pastoral sequence of flower images, but his elaboration of it is cut short by Guiderius:

> Prithee have done,
> And do not play in wench-like words with that
> Which is so serious. Let us bury him,
> And not protract with admiration what
> Is now due debt. To th'grave.

'that which is so serious . . .' When words have done their best, the ineluctable fact remains. The lines express a harsh truth, and the superb lyric, 'Fear no more the heat o' the sun', brings this movement of the scene to an end.

> Golden lads and girls all must,
> As chimney-sweepers come to dust,

as must also the tender Fidele (or so it seems) and the crude Cloten who are to be laid side by side in death.

Act V, sc. iv has also its elegy. The gaoler is a jovial character, and, unlike some of his companions in law-enforcement in Shakespeare's plays, he has a fair command of language.[5] He speaks of Posthumus's approaching execution:

> A heavy reckoning for you sir: but the comfort is you shall be called to no more payments, fear no more tavern-bills, which are often the sadness of parting, as the procuring of mirth: you come in faint for want of meat, depart reeling with too much drink: sorry that you have paid too much and sorry that you are paid too much: purse and brain, both empty: the brain the heavier for being too light; the purse too light, being drawn of heaviness. O, of this contradiction you shall now be quit. O, the charity of a penny cord! it sums up thousands in a trice: you have no true debitor and creditor but it: of what's past, is, and to come, the discharge: your neck, sir, is pen, book, and counters; so the acquittance follows.

The speech is a version of 'Fear no more the heat o' the sun', as Falstaff's prose address to honour in *Henry IV* part i (V, i, 130–40) is a version of Hotspur's enthusiastic apostrophe:

> By heaven, methinks it were an easy leap,
> To pluck bright honour from the pale fac'd moon . . .
> (I, iii, 201–2)

---

[5] Anne Righter, in her introduction to the Penguin *Tempest* lists Launce and Speed, Touchstone, Dogberry, Feste, Lavatch, and the grave-digger in *Hamlet* as 'corrupters of words', i.e. they deal in quibbles and verbal errors and games with words. She points out that Stephano and Trinculo in *The Tempest* depend on situation not language for comic effect although: 'They too play with language but with on the whole a feebleness of invention that betrays how much, for Shakespeare, the life has gone out of this particular kind of verbal exercise'. The gaoler is not a corrupter of words but there is a good deal of verbal energy and play in what he says.

One speech does not cancel the other in either instance. All the speakers speak truths and the gaoler of *Cymbeline* can strike deep notes when he warns Posthumus, 'look you, sir, you know not which way you shall go':

POSTHUMUS: Yes, indeed do I, fellow.

FIRST GAOLER: Your death has eyes in's head then: I have not seen him so pictur'd: you must either be directed by some that take upon them to know, or to take upon yourself that which I am sure you do not know, or jump the after-enquiry on your own peril: and how you shall speed in your journey's end, I think you'll never return to tell on.

'I'll jump the life to come', Macbeth boasted, but the gaoler would have reminded him, 'on your own peril'.

In these scenes Imogen and Posthumus are brought as near to death as may be without final dissolution, and they are both mourned. At the end they will seem to each other to be raised from the dead, a situation which sets the seal upon the reconciliation development of the narrative base. From conflict and negation come concord and affirmation. Estrangement and enmity are overcome: life is reborn.

The episodes and speeches which cluster round images of death make a strong centre of imaginative activity and they also conduct the story to its nadir before the final ascent into peace and amity. There are many entanglements to be unravelled in the last scene but to assure us that even at this late stage all will be well, Shakespeare provides a supernatural intervention and a prophecy. It is appropriate that the ghosts should appear to plead on behalf of Posthumus, for his role has been a fragmentary one and interest in him needs to be built up so that he can take his proper rank as hero in the finale. His family's prayers and Jupiter's response neatly fulfil two functions: that of bringing Posthumus forward as a centre of attention in time for his reunion with Imogen, and that of providing some supernatural authority for the series of happy reversals of unhappy events which is about to take place. The playwright, of course, can make happen what he will, but when the playwright has on his hands so much complication as Shakespeare has here, he may well be glad to pass some of the responsibility to a less challengeable power. There is a third function of the vision also. Prophecies provide programmes in other plays, and although Jupiter's 'tablet' appears too late to afford a framework for the whole play it does at least firm up the last scene. It promises the audience that the dramatist sees his way clear and the audience, for its part, can afford to relish whatever suspense and excitement he can squeeze out of the last complications, without real anxiety over the outcome. We can also enjoy the final satisfaction of hearing Philarmonus set out for us how the prophecy has been accomplished, point by point. So many stories in the air: the juggler/dramatist proudly displays them at the end, all safely caught. The last Act reminds us of everything, so as to ensure that we savour to the full the resolution which has been arrived at. There is a similar technique of restatement of the complications before resolution in *Measure for Measure* and *All's Well that Ends Well*, but there aspects of the plays which have been important in our experience of them are not included in the recapitulation, so that the endings leave us dissatisfied. Unlike those of the earlier plays, however, the story elements of *Cymbeline*, many and divers as they are, keep within the bounds which the narrative as a whole allows them. Whatever we may miss in *Cymbeline*, at least all the story-teller's debts are paid off at the end.

Dr Johnson was hard on *Cymbeline* and a modern critic must blench at the language he uses. Yet Johnson could make superb recognition of Shakespeare's genius: he evidently missed the marks of it here. Up to a point, at any rate, we may even say he was right. Supreme examples of Shakespearean creativity occur when he draws deep upon the resources of his imagination and experience. The over-provision of action in *Cymbeline* removes the need for that kind of activity here. The play contains great moments, for he touched nothing that he did not enhance, but Shakespeare is too busy managing the story lines for the great creative forces to be fully engaged. He did not repeat the method which he adopted in *Cymbeline*. When he turned to a fresh handling of the reconciliation story in *The Winter's Tale*, experience had given him greater confidence in handling the pattern of events and it is a striking feature of the second version, compared with the first, that the amount of action is considerably reduced.

As in *Cymbeline*, the initial situation in *The Winter's Tale* is developed speedily, forcefully, and economically. Leontes' jealousy is no sooner shown to us than it is full-blown. By Act III, sc. ii,

Polixenes, the boy-hood friend, has been forced to flee for his life, Mamilius is dead, Hermione apparently dead, the baby despatched to death, and Leontes has already recovered from the dreadful delusion, in the grip of which he has destroyed his family and ruined his life. The potential for destructive violence implicit in the narrative formula is allowed fuller development than it was in *Cymbeline*. In *The Winter's Tale* Leontes appears, not only to himself but to the audience also, to have executed a terrible act of revenge, and we are given the moment when his delusion falls from him and he realises what he has done and the remorse to which he has condemned himself.

A Roman invasion and the discovery of long-lost heirs to the throne can be brought into service in *Cymbeline* to reunite Posthumus and Imogen and to confirm their marriage, but no such expedients can mend the broken family of Leontes. Death appeared in the earlier play to mark the end of the road down which suspicion, malice and hostility were leading the characters but only the queen and Cloten died in reality and for them it was 'poetic justice'. In *The Winter's Tale*, Antigonus, a good man, and Mamilius, a guiltless child, both die, to say nothing of the mariners who are not at all implicated in the action except that they have taken Antigonus to Bohemia. Hermione also appears to die and is, in fact, dead to the world for sixteen years. A god intervenes to clear Leontes' eyes of his gross self-deception and to hint that the baby sent to destruction may be found, but Apollo does not arrest the sequence of evil consequences from Leontes' mad jealousy. The downward movement of the play continues till midway through Act III, sc. iii.

The first half of *The Winter's Tale* constitutes a powerful handling of the crime-and-its-consequences story. Leontes' crime stems from a mind temporarily but catastrophically diseased. He fills the roles of both criminal and avenger for the crimes he commits he enacts in the name of vengeance. Retribution overtakes him in the form of deep remorse for what he has done and irreconcilable grief for what, by his own act, he has lost. The alternative aspects of the crime-and-its-consequences story are thus given clear and strong development before Shakespeare moves his play on towards the third possibility: reconciliation. But here in this play violence and remorse have been too strongly stressed for everything to be smoothed out, as the more diversified but less deeply studied stories of *Cymbeline* could allow. Mamilius and Antigonus remain dead, sixteen years must pass.

By the middle of Act III Shakespeare has left himself with the situation which he took pains to avoid in *Cymbeline*; that is, the cause of initial estrangement has been removed and only reunion remains to be achieved, with all the risk of anti-climax which this closing movement involves. The end of Act II of *Cymbeline* shows Posthumus full of threats and venom. Acts III and IV make use of the full range of story materials drawn on in the play and we do not see Posthumus again till the beginning of Act V when his mood has quite changed and he no longer thirsts for vengeance. If we turn to see what Shakespeare does with the fourth Act of *The Winter's Tale* in replacement of the episodic variety of *Cymbeline*, we find that the answer is that he there performs one of the characteristic feats of his creative imagination, producing out of his resources a copiousness of life and sympathy of which it might well be said 'Here is God's Plenty'.

In Act IV we are to learn of the love of Perdita and Florizel, to see Polixenes' threats to this love, and to be party to Camillo's plans for a return to Sicily. In other words, preparations are to be made for the reunion of Leontes with the daughter whom he thinks he has killed. Thus the hint dropped by the oracle will be justified and the (apparently) only repairable breach, of all those made in the early part of the play, will be mended. The plotting is neat enough in itself but Shakespeare is evidently aware that the predictability of the dénouement threatens slackness of pace and loss of interest. He does what he can to diminish the threat. Apollo's words are conditional only: 'the King shall live without an heir, *if* that which is lost be not found': Time himself refuses to prophesy about Perdita: 'What of her ensues/I list not prophesy'; but the dramatist's major effort goes into the pastoral scenes of Act IV which must do more than merely prepare the ground for the dénouement if they are to retain the eager interest of the audience.

In scene ii we are introduced to Autolycus, a totally new character who enters singing of daffodils and tells us he was once a courtier but has given that up to become 'a snapper-up of unconsidered trifles' which the foolish and unwary leave in his way. We meet the clown again, whom we last saw telling his father of the bear's attack on Antigonus: 'to see how the bear tore out his shoulder-bone, how he cried to me for help, and said his name was Antigonus a noble-man'. Here it is Autolycus who, pretending he also has been attacked, though by a robber not a bear, cries to the clown for help and receives his ready sympathy:

CLOWN: Alas, poor soul!
AUTOLYCUS: O, good sir, softly, good sir! I fear, sir, my shoulder blade is out.

The scene alerts us to a change of mood and sends us with 'a merry heart' into scene iv. It is in the first part of this scene that the triumph of Act IV comes, as moods and styles and manners are mingled and harmonised with an apparent ease and inexhaustibility of invention, which perhaps obscure recognition of what a stupendous piece of work it is. No plot movement takes place in this scene until Polixenes removes his disguise at line 404, but the play is not only sustained but made rich beyond measure by what precedes and immediately follows Polixenes' dramatic explosion of wrath. This work of a dramatist in full and confident enjoyment of his powers combines literary pastoral and the true life of the country-side, Florizel's and Perdita's classical allusions and the Shepherd's reminiscences of his old wife—'her face o'fire with labour and the thing she took to quench it'. It combines exquisite lyric with the prose humours of Autolycus and the clown. It combines the ominous courtly sophistication of Polixenes with the artless queenliness of Perdita. It combines the brave young love of Florizel and Perdita with the old man's despair:

> You have undone a man of fourscore three,
> That thought to fill his grave in quiet, yea,
> To die upon the bed my father died,
> To lie close by his honest bones; but now
> Some hangman must put on my shroud, and lay me
> Where no priest shovels in dust . . .

It keeps the interest of the audience by changing the focus of attention from one group to another, by changes in the manner of speech, by changes from intense and refined feeling to broad comedy, to quasi-philosophical discussion, to dramatic dialogue. The moment when Polixenes unmasks himself and his anger explodes upon the young lovers is deferred, adding a touch of anxiety and suspense to the audience's enjoyment of the varied speech and movement which the scene provides.

When the king has stormed out with a final brutal threat to Perdita, Florizel keeps a stunned silence while Perdita and the Old Shepherd reproach him. When he speaks at last, he speaks finely:

> Why look you so upon me?
> I am but sorry, not afeared; delayed,
> But nothing altered: what I was I am.

His language takes on the heroic proportions of Macbeth and Lear as he assures Perdita that her place as his chosen bride is secure:

> It cannot fail but by
> The violation of my faith; and then
> Let Nature crush the sides o'th earth together
> And mar the seeds within!

After this the scene becomes immersed in the business of preparing the dénouement by means of Camillo's somewhat complex plots. It ends eventually with Autolycus parodying courtiers, kings, and plotters all, but nevertheless making himself useful to the cause of youth and happiness.

Act IV has contributed a splendid middle section for this play but the problem of maintaining interest in the ending is now, if anything, more severe than ever. All is prepared for the reunion of Leontes and Perdita and of Leontes and Polixenes through the love of their children. Shakespeare is certainly capable of making these scenes of reunion moving and it is possible that he actually did so. Simon Forman, the astrologer, saw *The Winter's Tale* at the Globe Theatre on 15 May 1611 and left an account of it which takes the story to the point where Perdita is recognised as Leontes' daughter. If he saw the statue scene where Hermione, thought to be dead, comes to life, it is strange that he did not trouble to note this striking climax of the play and his omission of any reference to it leaves room for the suspicion that there was an earlier version of the play in which Hermione did *not* come to life. But if indeed Shakespeare did once end the play with the reunion of father and daughter, he must soon have changed his mind, discarded what he had written, and chosen instead to subordinate the expected scene to the quite un-expected resuscitation of Hermione. Whether or not the statue scene represents second thoughts, its unexpectedness is certainly a brilliant stroke. When in Act V, sc. ii the gentlemen of the court *narrate* the scene of recognition and mutual joy, which the audience must all along have expected to witness for themselves, there could be no premature leaving of the theatre then, for what could the dramatist possibly have in store beyond the ending everyone has been expecting? Anticipation of some quite unforeseen excitement connected with Julio Romano's statue, standing in 'that removed house', is at once kindled. 'Shall we thither?' asks the Second Gentleman and the First Gentleman answers for all when he says: 'Who would be thence that has the benefit of access?' The statue scene, like the sheep-shearing, is one of the marvels of *The Winter's Tale*. The awe and mystery, and the grief and regret which are the setting of them, are heightened by Paulina's apparently matter-of-fact warnings that the paint on the seeming statue is not yet dry; but the tragedy of the lost years which no repentance can reclaim is brought out most poignantly by Leontes' half complaint and the assent to it of the devoted friend:

LEONTES: But yet, Paulina,
    Hermione was not so much wrinkled, nothing
    So aged as this seems.
POLIXENES: O, not by much!

Posthumus and Imogen had thought each other dead in *Cymbeline* and their finding of each other alive after all typifies the emergence of peace and love out of the evil and enmity of the play. The image of rekindled life is set on stage much more daringly and very much more movingly in *The Winter's Tale* and Shakespeare has even cheated a little to safeguard the full effect of this sensational climax. The apparently ghostly figure of Hermione appeared to Antigonus, as he tells us in Act III, sc. iii, to direct him about the disposal of the baby and this, by all the rules of convention and fair play, should mean that she is really dead; but we may lay the blame upon poor Antigonus whose judgement is much disturbed by the unhappy situation in which he finds himself.

Far from our nerves being relaxed as the play ends, they are rather tightened as the statue, incredibly, fearfully, warms to life before our eyes and then is heard to speak and bless the kneeling Perdita. Nothing could be further from anti-climax. Shakespeare has found such a way to handle the last movement of his reconciliation story that, instead of coming too quietly, too expectedly to rest, the play suddenly reaches for new sensation, new effect, when it would seem that, by all ordinary calculation, the material can have no more to give.

In its pushing beyond the limit of expectation and its production of a staggering *coup de théatre* when all seems set for a different ending, *The Winter's Tale* is close to *King Lear*, where also a reconciliation development of the story is involved. This point will be taken up again. For the present, it is the difference of the handling of the plot pattern from the earlier version in *Cymbeline* which is to be observed. The reduction of the number of story lines, the bravura display in Act IV, sc. iv, the tremendous climax of the ending—these give Shakespeare opportunity for some of his greatest imaginative feats. It is surprising, perhaps, given the superlative success of *The Winter's Tale*, that he evolved yet a third treatment of the pattern. It is astonishing, and yet at the same time typical of his genius, that *The Tempest* should be as different as it is from the other two.

When we consider the handling of the story in *The Tempest*, it is at once evident that it has many curious features. First and most obviously, Shakespeare here observes the neo-classic unities of time, place and action, as he has not done since *The Comedy of Errors*. Coming to the play, as he appears to have done, after *Cymbeline* and *The Winter's Tale*, it is easy to suppose that he may have seen some attractions in the neo-classic prescription. *Cymbeline* gave what may be described as a spatially extensive treatment to the reconciliation plot, with many centres of action and a variety of locations. *The Winter's Tale*, on the other hand, was temporally extensive, sixteen years being allowed to lapse between the first and second halves of the play. In the earlier play a technique of abundant continuous action was adopted; in the later, a quite different two-part arrangement was employed. To start the action near the end of the story and tell only in retrospect what led up to it represents a third method, the technical problems of which challenge a dramatist and may offer him also, perhaps, a new opportunity. So far so good. It is at this point, however, that the more remarkable aspects of Shakespeare's work on the story appear.

We observe, to begin with, that *The Tempest* makes little use of the dramatic possibilities afforded by the method of starting the action at the period of crisis. No antecedent history, in this play, brings the characters to flash-point where passion erupts in dramatic event. Instead of the characters meeting and striking sparks off each other, they are separated into groups which have no contact and the principal figure, Prospero, does not reveal himself to most of those involved until the final scene. Nor is Shakespeare interested in following the example of Garnier, Daniel, Greville and others who used the neo-classic framework for discussion, reflection and analysis rather than for action. Prospero speaks one speech which reflects directly on life but this has nothing in common with the French Senecan style. Though there is little dramatic action or reflection, however, there is a good deal of music and dancing and there are striking visual effects, notably the banquet and the masque.

Is the play itself to be thought of less as drama than as masque? Enid Welsford has suggested that this is so and that the play 'expresses, not uncertainty, ended by final success or failure, but expectancy crowned by sudden revelation. ... The plot of *The Tempest* leads up, without hesitation or uncertainty, to that moment when Prospero gathers his forgiven enemies around him, draws back the curtain from before the inner stage, and discovers Ferdinand and Miranda playing at chess'.[6] Yet *The Tempest*, emblematic as it sometimes seems to be, and though it eschews dramatic possibilities which offer themselves, is nevertheless too dramatic to be entirely a masque and also too complex to be resolved by an image of courtly harmony.

Possible depths of meaning in *The Tempest* were much in Professor Frank Kermode's mind when he prepared his Arden edition in 1954: 'There can be no question', he writes in the introduction:

that the tragicomic form of the last plays was dictated by the nature of the fables treated, and that these were chosen because they lent themselves to the formulation of poetic propositions concerning the status of human life in relation to nature, and the mercy of providence which gives new life when the old is scarred by sin or lost in folly. (p. lxi)

[6] *The Court Masque* (Cambridge, 1927), reprinted 1962, pp. 339-40. *The Tempest* is discussed in Chapter XII, passim.

These firm assertions are supported with learning and expounded in detail but the confidence shown is not reflected in the more recent New Penguin edition (1968). '*The Tempest*', according to Anne Righter, 'is an extraordinarily secretive work of art'. It raises questions which it does not answer about the nature both of its characters and of its events, whether these are enacted in the course of the play or merely referred to. 'Its very compression, the fact that it seems to hide as much as it reveals, compels a peculiarly creative response', which has taken the form of adaptations, or of original works inspired by the play. The stimulus to independent creation has also had a great effect on critical accounts of the play:

> To talk about *The Tempest*, even to try to describe it, without adding to it in terms of motivation, psychology, themes, or ideas, is extremely difficult. As with one of the seminal myths of the classical world, all interpretation beyond a simple outline of the order of events, a list of the people taking part, runs the risk of being incremental. Criticism of the play is often illuminating in itself, as a structure of ideas, without shedding much light on its ostensible subject. It may falsely limit Shakespeare's achievement. Troubling, complex, exasperating, the original is infinitely greater and more suggestive than anything that can be made out of it. (p. 22)

These comments may apply, though the Penguin editor does not say so, to Professor Kermode's exposition in the Arden.

Though to avoid all the pit-falls is scarcely to be hoped, an attempt to consider *The Tempest* on lines used for other plays may still yield some profit. Three variations on the basic crime-and-its-consequences story, revenge, retribution, reconciliation, have been considered in this chapter and, approaching *The Tempest* from this point of view, it is observable at the outset that this time there is no doubt that a crime has actually been committed. In *Cymbeline* Posthumus believed that Imogen had been unfaithful to him but he was wrong.[7] Leontes is similarly wrong in *The Winter's Tale*. The vengeful acts

---

[7] There are, typically, a number of potential 'criminals' in *Cymbeline*. The queen schemes various kinds of evil, including murder, and so does Cloten but their plans are disrupted before they have gone too far. Iachimo's traducing of Imogen is a crime actually perpetrated but it is not known to other characters until the last scene of the play.

which both perform are consequently quite out of place and their attempts to wreak vengeance become themselves a 'crime' which has to be expiated and forgiven. Alonso and Antonio did, however, conspire to deprive Prospero of his dukedom and did send him out to sea with his baby daughter, in an un-seaworthy boat. Prospero has, therefore, not only motive but also justification for revenge and, when the play starts he has opportunity as well. Retribution is similarly an important element in the play. Alonso suffers deeply and he fully accepts that all nature speaks against his sin:

> O, it is monstrous, monstrous!
> Methought the billows spoke, and told me of it;
> The winds did sing it to me; and the thunder,
> That deep and dreadful organ-pipe, pronounced
> The name of Prosper: it did bass my trespass.
> Therefore my son i'th'ooze is bedded, and
> I'll seek him deeper than e'er plummet sounded,
> And with him there lie mudded.
>
> (III, iii, 95–102)

Nevertheless, although these two elements of the story have scope to work, the possibilities of action stemming from them are not developed very far. Prospero exacts no vengeance: we are made most aware of Alonso's sufferings by his inertia and his silence.

By the end of Act I, the story up to date has been told and a new development, the love of Ferdinand and Miranda, has been initiated. Act II, in a long opening scene, allows us to see for ourselves the characters of the nobles from Italy who have arrived on the island. It also brings to immediate life before our eyes the original crime of usurpation and (intended) murder, in the re-enactment of it by Antonio and Sebastian. Antonio, who had won power for himself at the expense of his brother and was willing to take his brother's life, urges Sebastian to seize the crown of Naples by murdering *his* brother. The intervention of Ariel prevents a full repetition of the crime but, to underline the situation, Caliban, Stephano and Trinculo proceed to make a grotesque parody of the ambitions of court life. Caliban's switch of allegiance and Stephano's aspirations to kingship do not grow as far as murder till the second scene of Act III but the seeds are sown in Act II, immediately after the abortive attempt of Antonio and Sebastian. Act III opens with a love scene and then shows us Caliban instructing his new associates in how to kill Prospero. Stephano and Trinculo are drunk and not to be taken seriously. Caliban, however, is in earnest. Scene ii presents the banquet which vanishes to a clap of harpy's wings and it brings Alonso to confession and causes some disturbance of mind even to Antonio and Sebastian. Act IV presents the wedding masque and disposes of Caliban's plot. In Act V Prospero reveals himself and Alonso begs his forgiveness. In addition to our interest in these events as they unfold, we are entertained by comic capers and touched by the courtly grace of Ferdinand's and Miranda's wooing. One or two moments create a slight dramatic tension—when Antonio and Sebastian are poised with drawn swords over the sleeping Alonso and Gonzalo before Ariel enters to frustrate them, and when Prospero suddenly remembers the 'foul conspiracy' against his life and breaks off the masque; but the play does not deal in scenes of vigorous excitement and powerful passions.

The action of *The Tempest* has, in fact, the peculiarity that it is an almost entirely retrospective one. Its effect is to cancel a previous story whose events took place twelve years before the play opens. This earlier story was a strong and active one, involving violation of duty in the state and in the family, such a story as might make an apt scenario for a typical Jacobean tragedy, Caliban's reported attempt to rape Miranda supplying the otherwise missing element of sexual corruption. Alonso and Antonio believe that the story, whose development they controlled, has ended with the deaths of Prospero and Miranda. *The Tempest* shows this closed book being opened again and Alonso and Antonio being forced to live through a continuation of it, this time under the control of Prospero. The re-enactments of plotting to supplant a ruler and to dispose of him are this time frustrated. Caliban's offer of Miranda to Trinculo repeats the idea of sexual violation but Ferdinand's fervent promises of self-restraint purify this reminder of a tarnished world. His vows contribute to setting right what was wrong, just as Prospero's resumption of his dukedom restores the right order in society and the marriage of his daughter to Alonso's heir cancels old treachery with new pledging of faith. *The Tempest* re-orders the past but, apart from the one forward movement represented by the marriage of the young people, nothing, in this backward-looking story, is projected into the future. Years before, in *As You Like It*, usurpation and the enmity of brothers had already provided the initial impulses of action and in the forest of Arden each of the characters had made some discovery about himself, as the courtiers in *The Tempest* do on the island. But, in *As You Like It*, a future is prepared which Jaques allows us to foresee. Addressing the Duke, Orlando, Oliver, Silvius and Touchstone in turn, he makes his forecasts:

> You to your former honour I bequeath;
> Your patience and your virtue well deserves it;
> You to a love that your true faith does merit;
> You to your land, love, and great allies;
> You to a long and well-deserved bed;
> And you to wrangling; for thy loving voyage
> Is but for two months victual'd. . .
>
> (V, iv, 180–6)

By contrast, *The Tempest* permits us only one distinct glimpse into the future and Prospero's tone has none of Jaques' buoyancy:

> in the morn,
> I'll bring you to your ship, and so to Naples,
> Where I have hope to see the nuptial
> Of these our dear-beloved solemnized;
> And thence retire me to my Milan, where
> Every third thought shall be my grave.
>
> (V, i, 306–11)

As You Like It seems to offer some appropriate comparisons but there are reminiscences of other earlier plays in *The Tempest* also. The love of Ferdinand and Miranda recalls the lovers of *Romeo and Juliet*. Ferdinand, like Romeo, has admired women before, but he finds Miranda's superiority to the rest overwhelming. Miranda, like Juliet, comes fresh to the experience of love and, like her predecessor, gives herself to it with unreserved generosity. She refuses to quibble or prevaricate—'But this is trifling'—and cuts through the conventions of amorous delay to speak plainly: 'I am your wife if you will marry me' (III, i, 83). There are echoes also of *Hamlet*. It is Prospero's custom, as it was King Hamlet's, to sleep in the afternoon and it is then that Caliban intends that he shall be murdered, not by poison in the ear, but by violence. Antonio is a brother, like Claudius, who has murdered for a throne—that Prospero is not in fact dead is not due to failure of Antonio's will. Unlike Claudius, however, he has no conscience. 'But, for your conscience?' asks Sebastian, when Antonio boasts to him of the rewards of supplanting Prospero, and Antonio replies, coolly ironic:

> Ay, sir, where lies that? If 'twere a kibe,
> 'Twould put me to my slipper; but I feel not
> This deity in my bosom . . .
>
> (II, i, 267–9)

Alonso, on the other hand, who shares Antonio's guilt, can do what Claudius could not, give up his ill-gotten gains in a gesture of genuine repentance. 'Thy dukedom I resign', he tells Prospero, 'and do entreat/Thou pardon me my wrongs' (V, i, 118–19). Prospero himself is a manipulator figure, akin to Ulysses in *Troilus and Cressida*, or the Duke in *Measure for Measure*—or Iago in *Othello*. But at that point it is evidently necessary to pause because in important respects Prospero is very unlike those who have fulfilled an apparently similar role before him.

In noting one further feature which *The Tempest* has in common with other plays, the difference in Prospero's role comes into prominence: that is, that *The Tempest* makes use of a programme. Curses and prophecies and oracles, and instructions of one character to another, have provided programmes in earlier plays and served the purpose, among others, of giving the audience a firm grip on the development of the action while leaving Shakespeare free to exploit the possibilities which offered themselves on the way. The exceptional feature of *The Tempest*, from this point of view, is that the programme is never revealed. Clearly there is one, and it is Prospero's, long meditated and ready to be put into action whenever the propitious moment arrives. He has calculated the time needed to effect it (I, ii, 240–1) and can brook no delay or hesitation in carrying out his instructions. Ulysses lays his plans in public but a villain like Iago decides in soliloquy what his next move will be. Both take advantage of opportunity and respond to situations as they arise. Both, as plotters, ultimately fail, since there are stronger influences upon Achilles than Ulysses' devices for stimulating him into action, and Iago's lies are in the end exposed, as, from moment to moment, there was always the possibility they might be. But there is no element of risk or experiment in Prospero's manipulation. When he soliloquises, it is not to size up the situation in order to determine what he must do next but rather to comment with satisfaction on the way his plans are working out. Perhaps it was possible that Ferdinand and Miranda might not have fallen in love but the play discourages us from pursuing this. 'They are both in either's powers', Prospero comments, 'It works'—there seems scarcely to have been any doubt that it would. So completely is he in control of the situation that he feels it desirable to invent a totally illusory obstacle to make the situation more interesting to the lovers themselves. The course of love could have run quite smooth and, in fact, after the slightest of (contrived) setbacks, we find that Prospero has already 'relented' and, in some scene that we did not see, joined the lovers' hands. It is true that at the point when Prospero breaks off the masque and the later moment (V, i, 17–30) when he declares his resolution to abjure vengeance, there seem to be faint indications of a temporary loss of control over events or of indecision. Yet the first cannot amount to much, since Prospero has evidently already worked out a method of dealing with Caliban and his companions and need only remind Ariel of what has to be done. The plot against his life has never been a real danger for he is fully aware of it. The apparent hesitation in Act V, sc. i as to what he shall do with his 'prisoners' is more debateable but it seems unlikely that Prospero ever intended any harm to the men he had brought to the island. 'I have done nothing but in care of thee', he tells Miranda (I, ii, 16). Her marriage to Ferdinand will return her to Italy and restore her to her rightful position. That she should become the wife of his heir will neatly pay back Alonso for his greed towards Prospero's dukedom in the past. To go further in retaliation, at least towards Alonso, would be to risk Miranda's happiness and indeed, her tender heart, which suffers with those she sees suffer, would no doubt be gravely bruised by serious violence towards any of the ship's company.

We may say, then, that Prospero has a programme and that he has far more power to carry it out than any of his fellow-manipulators in other plays. The audience, however, is not made privy to this programme and is deprived of the guide-lines which are elsewhere offered. The initial choice of a magician as central figure must be, at least in part, responsible for this. The audience has to be kept interested, even as Ferdinand and Miranda need to be, for if everything is too clearly seen to be arranged in advance, without obstacle, doubt or question, there would be no drama at all. It is essential that Prospero should be a somewhat enigmatic figure who does not take us into his confidence and who leaves us to guess at what may be in his mind. Though we feel the controlling influence of the programme, it is never set out for us and a much-used device is cleverly adapted in this way for the support of a new narrative situation.

When we look back at *Cymbeline* and *The Winter's Tale*, it is astonishing to recognise how much responsibility is imposed upon the figure of Prospero. In other plays the gods took a hand, to rebuke mortals or to make their ambiguous promises, but in *The Tempest* the gods themselves are stage-managed by Prospero and employed to celebrate his daughter's betrothal. In all three plays those who are thought to be dead come to life, and in *The Tempest* this power of restoring to life is also vested in Prospero. As he tells us: 'graves at my command/Have waked their sleepers, oped, and let 'em forth' (V, i, 48–9), and in the course of the play he brings Alonso and Ferdinand back, as it were, from the dead. As Ferdinand puts it, he has 'received a second life' of his 'second father' (V, i, 195). If we go back to *Hamlet*, with which *The Tempest* has common elements, we find that Prospero assumes the roles both of Ghost, in that he devises the programme, and of Hamlet in that he undertakes the burden of setting right the evils of the world.

This economy, to call it that, combined with the formal neatness of the unities, would seem to make for a very tightly constructed play indeed, and one in which all ends are firmly tied in. But, as has already been suggested, there are elements of the play pulling against any such result. The deep reserve of Prospero, a necessary trait to counter his undramatic control of events, is one of them. In addition, Shakespeare has further increased our interest in him, and at the same time intensified our uncertainties, by making him a passionate man. His recapitulation of the past, for example, when he first tells Miranda his own and her history, is pulled about by the pressure of his emotions as he relives the experiences of twelve years before. His harshness to Ferdinand, explained though it is, seems severe as, to leave Caliban aside, does his treatment of Ariel in Act I, sc. ii. His speech to Ferdinand, on the breaking up of the masque, shows him to be a philosopher but strong feelings of rancour and contempt, barely controlled by a pre-determined purpose, burn through his words of forgiveness to his brother in the final scene. Such qualities in the mage dedicated to virtue rather than vengeance add fuel to curiosity and invite speculation to play over character and event. Having devised a narrative scheme which should, to all appearance, allow for a perfectly rounded and self-contained unity, Shakespeare has, it seems, deliberately allowed cracks to open up through which we catch sight of areas beyond the action of the play and these tease us and remain inexorably beyond our exploration.

To embody his magic powers and, again, to give dramatic vitality to his role as magician, Shakespeare has given to Prospero the antithetical pair, Ariel and Caliban, one a bright being of light and air, the other a black agent, born of a witch and a devil. One truly serves him for a while, in expectation of being granted his freedom, the other serves also, but only for fear of the penalty of doing otherwise, and he will thwart Prospero or murder him if he can. The invention of these two is another neat and clever means of strengthening the interest of Prospero's role as magician and controller of events but this also, in the course of the play, leads out into regions far beyond the immediate area of the action. Caliban proves able to state a case of his own and arouses our guilt, if not our sympathy. In Ariel too, we seem to recognise an independent life and character which puzzle us out of thought. Ariel is an even more remarkable creation of the dramatist than Caliban since Caliban's motivations are in all their aspects humanly recognisable, whereas Ariel is essentially detached from all human conditions.

As for reconciliation, the end to which, it would seem, all the play has been tailored, when it comes it comes in more ambiguous form than it did in *Cymbeline* or *The Winter's Tale*. There have been deaths by the way in *The Winter's Tale* but by the end all enmity is purged. Harmony and thanksgiving conclude *Cymbeline* also but the absences from the final scene in that play are of particular interest in relation to *The Tempest*. Cloten was butchered in the act of pursuing murder and rape. The queen died, repenting nothing but that 'The evils she hatch'd were not effected' (V, v, 60). Shakespeare makes no attempt to assimilate them into the concord of the last scene but, in *The Tempest*, no one is omitted, not Caliban who would have relished Cloten's plan, nor Antonio, whose state of mind we have no reason to believe is any different from that of the queen. Caliban will 'be wise hereafter, and seek for grace' (V, i, 294–5): here, perhaps, is a victory in that he is reconciled to Prospero's mastery, but there appear to be no concessions from Antonio. Even Sebastian, who would seem to be made of more penetrable stuff than his companion, since at least he recognises that conscience may have a claim, even he fails to make any gesture either of sorrow for past misdeeds or of present goodwill. Nothing has weaned him from his partnership with Antonio. The unassimilated and un-assimilable remain on stage to the last in *The Tempest*.

When we review the various measures which Shakespeare adopted in the two earlier plays to bring the crime-and-its-consequences story to a resolution in reconciliation rather than revenge or retribution, the much less firm tone of the ending of *The Tempest* seems all the more remarkable. The action of the play has been pared down to a minimum so that only the last part of a whole sequence of events is presented. A magician figure is at the centre of events, who can, and does, by his power, prevent any untoward complications developing as he conducts matters to a conclusion. Why, then, with all things in favour of such an eventuality, does Shakespeare not arrange that Antonio and Sebastian clearly repent and receive the hand of friend-ship? Why does he not allow Prospero to seem more cheerful than he does as events draw to a close? Why are we deprived of the story-teller's valedictory assurance that back in Naples and Milan the three men of sin will really lead 'a clear life' or, if they do not, that they will come to 'lingering perdition' as Ariel warned them in Act III, sc. iii? To compare the handling of the story material in *The Tempest* with that in *Cymbeline* is to feel with particular force the situation in the later play. Not only is the number of story lines reduced to a single action, but in *The Tempest* Shakespeare the story-teller very conspicuously does *not* pay off all his debts.

The unanswered questions about the ending lead us back to the role of Prospero. Making him a magician has been part of Shake-speare's solution to the technical demands of the reconciliation plot, by means of a treatment which concentrates attention on the last movement and condenses the time scale. Some agency is required to produce the resolution and, if time is not available and a totally arbitrary supernatural intervention is unacceptable, a magician with a personal involvement in the action to be resolved is an excellent device. That it is one which presents problems in terms of the main-tenance of dramatic interest has already been suggested. In comparing him with other figures who fulfil ostensibly similar roles as plotters or manipulators within other plays, some distinctions have also been made. The implications of Prospero's function may now, perhaps, be taken a little further.

The play has been discussed so far in terms of how Shakespeare handled the material in order to tell his story of malice and hostility and its issue in reconciliation between the opposed parties. But the angle can be changed and attention focussed instead on Prospero as story-teller, rather than on Shakespeare. Within the play, it is Prospero who sets the story in motion and who organises the development of events. He arranges for the enactment of a story which he has worked out and he produces some scenes with special care—for example his own appearance as Duke of Milan, to the astonished courtiers in Act V, sc. i, and his revelation of Ferdinand and Miranda at chess. The relation of Prospero's role as dramatic story-teller to that of Shakespeare is a consideration which repays attention.

Bradley's recognition of a 'curious analogy' between the development of Iago's plots against Othello and the processes of dramatic composition has already been noted (p. 19). Iago and others may well be seen as in some degree the dramatist's surrogates within their respective plays, but it is Prospero who is most commonly identified with Shakespeare himself. He has unprecedented control over the play in which he appears and, so to speak, 'composes' it from within. In his abjuring of his 'rough magic' it is possible to see a parallel with Shakespeare's retirement from the theatre and his renunciation of his own art. When Prospero in the epilogue asks for the audience's indulgence to set him free, some have thought that we are listening to Shakespeare's request for his own release. His 'project', like Prospero's, has been to please and he has pleased so well that he can now retire to Stratford and the life of a gentleman.

The Tempest is usually regarded as Shakespeare's last play but as to why there were no more opinions differ. He may, indeed, not have renounced his art at all but have intended to write more. Perhaps he was bored with the theatre and would have turned, had he lived, to non-dramatic poetry. Perhaps he had explored to its limits the world of dramatic illusion and it was his last play 'because in it even he had reached the point beyond which there could be no further dramatic development' (Anne Righter). Considering the play, and especially Prospero's part in it, in the context of the present study, a somewhat different version of the situation may be suggested.

The Tempest is in essence, when all is said, a brilliant piece of story-engineering with most clever and ingenious contrivances to ensure complete coordination and smooth running. Improvisatory skills do not need to be called on in the course of it but security is not bought at the price of clogging the works with too much action. With such a splendidly devised mechanism there should have been no difficulty in bringing all to rest at the most satisfactory of full stops. Shakespeare had not employed such a technique since *The Comedy of Errors*. In the years between, his stories had bulged, dwindled, burst their limits, taken new courses, *Hamlet* being the supreme exception in that creative genius found there a way to express itself fully within the frame adopted. In the late plays Shakespeare was exploring a different approach to material. The drive through to a dénouement by process of reconciliation does not allow the conditions for slow preparation and development of characters, nor for complex interactions between them. Management of the story pattern is in itself a matter of considerable difficulty. In *The Tempest* Shakespeare arrives at what seems to be the perfect solution to the narrative problems and, equally, within the play, Prospero arrives at a perfect way of cancelling out the old ending to his story and creating a new one. Yet, in the very act of fashioning the ideal structure, Shakespeare introduces doubts where none need have existed; at the moment of completion of his plans, Prospero remains in some degree unsatisfied. Dramatist and magician have made their arrangements with care and skill, but life with its unbiddable emotions, its unexpected blanks, its unwanted and uncongenial demands, forces its way in, blurring the edges of the narrative and refusing to be contained within the well-prepared formula. Prospero, who began his part by narrating to his daughter the story of her past and who continues to be responsible for the story throughout the play, evinces towards the end some disillusion with his role. He stages a superb celebration of his daughter's betrothal, a scene which is to crown his plans for her and see the fulfilment of his dearest hopes but, before the masque can be concluded, the bitter memory of 'that foul conspiracy of the beast Caliban and his confederates' breaks in and spoils his triumph. At the recollection, the characters of the masque fade away 'into air, into thin air' for the exquisite words of Iris and the 'graceful dance' of the reapers and nymphs are seen to compose, after all, only a partial truth. Over and against the masque there stands the anti-masque, performed in this instance to the accompaniment of Ariel's tabor—Caliban and his companions lifting up their noses 'as they smelt music' and pictured for us

> I'th' filthy mantled pool beyond your cell,
> There dancing up to th' chins . . .
> (IV, i, 182–3)

Prospero cannot exclude them. They force themselves upon his attention and oblige him to take account of them. He has in fact already made provision for them, but at this moment of pride and joy in the happiness of his daughter he resents the necessity of meeting their demands.

It might be expected that a story-teller with such power as Prospero has over his materials would be allowed to bring to an assured and undisturbed conclusion this one story, at least, so close to his heart as it is; but no such thing. The climax of the second narrative in his total scheme has still to come, the moment when he will face Alonso and the others in his old form as Duke of Milan and receive, according to the development he has planned, their repentance and submission.

> They being penitent,
> The sole drift of my purpose doth extend
> Not a frown further. . .
> (V, i, 28–9)

he tells Ariel. But as Caliban and the clowns marred the happy celebration of the culmination of the Ferdinand and Miranda story, so Antonio and Sebastian refuse to cooperate in bringing the second narrative line to its proper destination. Has Antonio really repented? It seems not. Can Prospero himself, faced with Antonio's intransigence, play the role he has envisaged as his own part? He makes the gesture of forgiveness but it carries less than entire conviction:

> For you, most wicked sir, whom to call brother
> Would even infect my mouth, I do forgive
> Thy rankest fault—all of them . . .
> (V, i, 130–3)

Shakespeare and Prospero are both implicated in the business of story-telling in *The Tempest*. For much of the play their functions are inseparable but when it comes to drawing the final line and writing the 'happy-ever-after', Shakespeare stays Prospero's hand. Gonzalo, the good old man, offers a conventional happy ending in his summing up of what has occurred (Act V, sc. i, 205–13). He has an innocent delight in the golden endings of fairy tale but the play itself presses on beyond this naïveté. Whether or not Gonzalo is justified in including Claribel's marriage in his enumeration of the causes of rejoicing, we can be certain that he oversimplifies the Antonio/Sebastian situation. Yet he is not the only one to remind us how strongly tempted story-tellers may be to cheat. Prospero himself succumbs when in his speech, ostensibly of forgiveness, to his brother he pretends that a situation of mutual reconciliation exists, even while the words he uses deny it and so also does Antonio's silence.

The narrative-drama of his time had led Shakespeare into telling many stories and sometimes he too had cheated for the sake of the design. He had, however, time and again, managed to accommodate both life and the needs of narrative. If the story had to be changed to make room for an unexpected growth, so it was. If some cutting short or sleight of hand was needed to bring matters to an acceptable conclusion, then he relied on adding a fresh touch of dramatic vitality to the ending and so carrying off the situation in the theatre. But in *The Tempest* growing points are allowed to develop which he neither cultivates for their own sakes nor prunes for the sake of the ending and, as a consequence, the incompatibility between life and the stories that story-tellers make out of it is thrown into sharp relief. Prospero cannot mesh in together all the parts of the material he works with: Shakespeare will not.

'... the tragedian in real life was not the equal of the tragic poet', writes Bradley, comparing the role of Iago as composer of the story in *Othello* with that of Shakespeare as dramatist. 'His [Iago's] psychology ... was at fault at a critical point, as Shakespeare's never was. And so his catastrophe came out wrong, and his piece was ruined'.[8] Out of the ruin of Iago's piece, however, Shakespeare constructed *his* ending of *Othello*, but in *The Tempest* he simply left things as they were. The greatest of his story-tellers, Prospero, has

[8] *Shakespearean Tragedy* (London, 1906), p. 231.

done his best but life has proved resistant to his ordering and the edges of his story have shaded away into ambiguity and uncertainty. Only death, as he more than once acknowledges, is the real rounder-off. We are left with the paradox that the most tightly-woven of Shakespeare's mature plays is also the only one that is, in the modern phrase, open-ended. The triumphant working of the last variant on the last pattern questions its own accomplishment and brings us back to those reflections articulated by Virginia Woolf's Bernard: 'there are so many, and so many—stories of childhood, stories of school, love, marriage, death and so on; and none of them are true . . . Life is not susceptible perhaps to the treatment we give it when we try to tell it.' As for the creative activity which has been stimulated into action by all the stories of his previous career, the conditions of its working here are different. The conversation piece of Act II, sc. i has already been discussed (pp. 91–4, as a superb example of Shakespeare's creative power operating without the aid of narrative materials. But the distinctive achievement of *The Tempest* is something different and expresses itself in the many suggestions of things which are not included in the play. The story does not open out, as so many stories before have done, but it is set against a background whose dimensions, we are repeatedly made to realise, are greater than its own. In arousing our sense of this disparity and stimulating our responses to it lies the particular work of creation in this play.

7
Hamlet:
The Triumph of a Programme

Though *Hamlet* and *King Lear* stand on twin peaks among the high points of Shakespeare's creative art, considered in relation to their handling of their stories they are very different from each other. Each shares with other plays characteristics which have already been described but it is a different selection of characteristics in each play. *Hamlet* works upon a programme as other plays have done but this time the programme is thought through and carried out with extraordinary attention to all its implications. The kind of supplementary creation, which in other plays had an unsettling effect on what seemed to be a clearly laid down line of action, here reinforces the 'main' story and the power achieved by this concentration of effort appears to be virtually inexhaustible. *King Lear*, on the other hand, is less tightly organised. It also generates immense power but this is achieved by means of Shakespeare's response to difficulties of kinds which he has been seen to experience elsewhere, in particular the problems presented by unevenly spaced action. Such problems call for special imaginative exertion and Shakespeare's imaginative activity in *King Lear* is altogether exceptional in its results, though the same sort of activity can be observed at work elsewhere.

The two plays draw together many of the threads of preceding discussions and at the same time the earlier commentaries help to bring into focus important aspects of *Hamlet* and *Lear*. For these reasons the two plays come last in this study but they will now be discussed in chronological order, *Hamlet* first and then *Lear*.

In all the writing about Hamlet, the question most frequently asked is: why did Hamlet delay? The answers offered may be psychological or philosophical, moral or religious, but basically the question itself relates to dramatic structure. Put baldly, it is: how does Shakespeare fill the interval between instigation to revenge and execution of vengeance?

That finding material for the middle of a revenge play of this type constitutes a real problem can be illustrated by reference to Kyd's *Spanish Tragedy*. Kyd, who was remarkably clever at perceiving and developing dramatic possibilities, recognised the potentialities of the Senecan revenge formula not only for theatrical excitement but also for providing a firm dramatic framework. A deed calling for vengeance initiates the action, vengeance is executed at the close. Both polar events are of a nature to generate excitement and the clearly marked points of departure and arrival provide for positive movement and a sense of direction, qualities much needed by the early Elizabethan dramatists as they sought for a dramatic structure more ambitious and satisfying than that provided by mere sequentiality of events. Kyd follows Senecan precedent by having the ghost of Andrea and the figure of Revenge describe to the audience those events preceding the opening of the play which will require to be revenged within the action, but he enlivens the whole situation by his own device of a second murder which takes place within the framework set up by the first revenge scheme. From then on we are much more concerned about the Horatio-Hieronimo-Bellimperia situation than we are about Don Andrea and his somewhat obscure affairs.

Kyd also recognised that Senecan declamatory rhetoric, designed to give strong expression to reactions in acute situations, could be humanised and personalised to suit a more modern temper and he created a language for Hieronimo which, like his other innovations, was full of potential for vigorous development. Yet we cannot help noticing that Kyd, with all his gifts and allowing for his *two* starts— one for Andrea, one for Horatio—has difficulty in filling the interval between murder and vengeance. In his treatment of Hieronimo he gives us, splendidly, a mind become distracted through grief and the frustration of justice and beginning to sink beneath the burden into madness, but even so he has to fill out with the Alexandro-Viluppo material and with elaboration (lively enough in itself) of Pendringano's fate. Here is the penalty, or the problem, of what may be called the two-event revenge plot. In plays where revenge is piecemeal (as in *The Revenger's Tragedy*), the problem does not arise. In *The Spanish Tragedy* it does and *Hamlet*, which is also based on the two-event plot, inherits the same difficulty.

Kyd reduces the distance between the beginning and the end of his play by, in effect, starting it twice. Shakespeare rejects Kyd's double crime idea (wisely, since Kyd's example shows how difficult it is to sustain equal interest in both) and he retains the usual Senecan situation in which the murder to be avenged has taken place before the play begins. But he defers statement of the original crime until near the end of Act I. Up to that time we cannot be certain, from what is put before us, that it is going to be a revenge play at all. The traditional ghost is indeed introduced in the first scene but only by report and at that point his significance is doubtful. Those who discuss him are inclined to believe that he comes to warn of some impending national disaster. He is clad in armour, a fact which puts Horatio in mind of the dead king's single combat with Fortinbras of Norway and of young Fortinbras's anger at the forfeiture of Norwegian land, which followed his father's defeat. He recalls that apparitions and omens preceded the death of Julius Caesar and one of his first questions to the ghost is whether he knows of any calamity impending to the country. A reasonable deduction to make from this first scene would be that the two young sons of the two dead kings will be taking up the quarrels of their fathers and that the audience is being prepared for a political and dynastic struggle, embellished by whatever personal matter the dramatist may see fit to add.

Scene ii establishes the identity of the reigning kings of Denmark and Norway and this corrects some natural assumptions derived from scene i. It also shows Claudius dealing efficiently with the threat of war from Norway. Otherwise, it sets the play off on a new tack. Claudius's first speech, politically adroit as it is, draws immediate attention to personal elements in the situation—'our dear brother's death'—and throws in a surprising complication—'. . . our sometime sister, now our queen . . . Have we . . . Taken to wife. . .'. Young Hamlet appears, and he alone among the company is dressed in mourning for the dead king who was his father. The sister-wife, the nephew-son, the uncle-father converse and Hamlet's first words ensure that the audience will not overlook the relationships between them:

KING: But now, my cousin Hamlet, and my son—
HAMLET: A little more than kin, and less than kind.
KING: How is it that the clouds still hang on you?

HAMLET: Not so, my lord; I am too much i' the sun.
QUEEN: Good Hamlet, cast thy nighted colour off,
        And let thine eye look like a friend on Denmark,
        Do not for ever with thy vailed lids
        Seek for thy noble father in the dust.

The king and queen speak apparently freely and open-heartedly. Gertrude is affectionate, Claudius considerate and generous. To assuage any sting that Hamlet may feel at his own failure to succeed to the throne he makes a public pronouncement:

> let the world take note
> You are the most immediate to our throne

and he adds assurances of personal esteem and goodwill:

> we beseech you bend you to remain
> Here in the cheer and comfort of our eye,
> Our chiefest courtier, cousin, and our son.

When the king and queen leave the stage, Hamlet may seem to have been won over but his outburst as soon as he is alone disposes of any impression of that kind which may have been created. The preceding exchanges and the situation at court, as it has just been presented, all stand in a different light by the time that Hamlet has finished his first soliloquy and Horatio and others have come to tell him of the ghost. Hamlet's first response is not, like Horatio's, political, but personal and moral: 'I doubt some foul play'.

Scenes i and ii have been full of story possibilities. Scene iii may reasonably be expected to identify the major lead out of all those which have been offered. Instead, however, of following up either the political or the family situations of the royal house, the scene takes up and expands what has appeared to be only a minor point in scene ii, Laertes' departure for France. In the course of it we meet a new character, Ophelia, and we hear a great deal about Hamlet. A puzzling feature of what we hear is that it does not appear to bear much relation to the young man we have already encountered. The Hamlet who spoke in soliloquy in scene ii and received news of the appearance of the ghost was one whose mind was full of foul images and who contemplated suicide, a man preparing to meet a ghost, 'though hell itself should gape'. The Hamlet whom Polonius and

Laertes speak of is one capable of thoughtless trifling, one whose wooing of a pretty girl may be dangerous for her but is a casual matter for him. The tone of the scene seems to belong to a different world from that which contains the ghost of old Hamlet and the sombre passionate figure of his son.

It is against the background of these three scenes that the interview between Hamlet and the ghost finally occurs and at this point that the motivating impulse of the play is first clearly defined as revenge. Shakespeare has thus, so to speak, held back the start of the story (whereas Kyd started twice) and he has used the opening scenes to provide an introduction to the complex world of political, familial and love relationships into which the ghost's disclosures are to be injected. Scenes ii and iii have already made it apparent that relationships and emotions are so much intertwined in this world that any new element will cause widespread reaction. The Senecan ghost, in these circumstances, is no longer merely a device for starting the play but is a dynamic actor on a scene already alive with character and tension.

The spirit of the dead king provides answers to some of the questions raised by earlier scenes. He also instructs his son to act. From the information he gives and Hamlet's acceptance of his instructions, the whole subsequent action of the play proceeds.

It is a characteristic method of Shakespeare's dramatic storytelling to lay down early in a play a programme for the development of the action which is to follow. This has been observed in relation to a number of plays in the course of this study and *Hamlet* provides the culminating example. The guiding formula is that provided by the exchanges between Hamlet and the ghost in scene v. From the implications of what is enjoined and accepted in this scene, Shakespeare draws out the matter which constitutes the action of his play until the moment when Claudius dies by Hamlet's hand.

The action of the play can be laid out as a matter of coherent and consistent development from Act I, sc. v and the following pages will attempt to do this. The detail required will indicate some of the richness of the play and the study will bring us round once more to recognition of the supreme creative power which, above all else, sets Shakespeare apart.

The ghost opens his mind freely to Hamlet; that is to say, he not only tells him the story of his murder and demands that Hamlet

avenge it but he reveals his own sense of the most dreadful implications of the murder. He emphasises sexual corruption in the relations
of Claudius and the queen, seduction matched by weakness and
leading to a marriage which he and Hamlet regard as incestuous,
and he emphasises also the particular villainy of sending him to his
death with all his sins on his head so that he has to expiate them by
his torments in the afterlife. He urges Hamlet to avenge murder
and cleanse the court of sexual impurity and he also instructs him to
distinguish between the two agents of these crimes. Hamlet must
not contrive anything against his mother.

What the ghost presents to Hamlet is an overwhelming tally of
crime and sin and the task of setting right what is so deeply wrong
is a terrible burden. The ghost's speech marks the end of his youth.
The young man who wrote verses to Ophelia and whom Laertes and
Polonius describe had already at least begun to sicken and fade
(though they have not noticed it) before they think fit to warn
Ophelia of him but at this moment, when the ghost delivers his
message, the last of Hamlet's youth dies. 'You, my sinews, grow not
instant old', he says. The old life he knew is dead with his youth,
and he must begin to live a new one:

> Yea, from the table of my memory
> I'll wipe away all trivial fond records,
> All saws of books, all forms, all pressures past,
> That youth and observation copied there,
> And thy commandment all alone shall live
> Within the book and volume of my brain,
> Unmix'd with baser matter. . .
>
> (I, v, 98–104)

The action of the play which follows will show what performance
of this vow exacts and it is soon plain that attention is to be claimed,
not primarily for violent and sensational events, but for a demonstration of what the shedding of an old life and the assuming of a new
will mean in these circumstances and for this particular young man,
Hamlet.

Our understanding of the situation is sharpened in the next two
Acts by, among other means, the introduction of various contrasts.
Immediately after the ghost scene at the end of Act I and the
sequence of Hamlet's reactions to the ghost's tale, ending with his

sober though reluctant acceptance of his duty, Act II opens with Polonius in the act of instructing his man, Reynaldo, how to set a watch on Laertes. This is a meaner—and sillier—Polonius than the one who gave Laertes his parting advice, and we see him now as a shallow moralist busied with petty designs to counter petty sin. Polonius has got the world and human nature by heart, or so he believes, and in his own view he knows all the tricks. He is untiringly busy but his attitude to life is essentially a stale and unprofitable one. He has, by his own account, known and done everything, including loving madly in his youth and acting Julius Caesar in his student days. Everything, as he handles it, loses its bright gloss and becomes 'a little soil'd i' the working'. Polonius is far from being a bad man. He means well but his imagination does not go beyond the proverbial wisdom of the worldly-wise. His view of human behaviour might, in other conditions than those provided by the play, pass as shrewd but, in the play as it is, his confident diagnoses of one situation after another are proved wrong. The effect of this, as we watch, is to enforce our recognition that the issues involved in the action lie at a profounder level than those one or two layers of motive and impulse which Polonius understands.

The inadequacies of Polonius within the world of the play point the contrast between that world as it is progressively revealed and the world of appearances which is commonly accepted. Hamlet's meeting with his old friends, Rosencrantz and Guildenstern (II, ii) offers another kind of contrast, this time between Hamlet as he was in days before his father's death and Hamlet as he is now—not simply oppressed, as in the Act I, sc. i, soliloquy, but burdened with knowledge and a fearful obligation. We have a brief glimpse of the genuinely carefree life of an earlier time as for a moment Hamlet recaptures the tone of his student days and spontaneous warmth of friendship and light-hearted banter dispel the sombre clouds he lives under now. But this is only for a moment. A word brings the clouds back and then again the extent to which Hamlet's new life sets him apart from all that belonged to the old world becomes sharply apparent. He would share at least some of his feelings with these old and loved friends of his boyhood if he could, but they cannot follow him when he tries to explain the effect on him of the revelation of evil which he has undergone. They can make only a frivolous response to his 'What a piece of work is man' speech and Hamlet recognises that confidence is hopeless. Yet for old friendship's sake he warns them against meddling. Only those who know what the stakes are should take part in the game which is to play. Others, like Polonius, and like Rosencrantz and Guildenstern, can only act the fool or become the villain's pawns. By Hamlet's advances to and then parrying of Rosencrantz and Guildenstern, and finally by his contrivance of their deaths, Shakespeare gives mordant expression to what is involved in Hamlet's promises to the ghost. He must 'wipe away' from his mind 'all pressures past that youth and observation copied there': the new obligation to the ghost cancels out all previous obligations.

His brutality to Ophelia in the central area of the play is an even more striking demonstration of the same thing. We never see Hamlet in his old relationship with Ophelia: we only hear about it from Act I, sc. iii onwards, but the effect of the ghost's revelations upon this relationship is shown to us early, in Act II, sc. i, when Ophelia reports to her father how Hamlet had appeared to her: 'As if he had been loosed out of hell/To speak of horrors. . .' Perhaps we are to understand that in this first interview with Ophelia, when he looked so long and intently into her face, he was wondering whether he could share the burden of his knowledge with her, or it may be that, distractedly bearing the weight of the new life which has fallen upon him, he sought her out to find in her an image of the former life now for ever inaccessible to him.

We know what kind of poetry Hamlet wrote when he was the young lover described by Polonius and Laertes in Act I, sc. iii. Doubt was then an idea to be used playfully:

> Doubt thou the stars are fire;
> Doubt that the sun doth move;
> Doubt truth to be a liar;
> But never doubt I love.
> (II, ii, 115–18)

Since then, distrust of all 'seeming' has entered deeply into his soul and Ophelia sees clearly how different he is, though she does not know the cause:

> O what a noble mind is here o'erthrown!
> . . .
> And I, of ladies most deject and wretched,

That sucked the honey of his musicked vows,
Now see that noble and most sovereign reason
Like sweet bells jangled, out of time and harsh,
That unmatched form and feature of blown youth
Blasted with ecstasy. . .

(III, i, 150–60)

Various elaborations of Hamlet's state of mind in regard to
Ophelia could be proposed: for example, that it is in relation to her
that the clash between his old and new selves is most distressing to
him and that his harshness is a product of his pain; or that he must
treat her and his own feelings for her with particular violence lest
love and pity deflect him from the mission he has undertaken.
Hamlet has become a new man and must henceforward look on all
things with new eyes. He has become a stranger to those who knew
him best[1] and it is necessary that he should keep his distance from
them lest they weaken or contaminate his purpose. His 'antic disposition' is both a sign of his alienation and also a device he adopts
deliberately to prevent others getting too close to his mind and thus
being in a position to loosen his grasp on what he must do.

What the ghost's commands involve, then, in terms of hitherto
close relationships, is one important aspect of the middle material of
the play. The bringing of Ophelia, Polonius, and Rosencrantz and
Guildenstern to their deaths constitutes a dramatic conclusion to this
line of deduction from Act I, sc. v and another aspect of the ghost's
communications to Hamlet has to be taken into account in considering their fates.

The ghost's theological persuasion has been the subject of some
enquiry and speculation. He is suffering, it would seem, in purgatory
for sins committed in his lifetime and it is a feature of his murder
which he specially emphasises that he was given no chance to clear
himself of sin before he died:

---

[1] Claudius, with his usual intelligence, sees and expresses the matter
clearly:

> Hamlet's transformation: so call it,
> Sith nor th' exterior nor the inward man
> Resembles that it was . . .   (II, ii, 5–7)

The change has occurred since I, v, when Hamlet was last seen.

Cut off even in the blossoms of my sin,
Unhouseled, disappointed, unaneled,
No reck'ning made, but sent to my account
With all my imperfections on my head.
O, horrible! O horrible! Most horrible!

(I, v, 76–80)

Whatever is doubtful about the theology, it is at least manifest that
the ghost sees the murder and its consequences as having a spiritual
dimension: there is a level of judgement beyond the human in which
he, a good man by earthly standards, may be convicted of 'foul
crimes'. If this is so, what then should be the judgement on Claudius,
a fratricide, who cuts off his brother's mortal life and sends him to
suffer the unspeakable torments of purgation in another world?

The emphasis placed by the ghost on these ideas draws attention
to their importance. In fact, they provide the background against
which the characters play out their destinies. The events which take
place have implications not only in this world, but in another also
and Claudius, for one, has no doubt that what will pass as acceptable
here will be exposed in its true colours in that 'undiscovered country'
beyond the grave:

In the corrupted currents of this world
Offense's gilded hand may shove by justice,
And oft 'tis seen the wicked prize itself
Buys out the law. But 'tis not so above.
There is no shuffling; there the action lies
In his true nature, and we ourselves compelled,
Even to the teeth and forehead of our faults,
To give in evidence. . .

(III, iii, 57–64)

To trace the developments from the ghost's insistence on sin and
judgement is to enter into a discussion of Claudius, primarily, and
of Gertrude and of Hamlet's attitudes towards them both. The fates
of Ophelia, Polonius, Rosencrantz and Guildenstern fall into place
in the course of the discussion.

Act II opens with Claudius and Polonius setting a trap for Hamlet,
with Ophelia as the bait. She is to appear to be reading a devotional
book and to be placed, as though by accident, in Hamlet's way.

Polonius, having planned the deception, is ready enough at the same time to wag a reproving finger at deceit:

> We are oft to blame in this,
> 'Tis too much proved, that with devotion's visage
> And pious action we do sugar o'er
> The devil himself. . .

His easy moralising does not touch his own conscience but it does touch the king's who turns aside to confess:

> O 'tis too true.
> How smart a lash that speech doth give my conscience!
> The harlot's cheek, beautied with plast'ring art,
> Is not more ugly to the thing that helps it
> Than is my deed to my most painted word.
> O heavy burden! . . .

This sudden break in Claudius's hitherto uncracked façade marks the beginning of a strong development of material round Claudius. By the end of the scene his language is sharper than it has been before. He has overheard Hamlet's conversation with Ophelia and he no longer accepts that the cause of Hamlet's behaviour is either love or madness. He recognises Hamlet clearly as a danger and he is no longer willing to attempt to pacify him or temporise with him: 'He shall with speed to England'. In the next scene Hamlet springs *his* trap for the king and, where Claudius failed, Hamlet succeeds. The king is caught and exposes his guilt to Hamlet. He has now twice confessed in this Act, once in his aside on Polonius's speech, and again by his response to the Mousetrap play. Alone in scene iii he knows that matters have come to a crisis for him: 'O, my offense is rank, it smells to heaven'. Like Milton's Satan, on Mount Niphates, hesitating for a final instant before he commits himself irredeemably to evil, Claudius reviews his course of life and whither it tends. He thinks with anguish of his state of sin and deprivation and he toys with the idea of repentance. But, like Satan, he knows that he cannot really repent. He is not prepared to give up the fruits of his sin, and heaven will not be hoodwinked. On earth justice can be shoved aside if the offender is rich and powerful enough, but not so in heaven: 'There is no shuffling, there the action lies/In his true nature'. Even so his heart is not yet entirely hardened. He continues to wish that he could repent even while his self-will is asserting itself to make repentance impossible. He prays at last for a miracle that self-will may be broken and that he may be made humble and capable of penitence. It is the crucial moment in his history, and of the two currents in his soul the impulse to self-will is the stronger. His thoughts remain below. His prayers will not be heard in heaven.

'Satan', so runs the argument to *Paradise Lost*, Book IV, 'falls into many doubts with himself and many passions, fear, envy and despair; but at length confirms himself in evil.' Dame Helen Gardner compares the treatment of Satan with that of Macbeth[2] and he can be considered also in relation to Claudius. And we may add that if Milton learned something from Shakespeare's portraits of damnation, so may have done also an altogether lesser writer whose efforts, though much inferior, are nevertheless of interest in relation to *Hamlet*. Heywood's *A Woman Killed with Kindness* was acted in 1603 and one or two touches in it seem to suggest that he had in mind in the writing of it a reproduction, scaled down to fit the dimensions of his domestic drama, of some of the features of *Hamlet*. Whether he was aware of it or not, some of his scenes do have that relation to the greater play and Heywood's cruder treatment throws into sharp outline points made more subtly by Shakespeare. The friend-betrayer and seducer, Wendoll, is a petty villain but, like Claudius and Satan, he too finds that 'villains, when they would, cannot repent' (II, iii, 52) and, like the mightier pair, after an effort of self-examination, he accepts his situation and plans to pursue, without further compunction, an unscrupulous career of self-advancement. All three of these figures are fully aware of their state when they finish their self-examination and turn to ruthless prosecution, without further hesitation, of their careers of evil-doing.

Act III, sc. iii is the climactic moment of Claudius's life. For a moment the balance sways uncertainly between repentance and obduracy but when he rises from his knees it is plain that he will not now turn back. Claudius has ripened for the damnation which the ghost plainly indicated that he deserved and it is by Hamlet's doing that this is so. His continual pressure on Claudius, in the first place by his unaccommodating behaviour, then by his growing eccentricity, and finally by the staging of the play, has forced

---

[2] 'The Tragedy of Damnation' in *Elizabethan Drama: Critical Essays*, ed. R. J. Kaufmann (New York, 1961), pp. 320–41.

Claudius out from behind his screen of 'painted words' and obliged him to recognise what lies at the bottom of his own soul. He dies at the end a confessed 'incestuous, murderous, damned Dane' (V, ii, 317).

Much comment has been directed to Hamlet's part in Act III, sc. iii and commentators have been greatly exercised over Hamlet's rejection of the opportunity to kill the king while he kneels in prayer. They divide, roughly speaking, into those who consider that it was temperamental inability to take action which held him back, i.e. weakness of character, and those who are appalled by the reason he gives for withholding—that he wishes to despatch Claudius while he is 'about some act/That has no relish of salvation in't', so as to be sure that 'his soul may be as damn'd and black/As hell, whereto it goes'. Both parties are inclined to think that the reason he gives for hanging back is not his real one. Yet Hamlet's respect for religious observance, even when performed by such a man as Claudius, is something we are surely meant to note and approve of, for it is contrasted with the attitudes of Laertes and Claudius himself in Act IV, sc. vii:

KING: . . . what would you undertake
          To show yourself in deed your father's son
          More than in words?
LAERTES: To cut his throat i' the church
KING: No place, indeed, should murder sanctuarize;
          Revenge should have no bounds. . .

As for the argument that Hamlet's own character is terribly blackened if he *really* wants to damn Claudius, the reply must lead us back to the development of the play from the programme in Act I, sc. v. For the prayer scene should be understood in terms of the material and movement of the play as a whole, not in terms of the psychology of Hamlet. The play becomes, as it progresses, not a story about how one man manages eventually to kill another man, but an account of a crisis which forces the protagonists to recognise and choose between absolutes which lie beneath the activities and motives of ordinary life and which may remain permanently hidden unless some particularly severe and unusual pressure forces them into notice. There is nothing forced or strained in this development of the story, given the light in which the ghost sees the crimes which have been committed and the terms in which Hamlet accepts the obligation to take action and to set things right. Thus Claudius chooses, with Milton's Satan:

> Farewell remorse! All good to me is lost;
> Evil, be thou my Good. . .
> *(Paradise Lost*, IV, 109–10)

Thus Hamlet chooses when he responds to the ghost's commandment to exorcise evil from the state of Denmark:

> thy commandment all alone shall live
> Within the book and volume of my brain.
> (I, v, 102–3)

Those who palter with the choice, like Rosencrantz and Guildenstern, or who are incapable of recognising what the situation demands, like Polonius, are crushed between the opposing forces:

> 'Tis dangerous when the baser nature comes
> Between the pass and fell incensed points
> Of mighty opposites. . .
> (V, ii, 60–2)

Ophelia is crushed too, or perhaps pulled apart would be an apter metaphor. In her innocence she knows nothing of the forces and antipathies engaged but feels only the pull of her affections and loyalty to her father and the contrary pull of her feelings for Hamlet. It is true that Hamlet's insistence on his mission brings pain and disaster to all these persons who are by no means wicked. It is part of the tragic force of the play that it should be so. It is also part of the nature of the conflict that there should be no truces and no compromise.

It is an essential and emphatic element in the ghost's presentation of the data of the play in Act I, sc. v that Claudius is seen to be damnable and it is right, therefore, that Hamlet should wish him to be damned. That he does so is not a reflection on Hamlet's own character but a crucial necessity of his role. The evil which is masked under a smiling front must be exposed and must be destroyed. The severity of the situation is such that there is no room for what Troilus, with less justification, calls 'the vice of pity'. Pity, like the pitiful Ophelia, may be an invitation to weaken in the struggle and may lead to betrayal of the cause. Though a man becomes more than himself in this struggle, he may also become less than humane and the uncompromising aspects of Hamlet's activities have caused some distress to recent critics.[3] Eleanor Prosser, for example, in her book, *Hamlet and Revenge* (Stanford and London, 1967) sums up her conclusions in this way: 'despite our sympathy for Hamlet's agony the savage course on which he embarks is intended to appall us' (p. 252). Her comment, and others of a similar sort, seems to be based on a misunderstanding of the level at which the story material is being treated in this play. A revenge plot is its framework but in the presentation of the situation into which the ghost's revelations are cast and in the working out of the implications of these and the instructions to Hamlet, Shakespeare is dealing with action at what may be taken to be its ultimate roots. If Claudius is evil and Hamlet is dedicated to destroying evil, the considerations which are fitting to less drastic circumstances may here be inappropriate. As a revenge play *Hamlet* takes an almost entirely subterranean course. The flashes of violent action which occasionally burst to the surface—the deaths of Ophelia, Polonius and Rosencrantz and Guildenstern—are incidental eruptions which testify to the great energies engaged. 'Accidental judgements, casual slaughters', Horatio calls them (V, ii, 374). They are not part of a linked and deliberate scheme of murder as the deaths in *The Revenger's Tragedy* are, nor diversionary incidents as episodes in *The Spanish Tragedy* are. Only in Act V does action come to the surface to be resolved by sword-play and stabbing. The court assembles again as in Act I, sc. ii, but this time it will not disperse until murder and treachery have been finally unmasked and Denmark cleansed of the 'something rotten' which polluted it.

Shakespeare's comprehensive mind is nowhere more fully engaged than in this play. If it had not been so, *Hamlet* might have been more schematic. Possibilities of misreading would then have been reduced but so also would the marvellous richness. The treatment of Claudius is a case in point for though Claudius devotes himself to and becomes identified by Hamlet with an evil principle, he remains for the audience a man. The physical repulsiveness which Hamlet

[3] See for some examples of varied opinions and a discussion, Patrick Cruttwell's essay ' "Sweet Prince" or "Arrant Knave" ' in *Hamlet* (Stratford upon Avon Studies, 5, 1963), ed. J. R. Brown and B. Harris.

sees in his uncle is not seen by others in the play any more than they see the moral ugliness so blatant to Hamlet's opened eyes. The audience also should see a well-looking man, no monster but one with whom Gertrude could plausibly fall in love and one who is capable of giving love in return. In a moment of insight comparable with his self-analysis in Act III, sc. iii, Claudius speaks of his feeling for Gertrude and describes his love for her as 'my virtue or my plague' (IV, vii, 13). Love in itself is a virtue but, as Claudius has loved, murder and incest have been the results. In a corrupted soul, even virtue is corrupted. Nevertheless, the audience may, though Hamlet may not, indulge itself in some pity for Claudius on account of his evident feeling and consideration for the queen. Yet the judgement of the play upon him and his love is inexorable. Gertrude's death by the poison he has prepared is a striking image of the un-wholesomeness of his passion.

The ghost's instructions concerning the queen relate as directly to his ideas about sin and judgement as do his words concerning Claudius. 'Leave her to heaven', he bids Hamlet, specifically pro-hibiting him from wreaking punishment upon his mother. There is again a dim echo of the situation in *A Woman Killed With Kind-ness*. Wendoll, the false friend and seducer, refuses the opportunity to become a better man through heart-felt penitence when his mis-doings are found out and, instead, he deliberately enters on a down-ward path. In contrast, Ann, the erring wife on whom her husband refuses to exact vengeance, takes to heart her sin, does self-inflicted penance for it, and dies forgiven by heaven and earth, an edifying example to all. The situation in Heywood's play is pallid, largely because Ann herself scarcely becomes more than a type-figure, first of a frail, easily-misled female, and then of a penitent sinner. The woman 'left to heaven' in Shakespeare's play is scarcely more clearly defined but she gains life from those who surround her, especially her son. Dramatic interest also gathers around her in relation to Claudius.

Claudius is an intelligent, able and self-aware man, full of qualities which might have made a hero—hence arises in relation to him what Helen Gardner has called 'the tragedy of damnation'.[4]

---

[4] Much of what she says in her article (op. cit., p. 181) is relevant to Claudius though we do not know enough about his earlier life to be able to match him fully to the pattern she describes: 'the deforming of a

Gertrude likewise has qualities of a traditional heroine, for she is affectionate, unassertive, unintellectual, tender-hearted. Shakespeare has, it is true, submitted these qualities to unusual strain for Gertrude appears to be a quite remarkably unthinking woman. She seems never to have reflected either upon her own actions or those of other people and never to have suspected that there might be anything questionable in the events in which she has been involved. '...frailty, thy name is woman', Hamlet exclaims in Act I, sc. ii, remembering how quickly his mother fell to the blandishments of Claudius. So indeed did Ann Frankford, whose husband was young and handsome and loving, fall with scarcely a struggle to the love-talk of Wendoll—though she does have the percipience to see that she may be entering 'the labyrinth of sin' (II, iii). As with Gertrude, realisation of the full enormity of what she has done comes rushing on her like a flood in the scene where her husband surprises her with her lover (IV, v) and, Wendoll having fled, faces Ann alone. 'I'll debate with thee', he says:

> FRANKFORD: ... Was it for want
> Thou play'dst the strumpet? Wast thou not supplied
> With every pleasure, fashion, and new toy
> Nay, even beyond my calling?
> MRS FRANKFORD: I was.
> FRANKFORD: Was it then disability in me?
> Or in thine eyes seem'd he a properer man?
> MRS FRANKFORD: Oh, no.
> FRANKFORD: Did I not lodge thee in my bosom? wear thee
> Here in my heart?
> MRS FRANKFORD: You did.
> FRANKFORD: I did indeed.
> Witness my tears I did.
> (IV, v, 105–14)

---

creature in its origin bright and good, by its own willed persistence in acts against its own nature'. I think, however, that Professor Gardner underestimates how much we *are* shown of Claudius when she writes, in the same essay, 'The predicament of Claudius is direr than Hamlet's but Shakespeare pays little attention to it. We are held enthralled instead by the voice of Hamlet...' I have tried to show that what Hamlet says is often misunderstood because insufficient weight is given to the degree and kind of attention which Shakespeare indeed pays to Claudius.

These two 'typical' women have much in common, both in their frailty and their susceptibility to admonition. Like Chaucer's Criseide, they are 'sliding of corage'. In an often-used image, they are soft wax, by nature adapted to receive the impression of a stronger nature. But since neither of these is an actively wicked woman, only a passive receiver of evil influence, each is capable of abiding finally by the good when the issues are put starkly before her.

The last idea with which Frankford stings his wife's conscience is the injury done to their young children. Gertrude is an older woman than Ann and it is her grown-up son himself who performs the role that the husband fills in the other play. His own sense of injury is apparent in almost the first words he speaks in the scene: 'would it were not so, you are my mother' (III, iv, 16). Like Frankford, Hamlet insists that no deficiency in the husband could explain and excuse the wife's infidelity. King Hamlet lacked nothing in appearance or character or love of his wife which might have accounted for Gertrude's easy descent to his brother. This being so, her sin stands out in dreadful clarity:

> Such an act
> That blurs the grace and blush of modesty,
> Calls virtue hypocrite, takes off the rose
> From the fair forehead of an innocent love,
> And sets a blister there, makes marriage vows
> As false as dicer's oaths.
> (40–5).

'How smart a lash that speech doth give my conscience!', exclaims Claudius in Act III, sc. i, responding unexpectedly to one of Polonius's moral platitudes. To rouse the much more dormant Gertrude, Hamlet needs stronger language and the whole scene in the queen's closet is conducted in a whirl of emotion and verbal excitement. The difference in style and manner from the treatment of Claudius adds dramatic variety to the play and, in addition, Hamlet's fierce, non-naturalistic contrast between the two brothers emphatically draws attention to the profound opposition built into its structure between the good man and the polluted, destructive other:

> See what a grace was seated on his brow,
> Hyperion's curls, the front of Jove himself,

> An eye like Mars, to threaten and command,
> A station like the herald Mercury
> New-lighted on a heaven-kissing hill;
> A combination and a form, indeed,
> Where every god did seem to set his seal,
> To give the world assurance of a man:
> This was your husband.—Look you now, what follows:
> Here is your husband, like a mildew'd ear
> Blasting his wholesome brother. Have you eyes?
> Could you on this fair mountain leave to feed,
> And batten on this moor? . . .

At once the queen sees what her easy acceptance of the course of events has hitherto blinded her to:

> O Hamlet, speak no more.
> Thou turn'st mine eyes into my very soul,
> And there I see such black and grainèd spots
> As will not leave their tinct.

Gertrude's behaviour after her interview with Hamlet is not markedly different from what it was before. No new antipathy to Claudius reveals itself in her words or her actions but though in the very next scene she addresses him as 'mine own lord', and no suspicion crosses his mind that something has come between them, she does, in fact, at once lie to him in her account of Hamlet's murder of Polonius, making it out to have been an act of clinical madness. Her reluctance to see the mad Ophelia indicates the disturbance in her own mind but all is calmness when, at the end, with characteristic quietness and lack of demonstration she marks her divorce from Claudius and her cleaving to her son by disobeying her husband's injunction not to take the poisoned cup: 'I will, my lord; I pray you pardon me' (V, ii, 283). As she dies, she warns Hamlet of the treachery:

> O my dear Hamlet!
> The drink, the drink! I am poisoned.
> (301-2)

'If thou hast nature in thee, bear it not', the ghost urged Hamlet, recounting the facts of his 'most horrible' murder:

> Let not the royal bed of Denmark be
> A couch for luxury and damnèd incest.
> But howsomever thou pursuest this act,
> Taint not thy mind, nor let thy soul contrive
> Against thy mother ought. Leave her to heaven
> And to those thorns that in her bosom lodge
> To prick and sting her. . .
>   (I, v, 82–8)

The business of the play shows both how Hamlet executes these missions and what is involved in the doing of it. The moral dangers which threaten Hamlet himself in this situation are acknowledged in the ghost's warning: 'Taint not thy mind'. That he may become inhumane, in striving to look beyond pity to absolutes in relation to which compromise would be defeat, has already been suggested. But Shakespeare seems to take care to demonstrate that, in spite of the dire situation in which he is placed, and whatever the pain inflicted or suffered, Hamlet's human feelings do not atrophy. He weeps for the death of Polonius (IV, i, 27) and at the death of Ophelia he bares his heart:

> I loved Ophelia. Forty thousand brothers
> Could not with all their quantity of love
> Make up my sum. . .
>   (V, i, 263–5)

This downright statement at Ophelia's graveside is the only such direct expression of tender feeling which the play allows him. It is instantly followed by a semi-hysterical outburst. The speeches indicate both the strength and reality of Hamlet's attachment to Ophelia and also the terrible strain he is under for most of the play in suppressing his personal disposition in the service of a cause which claims the sacrifice of individual hopes and choices. 'The time is out of joint', he realises at the end of Act I and adds with a rush of anguish as he forebodes what this will mean to him: 'O cursed spite,/That ever I was born to set it right'.

In soliloquies, the state of his own mind engages a great deal of Hamlet's attention. That he has been urged to act and has not yet acted is a thought that oppresses him. Is he a coward? The word recurs, in II, ii, 565—'Am I a coward?'; in III, i, 56–89, when he speaks of the common heritage of sin which makes 'cowards of us all' in the face of death; and in Act IV, sc. iv when he wonders whether his delay has been produced by

> thinking too precisely on th' event—
> A thought which, quartered, hath but one part wisdom
> And ever three parts coward. . .

To defeat 'cowardice', he whips himself up to frenzy:

> Bloody, bawdy villain!
> Remorseless, treacherous, lecherous, kindless villain!
> O, vengeance!
>   (II, ii, 575–7)

> Now could I drink hot blood
> And do such bitter business as the day
> Would quake to look on. . .
>   (III, ii, 380–2)

> O from this time forth,
> My thoughts be bloody, or be nothing worth.
>   (IV, iv, 65–6)

But, in fact, action on this level is not what is called for. The struggle in which Hamlet is engaged is one in which the final killing of Claudius must be only an outward and visible sign, or a culmination, of what has been achieved by other means. His mere death is not the be-all and end-all of the play. Hamlet tries to force himself to simple murder but is continually forced back to something else:

> The play's the thing
> Wherein I'll catch the *conscience* of the king.
>   (II, ii, 600–1)

> O heart, lose not thy nature; let not ever
> The soul of Nero enter this firm bosom.
>   (III, ii, 383–4)

The 'bloody thoughts' of Act IV, sc. iv remain uncountered and they are followed by the deaths of Rosencrantz and Guildenstern. But when we next see Hamlet he is in the churchyard and at his least terrible, brooding with mingled irony and sympathy on the dead bodies around him and on the human lot. By Ophelia's coffin his talk is of love, borne both to her and to Laertes.

In his soliloquies Hamlet constantly tests himself to find whether or not he is sticking to his task. He dreads that he will give up, and half way through the play the ghost reappears to reinforce his resolution (III, iv). Towards the end he achieves a greater composure and it is a striking feature of the dénouement that he enters what is to be the final scene in no bloody frame of mind. One result of Shakespeare's method of handling the revenge plot in this play is to be noted here: that is, that Hamlet is cleared of the stigma of cold-hearted butchery and of underhand plotting. From Act IV, sc. i onwards, at the latest, Claudius knows his enemy and takes steps to remove him. It is he who plots by cowardly and underhand means to kill Hamlet and Hamlet himself comes to the duel with Laertes 'Most generous and free from all contriving' (IV, vii). The explanations of secret machinations which commonly occur at the end of revenge plays fall in this one to be given, not by Hamlet, but by Laertes, on his own behalf and the king's. It is Laertes who has assumed the role of unscrupulous pursuer of blood-vengeance, regardless of all restraints of humanity or religion:

> To hell allegiance! Vows to the blackest devil!
> Conscience and grace to the profoundest pit!
> I dare damnation. To this point I stand,
> That both the worlds I give to negligence,
> Let come what comes; only I'll be revenged
> Most throughly for my father.
>   (IV, v, 128–33)

And it is Laertes who, egged on by Claudius, is willing 'To cut [Hamlet's] throat i' the church' (IV, vii, 126).

By the striking demonstration in the graveyard scene that Hamlet's feelings remain alive and by relieving him of the odium of the bloody-minded avenger, Shakespeare appears to have indicated with great clarity that Hamlet had finally won through with untainted mind in spite of all the temptations from within and from without that have attacked him. We should have no reservations about Horatio's epitaph, 'Now cracks a noble heart' (V, ii, 351).

To the end Hamlet can still believe in love and offer friendship and his influence works for good. Before the duel he apologises to

Laertes and addresses him as the brother he would have been if Ophelia had become Hamlet's wife. The gesture is a touching one in personal terms but its significance extends beyond that. Brotherhood is a common symbol of the ties of shared experience that bind humanity and it further suggests loyalty, affection and mutual support. In Shakespeare's plays there are many brothers, but the most striking examples draw on the usual responses not to restate them but to lend impact to situations in which the expected values are denied. The relations between Richard of Gloucester and Clarence, Oliver and Orlando, Don Pedro and Don John, Edmund and Edgar, Prospero and Antonio, imply a breaking of bonds between man and man and constitute a threat to all grace and order. King Hamlet's murder by his brother was the act which set the whole play in motion, a murder 'most foul, strange and unnatural', and yet his son, who has seen the face of evil, in spite of all and nearly at the end of the play, offers brotherhood as a token of reconciliation and trust. The offer would seem to suggest that humanity has won, civilisation triumphed over the jungle.

But this is not quite the end, of course. Laertes accepts Hamlet's offer of love and vows not to wrong it. Hamlet responds with an open heart and turns his attention to fencing: 'I . . . will this brother's wager frankly pay'. It is all deeply ironic. Laertes vows love and loyalty while committed to hatred and treachery. The 'brother' who has wagered on the match is Claudius who primed Laertes for the murder of Hamlet. With Claudius still alive, evil still works between man and man. The 'brothers', Hamlet and Laertes, kill each other. Yet the final word is not ironic. With the king's death, Laertes shakes himself free of his influence and begs Hamlet—'noble Hamlet!'—to 'exchange forgiveness' with him and Hamlet accedes. After this last trial, and at great cost, brotherhood, it would seem, in its proper meaning, has in the end been restored.

At the beginning of the last Act of the play occurs the scene with the grave-diggers, men who make their living by death. Hamlet had longed for death in his first soliloquy but the ghost's hints at 'the secrets of my prison-house' (I, v, 14) may have contributed to sharpen his fears of 'The undiscovered country, from whose bourn/ No traveller returns' in III, i, 79–80. In these speeches there is a solemn and fearful treatment of death but after the murder of Polonius Hamlet indulges instead in a vein of black humour:

KING: Now Hamlet, where's Polonius?

HAMLET: At supper.

KING: At supper! Where?

HAMLET: Not where he eats, but where a' is eaten; a certain convocation of politic worms are e'en at him. Your worm is your only emperor for diet: we fat all creatures else to fat us, and we fat ourselves for maggots. . .

(IV, iii, 17–23)

He adds, for the special benefit of the appalled Claudius, an explanation of 'how a King may go a progress through the guts of a beggar'. His reflections in Act V, sc. i arrive at a similar point:

Imperious Caesar, dead and turned to clay,
Might stop a hole to keep the wind away

(207–8)

but here he is simply making a wry acknowledgement of the likely fate of 'this quintessence of dust', however exalted in his life-time a man may seem to be. The wit is not black and bitter at this point.

Earlier in this scene (V, i), the clowns have practised their grave-yard humour and have sung cheerfully while they dug a grave for 'the fair Ophelia'. She died by water and will therefore rot quickly —unlike the tanner for 'your water is a sore decayer of your whore-son dead body' (167–8). One effect of the comic as opposed to the serious treatment of a theme may be a kind of liberation and Hamlet's encounter with the grave-diggers can be taken as an example of comedy's capacity to offer 'relief' of a more genuinely salutary nature than that provided by simple release of tension. The essential function of comedy in Shakespearean tragedy is to change the perspective.[5] Instead of the magnifying and isolating effect of tragedy, it draws men together and individual events dwindle to less than dominating proportions. The famous comic interlude in *Macbeth* reminds us that at Inverness there are not only the demonic figures of Macbeth and Lady Macbeth, reeking of blood in the terrible darkness, but also the earthy, rumbustious porter who, by what he says and the way he says it, offers a guarantee that life and humanity and justice will prevail. Similarly, when the grave-diggers sing at their work and accept so imperturbably the grim facts of

[5] See also pp. 30–7 above for a discussion of tragedy in Shakespearean comedy.

human mortality, the personal anguish of the *Hamlet* situations recedes for a moment as they are seen to be no more than episodes in an endlessly repeated process of life and death. The clown's eye view eliminates metaphysics. Seen under that influence, the graveyard provides material for ironic comment on human pretensions but it discourages the grand egotism of the heroic gesture.

The widening of perspective in this scene somewhat displaces Hamlet from the centre of the stage—to the grave-diggers he is no more than any other man and they make small account of him. He makes a last assertion of his role as the observed of all observers when he rants hysterically at Ophelia's grave side (266–78) but quickly drops his tone and speaks in a different mood to Laertes:

> What is the reason that you use me thus?
> I loved you ever. But it is no matter.
> Let Hercules himself do what he may,
> The cat will mew, and dog will have his day.
>
> (283–6)

Later he expresses particular regret for having given way to 'towering passion' (V, ii, 75–80).

'It is no matter' . . . The comic spirit at its healthiest can invigorate, by freeing men from over-preoccupation with themselves and by helping them to take experience in their stride; but if it slips into cynicism, instead of releasing energies, it may sap them by reducing the most solemn moments to triviality and by making all feeling and effort seem laughably vain. What follows after the graveyard scene demonstrates that the new tone in which Hamlet speaks to Laertes at its close does not, whatever else it does, presage a lapse into nerveless indifference. On the contrary, the Hamlet who takes unclouded pleasure in telling Horatio how he has dealt briskly with Rosencrantz and Guildenstern, and who enters with spirit into the conversation with Osric, seems a man refreshed and alert, full of zest and vitality. He readily accepts the apparently innocent invitation to display his fencing skill in competition with Laertes, behaving no longer like an outsider, a man among men but alienated from them, but like one who accepts his kinship and is content to work out his destiny among them.

Together with this current of feeling, there is another new element in Hamlet's attitude as the play moves towards the end. He

speaks more than once of his sense that responsibility no longer
rests with him:

> There's a divinity that shapes our ends
> Rough-hew them how we will.
>
> (V, ii, 10–11)

Heaven ordained that he should have his father's signet in his purse
to stamp the fatal order for Rosencrantz and Guildenstern and
heaven will provide for all in good time:

> There is a special providence in the fall of a sparrow. If it be
> now, 'tis not to come; if it be not to come, it will be now; if it
> be not now, yet it will come. The readiness is all. (212–16)

Not to promote events but to be ready when the time comes is now
his only care—'I am constant to my purposes', he tells the Lord who
comes from Claudius, 'they follow the King's pleasure. If his fitness
speaks, mine is ready; now or whensoever, provided I be so able as
now' (202–4). To his ears the king's fitness does indeed speak loud:

> Does it not, think thee, stand me now upon—
> He that hath killed my king, and whored my mother,
> Popped in between th' election and my hopes,
> Thrown out his angle for my proper life,
> And with such coz'nage—is't not perfect conscience
> To quit him with this arm? and is't not to be damned
> To let this canker of our nature come
> In further evil?
>
> (63–70)

Except for the attempt to have Hamlet himself killed, the count
against Claudius at this stage is, in one sense, no more than it was in
Act I. But what Claudius had done before the play started has been
not merely recalled but most fully realised during the action of the
play and its implications have been recognised by Claudius himself,
and by Gertrude, and by Hamlet. By now Hamlet thoroughly
knows Claudius's evil and has brought him to damn himself; he has
woken Gertrude's conscience; and he has stood firm against evil,
without being blasted by it. Thus the king's 'fitness' meets Hamlet's
at the end. The ghost's charges have been carried out. The action of
the play has unrolled through a deeper and deeper mining into the
situation from which it springs. From the struggle in the depths,

there emerges to the surface in the end the moment when Claudius dies by Hamlet's hand and, by that time, the death sets the seal on all that has been accomplished, becomes the self-evident, necessary and proper response to issues which have reached complete definition:

> is't not perfect conscience
> To quit him with this arm? And is't not to be damned
> To let this canker of our nature come
> In further evil? (67–70)

The structural principles of *Hamlet* are contained in the ghost's instructions and Hamlet's acceptance of them in Act I, sc. v; but Shakespeare's approach to the revenge situation which he crystallises in that scene and for which he has prepared the background in preceding scenes, can be further illuminated by considering the opposition of two words which recur frequently in the play: 'custom' and 'conscience'. There are nine references to custom in *Hamlet*, more than in any other play, and they occur in all Acts. Denmark, as we are made aware of it, is a place not easily given to disturbances, where custom asserts itself strongly. The sudden death of King Hamlet, the rapid re-marriage of Gertrude, the succession of Claudius to the throne in spite of the recall of young Hamlet and his availability for election—none of this, it would seem, has been allowed to disturb court life and make a breach in usual habits. Polonius and the others have fallen back easily into familiar rhythms and only Hamlet, obstinately wearing his black, is unwilling to accept that the new order is simply a natural continuance of the old. Hamlet is not a man to make observance of custom an excuse for failing to exercise individual judgement, as we see in relation to a much less important matter. 'Is it a custom?', Horatio asks, referring to the noise accompanying Claudius's revels, and Hamlet replies:

> Ay, marry, is't,
> But to my mind, though I am native here
> And to the manner born, it is a custom
> More honour'd in the breach than the observance.
> (I, iv, 13–16)

It is characteristic of the play that this apparently trivial and incidental detail should be given serious attention for custom is throughout treated as a moral issue of far-reaching consequences. It can harden the sensibilities, as it has made the grave-diggers indifferent to aspects of their trade which deeply distress others. 'Has this fellow no feeling of his business?' Hamlet asks as the grave-digger sings lustily at his work, and Horatio answers. 'Custom hath made it in him a property of easiness' (V, i, 66–9). But the strongest treatment of the theme occurs in Act III, sc. iv, when Hamlet brings his mother to face the monstrous truth of a situation she has been prepared to treat as within the bounds of normal behaviour.

'Peace; sit you down', he begins:

> And let me wring your heart; for so I shall,
> If it be made of penetrable stuff;
> If damnèd custom have not braz'd it so
> That it be proof and bulwark against sense.
>
> (34–8)

Towards the end of the scene he urges her to absent herself from Claudius's bed and encourages her to make the break with these words:

> That monster custom, who all sense doth eat,
> Of habits devil, is angel yet in this,
> That to the use of actions fair and good
> He likewise gives a frock or livery
> That aptly is put on. Refrain tonight;
> And that shall lend a kind of easiness
> To the next abstinence; the next more easy;
> For use almost can change the stamp of nature . . .
>
> (161–8)

The most important aspect of these references to custom is that they draw sharply to our attention the effort exerted by Hamlet when he stands against the current and refuses to allow the strong pull of custom to carry him along with it. 'Damned custom' can gloss over the ugliest situation and pressure is strong in *Hamlet*, from Claudius's first speech onwards, to allow it to do so. Hamlet's prime difficulty is, essentially, Shakespeare's difficulty as a playwright. Under the stimulus of sudden shock or outrage, a man may be capable of breaking through any restraint; but Shakespeare cannot allow Hamlet to kill Claudius under the immediate stimulus of the ghost's revelations in Act I. He chooses to keep the play going by exploring the situation in Elsinore from all points of view. While this is going on, Hamlet cannot be maintained continually at fever-pitch and, as time passes, 'that monster custom' asserts itself to make the monstrous itself appear acceptable. The point is made several times in the play that, circumstances changing, human purposes are infirm. The Player King addresses his much-protesting Queen on the subject:

> I do believe you think what now you speak;
> But what we do determine oft we break.
> Purpose is but the slave to memory,
> Of violent birth, but poor validity;
>
> . . .
>
> Most necessary 'tis that we forget
> To pay ourselves what to ourselves is debt.
> The passion ending, doth the purpose lose
>
> . . .
>
> This world is not for aye; nor 'tis not strange
> That even our loves should with our fortunes change.
>
> (III, ii, 181–96)

King Claudius also takes up this topic of the effect of time and circumstance upon feelings and intent, when he asks Laertes how far he is prepared to go in avenging the murder of Polonius:

> Not that I think you did not love your father;
> But that I know love is begun by time,
> And that I see, in passages of proof,
> Time qualifies the spark and fire of it.
> There lives within the very flame of love
> A kind of wick or snuff that will abate it;
> And nothing is at a like goodness still;
> For goodness, growing to a pleurisy,
> Dies in his own too much. That we would do,
> We should do when we would; for this 'would' changes,
> And hath abatements and delays as many
> As there are tongues, are hands, are accidents;
> And then this 'should' is like a spendthrift's sigh,
> That hurts by easing. . .
>
> (IV, vii, 110–23)

The fire of love or anger does not last. Other impressions supervene. The extraordinary emotion is overlaid by the ordinary, the customary. 'Heart-withering custom's cold control', as Shelley called it, cools the blood and dampens the responses.

These speeches bring home to us how much easier it would have been for Hamlet to let things go on as the first court scene suggests they were in a way to do, to accept Claudius's promise of the succession, to marry Ophelia, let the dead bury their dead, and let time do its office as the great healer. Then 'custom' would have triumphed; the untoward would have been averted.

But against the pressure exerted and the temptation presented by custom, Hamlet asserts conscience. He will rouse the conscience of the king that he may choose damnation, rouse the conscience of the queen that she may be saved, and he continually examines his own conscience to see how things stand in his own soul. 'Conscience doth make cowards of us all', he says (III, i, 83), recognising that as a mortal man he cannot but be a sinner and that therefore his own risks in this drama of damnation are fearful. He must do the right things and do them, moreover, for the right reasons. At the end, his conscience is satisfied. The deaths of Rosencrantz and Guildenstern do not weigh upon him (V, ii, 58); he has no further doubt that it is 'perfect conscience' to kill Claudius and would be damnable to let him live to perpetrate further evil, and, finally and incidentally, he has roused the conscience of Laertes who had himself, egged on by Claudius, been near damnation. 'Conscience and grace to the profoundest pit!', Laertes had exclaimed in Act IV, sc. v, 'I dare damnation. . .', but conscience asserts itself at the end. As he recognises the virtue of Hamlet and the villainy of Claudius, he confesses and asks forgiveness.

This chapter has described the action of *Hamlet* as it developed from the programme in Act I, sc. v and the discussion of the custom-conscience polarity has confirmed from another angle the essentially inward nature of the action. It is now time to consider the conclusions which emerge concerning Shakespeare's handling of narrative material in this play.

The programme device serves him well. It generates ample material for all five Acts for, although the programme is not set out until the end of Act I, the preceding four scenes have prepared the background for it and have consequently made the ghost's revelations more interesting and significant when they do come. What we already know of the world of Elsinore enriches our reception of the ghost's speeches, as we see in them the promise of exciting action pending in a scene already animated with striking characters deployed in a variety of piquant situations. The action as it develops, however, is not what might have been expected. There is an accidental killing, a madness and a suicide (the suicide taking place off-stage), it is reported that two others have gone to their deaths, and at the end there are four corpses on the stage: but, for all this, there are long periods of the play when no progress towards the prime objective of revenge plays, the execution of vengeance, seems to be made at all. It has been argued in these pages that those parts of the play in which the action seems to be suspended are in fact, in themselves, constituent parts of the action, for Shakespeare has chosen to develop his programme at a level where it is the movements of individuals faced with choice between moral imperatives—for good or evil— which are being dramatised. Physical activity, therefore, has place only as it derives from and relates to these movements. Yet, whatever the merits of the procedure Shakespeare decided on in his treatment of the revenge story, the inherent weakness of this method of handling the material remains: that is, the deficiency of what is normally understood as narrative progression. Shakespeare compensates for and almost entirely masks this by the brilliance and vitality of individual scenes—the episodes involving the actors, for example —and by the variety and energy of the language throughout. Yet he felt the need for more. The pulse of the basic story, the revenge motif, had to be kept beating. The audience must not be allowed to lose a sense of direction amid the winding paths taking them to the heart of the characters.

If, with these ideas in mind, we look again at Hamlet's soliloquies, their essentially functional nature in relation to the play as a whole stands out clearly and they can be seen to serve a number of purposes. In them Hamlet rouses and searches his own conscience; in them also he seeks to stimulate the impulse to action which is always in danger of dying as the lethargy of custom steals over it. The play tells us that all human passions weaken as new impressions supervene but Hamlet resists the operation of this process. He is bitter at the discovery of the impermanence of passion in himself and over and over again in his soliloquies he strains to whip himself up, to induce by auto-suggestion a feeling which is no longer spontaneous. It has been remarked above that Hamlet's prime difficulty as hero is Shakespeare's difficulty as playwright. For both of them the question is how to sustain the drive to a desired end throughout an interval in which, from the dramatist's point of view, interest may flag and, from Hamlet's, passion may dissipate. Shakespeare emphasises at several points in the play the weakness of the hold that extraordinary emotion and intention may have in the face of strong pressures exerted to encourage adjustment to circumstances. He concentrates this awareness in Hamlet's soliloquies and by this emphasis and concentration he transforms a narrative difficulty into part of the hero's own personal crisis. The effect of this single stroke is profoundly to deepen the character of Hamlet and so immeasurably to enrich the play; but the soliloquies have a more immediate dramatic usefulness too. As has already been noted, they keep the audience in mind of the basic concern of the story, Hamlet's committal to the killing of Claudius, and they also themselves serve in lieu of positive action in that direction. They create moments of high tension and appear to bring the story to the brink of a decisive movement forward. By doing so, they continually refresh the audience's expectation and suspense and channel off any incipient impatience. If the action as presented risks frustrating the expectations of the audience who may be looking for a more vigorous display of physical activity, there is Hamlet himself to complain of the want of it. This technique for neutralising a potentially damaging reaction and even making it useful to the play is several times effectively adopted by Shakespeare. He employs it in *Romeo and Juliet* (and even earlier, in *Venus and Adonis*) and in *Richard III* when, after the preposterous wooing of Lady Anne, Richard himself is made to ask: 'Was ever woman in this humour wooed?' (I, ii, 227), and thus to make acceptable what might otherwise endanger the audience's sympathy with the dramatist's purpose.

To many, the soliloquies of Hamlet have seemed to be the centre from which all the rest radiates. The demonstration attempted in this chapter has indicated that this is not so and that the generating impulses of the play are quite explicitly formulated and located elsewhere. But the figure of Hamlet himself, set within the structure of the play and used to shore it up at a weak point, becomes, by the mighty creative energy devoted to him, so vital, so fascinating, that the temptation is to allow him to dwarf his surroundings and to treat him as a drama—or the drama—in himself. This is, however, supremely a play in which every part of the material is animated. There are others in which some parts flicker only briefly into life, others in which some characters begin promisingly but afterwards go dead. In *Hamlet* the programme, as Shakespeare chose to develop it, allowed for the creation and organisation of a complex and crowded world and at the same time provided the inspiration for animating every part of it. To add the sensation, the suspense and the tension not afforded by the remarkable inward method of treating the revenge plot, the Hamlet of the soliloquies was developed and, out of the dramatist's need, a new element took its place in the consciousness of the world.

Whatever else has been said and may be said about *Hamlet*, then, analysis of the narrative situation has a contribution to make. The revenge story itself poses problems because it needs to be fed by sustaining material between the initial impulse to revenge and the final vengeance. Shakespeare chooses to meet these problems by detailed attention to a whole complex of relationships and interests and by tracing the impact of the ghost's communications on the intimate lives of all who become involved. This treatment provides material but little momentum. To meet the deficiency he infuses a special intensity into Hamlet and, by so doing, performs an act of creation over and above the mighty animating process which has taken place in the play as a whole. Some have found the creative energy which goes into Hamlet excessive, out of proportion to the play which ostensibly contains him. If this is so, the fault is the same as that which causes Shylock to burst the limits of his role in *The Merchant of Venice*: that is, the unpredictable and unpremeditated response of an immensely powerful creative imagination when it focuses upon a situation which, for one reason or another, specially stimulates it. *Hamlet* accommodates Hamlet infinitely more satisfactorily than *The Merchant of Venice* accommodates Shylock but in both plays, and however we fill up our account in the middle, what we should first and last celebrate is the glorious creative power, *Hamlet* offers us a double experience of this, in the play as a whole and in the special quality of Hamlet's soliloquies. Shakespeare did other very great things, but he did nothing greater.

8

King Lear

King Lear, for all its uniqueness, has much in common with other plays. Aspects of Shakespeare's experience as a dramatic story-teller which have been observed before will crop up again in this chapter and, in addition, it will be useful in the course of discussion to trace back to the beginning of his career a line of approach to the presentation of character and event which receives final and dismissive treatment in *King Lear*. The looking back which this entails, to a series of plays preceding *King Lear*, will offer one more illustration of Shakespeare's continual interest in and experiment with the dramatic possibilities of a subject or an approach and it will set *King Lear* in a line of development which is not usually given much recognition but which leads to a sharpened view of some features of this complex, moving play.

Among the connections which are often noted, that with *Timon of Athens* is the most convassed and likenesses and unlikenesses between the two plays have engaged the interest of many critics. The central figure of the man who falls from power and authority, and is deeply wounded by the ingratitude of those whose love and attention he has cause to expect, is an obvious common factor and there is some overlapping also in the modes of treatment. *Timon of Athens* has been briefly discussed in an earlier chapter in the context of Shakespeare's treatment of history but both plays can claim origins in historical record. *Timon* draws upon Plutarch's *Lives*, the principal source for his treatments of Roman history, and Shakespeare found an account of King Lear's reign in Holinshed's *Chronicles* which he used extensively for his English history plays. *Timon*, as was earlier noted, moves close to high tragedy towards the end and indeed it is more convincing as tragic drama than *Lear* is as a history play, despite Holinshed. Neither in *Lear* nor in *Cymbeline* does Shakespeare seem to have felt himself much bound by what his sources told him of ancient British history and he added to both later material from romance sources. There is some respect for the historical situation in *King Lear* in that, for example, the characters live in a pre-Christian world, but for his sub-plot Shakespeare turned to Sir Philip Sidney's great prose romance, *Arcadia*, and the fictional history of the King of Paphlagonia. No such addition of alien material takes place in *Timon of Athens* for, when Shakespeare sought there for a parallel to Timon, he found Alcibiades in the pages of Plutarch where he found Timon himself.

Both plays have a considerable satiric element. *Timon of Athens* has already been discussed from this point of view and in *Lear* also satire plays a large part. The Fool in the early Acts, and Lear himself later in his madness, direct satiric attacks, with more or less vehemence, upon the ways of society and individuals and there is, besides, a good deal of incidental satire on a range of targets. More will be said about this aspect of the play later, and also about the relation of *King Lear* to *Timon*, but first some other aspects of *Lear* will be considered for the light they may throw on the kind of play it is.

Shakespeare's conduct of his story once again offers a helpful approach. We may observe in the first place how rapidly the play progresses. The initial situation is established and the major developments grow out of it with speed and concentrated energy. Lear, flattered by autocratic power into a state of self-sufficiency where he need pay little attention to anything but his own will, makes his fatal mistake, accepts at face value the protestations of his wicked daughters and casts out Cordelia. Experience then teaches him that there are wills other than his own and that he has given away the power of controlling them. He becomes aware of others as he had never been before and recognises the wrongness of his previous judgement. With his new vulnerability and his realisation of it comes a new sympathy with the poor and the suffering. By what he has undergone and his understanding of its significance, he is ripe for reformation both as man and king.

This point in Lear's story has been reached early in Act III, sc. iv. The sub-plot, which parallels the folly and insensitivity of Lear by the story of Gloucester and his two sons, is not so far advanced at this point, but the main plot deriving from the original situation may be thought to be almost complete. All that remains is for the old king and his virtuous daughter to be reconciled and for the wicked sisters to be punished. The Gloucester-Edgar-Edmund story now develops rapidly and, whereas Lear's suffering and humiliation took place during Acts I and II at Goneril's and Regan's houses, when he was insulted and rejected by them both, Gloucester's comparable experience is his blinding in Act III, sc. vii. It is at once revealed to him, as it was to Lear, that he has misjudged his children. By the end of Act III, appropriate reconciliation and punishment are all that are left to be accomplished in the Gloucester story too.

The sub-plot is an addition to the Lear material which Shakespeare drew from a quite different area. Sidney's *Arcadia* weaves together a vast number of stories but, in Book 2 chapter 10, Shakespeare found one involving a father and a good son and a wicked son which might be adopted to match the father-daughters story of King Lear. Though he seized the idea and some of the details, he discarded much in Sidney's treatment of the episode that is in itself interesting and offers possibilities for development. Evidently at this stage of shaping his play he is concerned to achieve concentrated effect and opposed images of repudiation and loyalty, harshness and kindness are to stand out unblurred by distractions of any kind.

The force and energy of the early Acts are very remarkable but there is a price to be paid for this concentrated treatment. The first three Acts have gained some of their potency from the speed with which the events unleashed in Act I, sc. i drive so directly and inexorably through to their consequences. But by the beginning of Act IV the economy of the play appears to present a number of problems. Reconciliation on the one hand and punishment on the other need to be accomplished, but the intrinsic interest of these is likely to be considerably weaker than that of the events of the first three Acts. The stripping of the story to its essentials has given force and urgency to the treatment so far but left little reserve of narrative interest for the last two Acts.

Act IV, sc. ii initiates a new development in the story with the declaration of the adulterous love between Goneril and Edmund. The web is thickened by the rivalry between Goneril and her sister and finally both women and Edmund are destroyed by the double-dealing amongst themselves. It is a neat piece of plotting to tie the main and sub-plots together in this way and make the disloyal daughters and son the instruments of each other's punishment. The treatment of this late-developing intrigue, moreover, is very lively. Goneril and Regan express themselves in clipped, incisive speech, the fitting language of their inflexible, hard-set wills. The deadly clarity and conciseness of their private speech is strikingly contrasted with the rounded rhetoric of their public performance in Act I, sc. i, or even with the veiled threats of Goneril's first speech in Act I, sc. iv, before she comes quite out into the open. Edmund is equally terse. 'Yours in the ranks of death' is all that is permitted him as a love speech. Shakespeare needs to be economical with the time he allows for this situation to develop and with his masterly capacity for turning a necessity to advantage he makes the brevity itself telling. The bare dialogues reflect stark passions unadorned by sentiment and grace. The women's fierce instincts fasten upon Edmund and he, equally ruthless, performs cynically the minimum gestures of conventional gallantry to satisfy them and make them willing instruments of his advancement.

Goneril's letter to Edmund betrays them both and Edgar, himself ensnared by a letter at the beginning of the play, becomes his brother's executioner. Shakespeare extracts a variety of dramatic effects from the climactic moments of the love-intrigue. The audience will see dramatic irony in Edmund's cool calculations at the end of Act V, sc. i, for they know that the incriminating letter is in Albany's hands, like a time-bomb ready to explode and shatter Edmund's position. When he and Albany next meet in scene iii, the explosion is delayed as Albany first compliments Edmund on his 'valiant strain'. With the raising of the issue of the prisoners, Regan and Goneril are drawn in and thoroughly expose their own intentions towards Edmund and their mutual jealousy. Albany bides his time and when at last he speaks, his disclosure of his knowledge of the adultery is couched in terms of sophisticated irony. 'For your claim, fair sister', he says, addressing Regan:

> I bar it in the interest of my wife.
> 'Tis she is subcontracted to this lord,
> And I, her husband, contradict your banes.
> If you will marry, make your loves to me,
> My Lady is bespoke. . .

Lear and mad Tom have already inveighed against lechery in the play and Gloucester has paid heavily for his 'pleasant vices'; but here is a new turn to the treatment of the theme, not so much an echo of old moralities as an anticipation of the comedy of manners.

It is followed at once by an episode from romance or medieval chivalry. The trumpet sounds three times and on the third summons an unknown knight appears to undertake the challenge. The ritual of trial by single combat, in which right meets and defeats wrong, matches, up to a point, the ritual of the opening scene where, in an open competition, wrong defeated right. Edmund recognises the turn-round of events: 'The wheel is come full circle, I am here'. It only remains for the two women to die and Edmund, the spokesman once more, to underline how they stood and fell together:

> I was contracted to them both: all three
> Now marry in an instant.

Shakespeare finds ways to give variety and vivacity to the meting out of justice on the evil-doers but the achievement of reconciliation between Lear and Cordelia and Gloucester and Edgar does not lend itself to similarly dynamic treatment. Once Lear and Gloucester have been corrected in their earlier misjudgements of their children, there is no necessary impediment to reunion, but Shakespeare delays these moments, keeping Lear and Cordelia apart till the end of Act IV and reporting Edgar's revealing of himself to his father as late as Act V, sc. iii. The delays are somewhat arbitrary in both instances and Shakespeare himself seems to have felt that Edgar's motives for continuing to conceal his identity from his father needed some explanation. He does not take time to provide any, however, but simply makes Edgar confess that he has been at fault in it. Evidently he hoped that this would be enough to stave off over-eager enquiry into whys and wherefores.

An initial situation has developed rapidly to the point where the mistakes which precipitated disasters have been recognised and corrected. This sequence of events has been followed by the working out of another, by means of which the wrong-doers in the primary action have been punished. Interwoven with the punishment sequence, though with less time being devoted to it, is the movement of estranged fathers and loyal children towards each other. The fates of Edmund, Goneril and Regan follow the logic of familiar narrative patterns: the sinful, after initial triumphs, entangle themselves in further misdoing till they are trapped and destroyed by a representative of the good whom they have ill-treated. There is no equivocation about what happens to them and Edmund recognises the justice of his fate. A similar narrative logic leads to the happy union of Gloucester and Edgar and this also occurs, though Gloucester, harrowed by too much suffering, dies in the moment of joy. Lear and Cordelia are also united, but their story does not end there.

The conduct of the action in King Lear, as so far described, resembles the pattern of Shakespearean tragi-comedy, especially that of The Winter's Tale. In The Winter's Tale there is a similar rapid condensation of the early action so that the pressures exerted by Leontes' jealousy can be brought to bear at the earliest possible moment. The condensation of tragi-comedy is wanted in order to allow Time to work upon events and bring them out of the darkness of tragedy into the light of renewed hope and amity. This is not the purpose of the rapid and intense treatment of the initial situations in King Lear. No considerable lapse of time takes place from first to last and, in so far as one sequence of events in the second part of the play moves towards hope and reconciliation, the movement is thwarted in respect of both Lear and Gloucester. The speed with which events develop in the early Acts of King Lear could, in fact, on the showing so far, be described as a fault in Shakespeare's handling of his story, for it does not serve the obvious purpose that the condensation of The Winter's Tale does. On the contrary, the extension of the movements towards retribution and reconciliation in the second part of the play requires the exercise of ingenuity on the part of the dramatist and the acceptance of some implausibility by his audience, for the narrative material is running thin.

Shakespeare has paced his action in such a way as to give himself problems. The situation is in effect similar to that in The Merchant of Venice, where he used up a good deal of narrative material very quickly and invented a new and supplementary story for the last Act. There was not from the start so much narrative material on hand for King Lear as for The Merchant of Venice where Antonio, Portia, Jessica and Shylock were all capable of considerable development against distinctive backgrounds. The characters of King Lear are drawn more in the fashion of the dramatis personae in Timon of Athens, that is to say, with individual characteristics and backgrounds only very slightly suggested, so that if we should be curious about the world these characters inhabited before the play opened and about their ways of life, we shall discover little information to satisfy our curiosity. The characters are cut out sharply with bold, clear strokes and are not conceived in terms of a 'normal' daily life whose details may generate interest of its own as well as substantiating the people. The lack of history of the characters and the absence of tension between conflicting aspects of personality are factors which relate the play to *Timon* and also mark it off distinctly from *Hamlet*, *Othello*, and *Macbeth*, the other tragedies which surround it, and the narrative conditions are inevitably affected by these facts.

How far Shakespeare anticipated the exigencies of the narrative situation in *King Lear* it is impossible to say. He seems temperamentally to have welcomed the challenge of experiment with new methods and approaches. If difficulties arose in the working, he had a virtually inexhaustible resourcefulness to get him out of trouble. Narrative problems were a spur to creative invention, as has been noticed frequently in this study, and characteristic problems and responses lie at the back of the most astonishing scenes in the second part of *King Lear*.

'Do you suppose for one moment', Yeats asked Sean O'Casey, 'that Shakespeare educated Hamlet and King Lear by telling them what he thought and believed? As I see it Hamlet and Lear educated Shakespeare, and I have no doubt that in the process of that education he found out that he was an altogether different man to what he thought himself, and had altogether different beliefs.'[1] This is over-stated but it makes a good point all the same. *King Lear* especially, produces the terror and excitement of pushing into unknown and fearful regions and the dramatist himself may well have held his breath as they opened out before him. Some scenes, in particular, convey the experience of exploration in new, uncharted regions with special force and in identifying them we find ourselves looking at scenes where the 'story' as such counts for very little. Scenes in which Shakespeare 'does without events' have been encountered before and in some parts of *Lear* he does without them again but 'the gestures of easy conversation' are nothing to the purpose here. The account of *King Lear* which has been offered so far needs now to be amplified to take account of these scenes.

In tragi-comedy the events precipitating catastrophe may need to be concentrated into relatively short space in order to leave time for

[1] Quoted R. Ellmann, *The Identity of Yeats* (London, 1964), p. 42.

damage to be repaired and sympathy to be restored. The concentration of events in the story of *King Lear* up to an early point in Act III, sc. iv has no such function. Lear is brought through tribulation to the brink of rehabilitation only to be plunged into madness. This movement of fall, followed by tendency to recovery, followed by deeper fall is a recurrent phenomenon in the second part of the play. At the beginning of Act IV, Edgar congratulates himself on having attained the relative security of being: 'The lowest and most dejected thing of fortune', only to be confronted at once with the blinded Gloucester. Gloucester attempts to commit suicide and what appears to be a miraculous rescue gives him fortitude, as he believes, to bear all future affliction: but at once there occurs worse than he could have imagined, the entry of his master, Lear, mad. After promising comfort in Act V, sc. ii, Edgar returns immediately with news of Lear's defeat in the battle and of his and Cordelia's capture. After Edmund has repented in the last scene and revoked his order to the captain to kill the prisoners, Lear enters with the dead Cordelia in his arms. The process which these scenes exemplify is analogous to that in Donne's 'Nocturnal upon St Lucy's Day', where the poet mines deeper and deeper into the concept of deprivation and desolation, from an 'ordinary nothing' to 'a quintessence even of nothingness'. *King Lear* plays on the same word, not only in its language, but also in the visual images it presents. Edgar becomes 'nothing', without family or identity, an outcast of society; Kent becomes 'nothing', an unknown man condemned to the stocks; Lear becomes 'nothing', a madman raving in a hovel. Lear is sure, when he speaks to Cordelia, that 'Nothing will come of nothing', but by the end of the play the simple formula has come to contain all sorts of ambiguities and complexities and to open vistas whose horizons we cannot see. Similarly, the falling, steadying and again falling graph of the good characters' fortunes rouses our most sensitive hopes and fears.

The latter part of *King Lear* works out the basic situations in terms of punishment of the guilty and reunion of the innocent and enlightened, but the scenes in which 'nothing happens' in the literal sense are those which give the play the resonances whose vibrations make the mind quiver. The scene of Lear on the heath is one of these. Act IV, sc. vi is another, with mad Lear meeting blind Gloucester and talking to him in a mixture of piercing comment and blithe irresponsible, clown-like humour—'I remember thine eyes well enough', he tells him. The earlier part of the same scene is extraordinary in another way, for this is not so much an example of Shakespeare creating an astonishing effect in the absence of narrative event as one in which he builds deliberately towards the climax of a non-event. Gloucester's supposed leap from Dover cliff is elaborately prepared for by Edgar's scene-setting and culminates in Gloucester's prayer and what he intends to be his dying benediction on the son whom he has misjudged and whom he now fails to recognise. But there is no cliff, no leap, the preparations lack completion in action. There is in the end only the fear that Gloucester's hold on life will snap simply because of the shocks and strain that he has undergone.

In these scenes Shakespeare annexes for tragic effect more of the territory of comedy than he does anywhere else. The border-line always fascinates him, from the earliest plays where he juxtaposed tragic and comic—Egeon's grief and imminent death, for example, with the antics of mistaken identity in *The Comedy of Errors*—through subtler effects, as in *Much Ado About Nothing*, or, in tragedy, the laughter in *Hamlet*. But in these scenes of *Lear*, tragedy becomes farce and farce tragedy in continuous action and reaction. It is characteristic of the play that when, in Act IV, sc. vi, this effect has been made in the treatment of Gloucester's leap and something like quiet momentarily follows, then, with a sudden twist, the emotional pressure is doubled and we experience even more acutely that exacerbated state of sensibility when the grotesquely ludicrous and the unbearably pathetic are presented simultaneously to our sight. Lear, 'fantastically dressed with wild flowers', addresses the 'blind Cupid', tortured Gloucester, and Edgar's comment expresses the amazement that the scene must cause and the reaction to it:

> I would not take this from report: it is
> And my heart breaks at it.

The wonder is that we can echo Edgar's 'it is'. Bizarre and beyond anticipation as the scene is, Shakespeare's imagination encompasses it and our own receives it as a powerful spring of pity and terror.

To the narrative line of situation and development, followed by retribution and reconciliation, there are added, then, scenes which do not directly contribute to any of these ends. It is a characteristic of these scenes that they push situations a stage further than could be expected, so that Lear goes mad *after* he has repented of his errors, and Gloucester is confronted by his master in madness *after* he has attempted to commit suicide and become reconciled to endurance hereafter. Edgar, as he often does, makes the appropriate comments:

> O gods! Who is't can say 'I am at the worst?'
> I am worse than e'er I was...
> And worse I may be yet; the worst is not
> So long as we can say 'This is the worst'.
>
> (IV, i, 26–9)

The situation is not confined to these scenes but reaches its climax at what might be the culmination of the movement towards reconciliation and restoration in the last scene of the play. Lear and Cordelia have met at last in a deeply moving scene (Act IV, sc. vii), they have been captured by enemy forces and Edmund has planned their murder. But a strong counter-movement against villainy has asserted itself and Edmund repents and rescinds the order to kill them. It is too late for Cordelia, but Lear still lives to see and feel her death. His burst of passion wears itself out, he loses his grasp of what is passing and seems to lapse into a state of insensibility. Albany takes control of the situation and makes a conclusive speech which prepares for a sober but orderly end. But once more the play pushes on beyond what seems to be a boundary, as Lear revives and utters a great cry of protest and anguish. Like Gloucester's, his heart breaks and his final agony drains the others of energy and confidence in the future. Albany's speech, asserting control over the time to come, was spoken too soon: no one has the heart for anything like it now, for the framework of expectation has once again been shattered. The play leaves us to take the full impact of the situation without attempting to offer any accommodation of it.

The death of Cordelia has distressed many since the play was written and it is true that Shakespeare had the option of ending the play at the same point as the old play, *King Leir*, with the victory of Cordelia's troops and Lear's restoration to the throne. He might have thought it a more artistically satisfying conclusion that Lear should not renew his reign but should die in the hour of victory. In all the sources except *King Leir*, however, Cordelia's death, by suicide years after the events of her father's reign, is also reported. The time-gap and the new circumstances make such an ending unsuitable for the play but that Cordelia should die is an integral part of most versions of the Lear story. There is nothing arbitrary, therefore, in Shakespeare's decision to include her death in his play. Nevertheless, some have recoiled sharply from it and protested that the sufferings of Lear could well be enough for tragedy without the murder of the innocent daughter. If she has done no wrong, why should she be, wantonly as it seems, destroyed in this way? Taking up the point, others have argued that she *has* done wrong, has been too proud, too stubborn, too unyielding.

So long as the debate is in terms of 'poetic justice' and Cordelia's 'character', the parties are unlikely to convince each other. The analysis of the play which has been made in this chapter suggests, however, another line of argument for the artistic justification of the death of Cordelia. It is in line with all those other moments in the play when Shakespeare goes beyond what seems to be the culminating point of a scene or a sequence of events. The death of Cordelia is 'unnecessary' in the way that Lear's madness was unnecessary or Gloucester's meeting with him after his suicide attempt. This is the hall-mark of *King Lear*, that it pushes situations further than we could ever have expected, taking us, time and again, beyond what we thought to be the end and leaving us finally to face the realisation that there is no point at which the living can say 'This is the worst'.

Shakespeare did not necessarily set out to achieve such a result. He needed to create 'without events' in the second part of his play and he found the ways of doing so which have been described. As the play grew, its development generated an organic logic and the death of Cordelia became its natural outcome. The entry of Lear with Cordelia dead in his arms is a great theatrical stroke, giving a tremendous shock to the audience in the last minutes of the play when they might have expected no more than the passing away of a tired old man. When he wrote *The Winter's Tale*, Shakespeare took similarly startling measures at the end of the play to sting the audience to fresh attention and propel them into a new sensation. There he denied them the scene of reunion between Perdita and Leontes and gave them instead what they could never have expected, the coming to life of Hermione. An essential difference between that and the Lear scene, however, is that the resuscitation of Hermione confirms the movement towards reconciliation and new life in the later Acts of *The Winter's Tale*, whereas the death of

Cordelia gives a sudden terrible blow to any hope of a comforting conclusion which may be founded on Cornwall's death, Albany's change of side, Edgar's victory and Edmund's dying attempts to save the lives of the captives. Both scenes produce theatrical moments of remarkable power and stimulate deep responses but, paradoxically, though the reanimation of Hermione is a confirmatory event and the death of Cordelia is a frustrating one, yet, because of the characteristic movement of scenes in the later Acts of *Lear*, the death of Cordelia is more deeply lodged in the fabric of the play than is the coming to life in *The Winter's Tale*.

To consider *King Lear*, like other plays in the Shakespeare canon, as an evolving play is to throw emphasis on to the imaginative life which kindles into fresh energy in the process of creation. At earlier times in his career such a process produced irregularities in the surface and as late as *Measure for Measure* the development of Isabella does not take place without leaving signs of adjustment and redirection in the course of writing. But *King Lear*, though it sails near to great difficulties, achieves artistic coherence and all its elements are fused together by the compelling force of a growing vision of a world in which no foothold is secure. So it is that individual scenes can be singled out and each treated as a centre from which radiate significances binding together the whole play. Harry Levin examined the Dover cliff scene (in *More Talking of Shakespeare*, ed. John Garrett, 1959; reprinted in the Signet edition of *King Lear*) but there are others which can seem equally central. Part of a comparatively early scene, Act II, sc. iv, for example, which in its place appears to be perfectly self-contained and limited, may be seen, on later reflection, to epitomise far-reaching issues. Goneril and Regan bargained with their father at the beginning of the play, outbidding Cordelia for their share of his power and favour. The dispute over the number of retainers he should be allowed to keep is an ironically reversed auction, where the offers are constantly decreasing till they reach rock bottom.

GONERIL: Hear me, my lord.
           What need you five and twenty? ten? or five?
           To follow in a house where twice so many
           Have a command to tend you?
REGAN: What need one?

The last is a devastating question. It denies validity to all those 'needs' which cannot be quantified because they are not susceptible to rationalist calculation. They include the need for love, loyalty, and respect and the recognition of dignity in the aged, infirm, weak or subordinate. To recognise them is to accept restraints on one's activities, to know that there are some things that a man or woman 'must not' do and to deny them is to stop at nothing which the mind can frame. 'All with me's meet that I can fashion fit', as Edmund says (I, ii, 175) and he and Goneril and Regan are at one in their disdain for any of the natural pieties. The whole play could be discussed in terms of the testing of these pieties. Alternatively, one might take as the key-word, 'nothing', a word played with so much in the early Acts and illustrated, as has already been noted, by crucial images in the play. These images focus on Lear's comment on 'unaccommodated man'—'no more but such a poor, bare forked animal as thou art', he tells Edgar (II, iv). 'If it be man's work, I'll do't', the Captain promises Edmund, accepting the commission to kill Lear and Cordelia in the hope of reward, and begging a question the play advances towards time and again: what is it to be a man? Other key-words, other key-scenes suggest themselves and all bear witness to the esemplastic power of a great imagination working intensely within the rare and powerful pattern it is absorbed in creating.

So far Shakespeare's handling of his story has been described, the pace at which he presents events observed and the way in which they are developed. The 'lacunae' have been noticed particularly, that is, the scenes where no 'events' take place, and the consequences of his treatment of these have been suggested. Parallels with other plays have been occasionally noted since, to draw together Cordelia's death with Hermione's coming to life, for example, is to see something of the deep reservoir of possibilities which Shakespeare could discover on occasions when he is making use of an essentially similar technique. Satire is another technique employed in *King Lear* and it is one that has a particularly long and interesting history in his plays. To trace its course at this point, although it involves turning away for the time being from *King Lear*, will in the end enable us to take another view of the individual qualities of that play and bring us back to the question of the relationship between it and *Timon of Athens*.

In an earlier chapter, *Timon of Athens* was briefly described, alongside *Troilus and Cressida*, in the context of Shakespeare's treatment of history, or pseudo-history, and their adoption of a satirical mode was considered as one of the ways in which Shakespeare sought to bring this kind of source material to life for his own audiences. But Shakespeare's interest in and experiments with satire date back long before these two plays and he made abundant use of the comic possibilities of the mode when he wrote *Love's Labour's Lost*.

In *Love's Labour's Lost* the comic exposure of the deluded and unrealistic pretensions of the King of Navarre and his friends and the amendment of their vices by correction constitutes the principal business of the play. Subsidiary pretensions and affectations cluster about the main interest and serve to comment on it and illuminate it. Thus Don Armado presents himself as a magnifico and Holofernes himself as a weighty scholar. Their pretensions of character are reflected in their affectations of language, and style of speech throughout the play is both the medium and the butt of satiric comment. The entry of death, in the person of Marcade, appears in this context as the biggest satiric stroke of all, in one moment reducing the preening and posturing that has gone before to the level of child's play, culpably inappropriate in an adult world. The satirist's function is performed by many characters in the play but the major satirists are objects of mockery in their turn. All are implicated in the goings-on, all are trounced by the laughter which in this play sports with human follies not with crimes, until, at the end, even folly itself is shown to be in some lights a serious matter.

The comedy of *As You Like It*, like that of *Love's Labour's Lost*, is to a large extent based on satire and, as in the earlier play, satiric energy is widely diffused. Rosalind satirises romantic sentimentality and Touchstone romance itself. Characters use parody against each other, as Jaques parodies Amiens' pastoral idyll in Act II, sc. v and Touchstone parodies Orlando's love-lyrics in Act III, sc. ii. Action is arranged to make heroics look a little foolish, as when Orlando dramatically bursts in upon Duke Senior's peaceful meal in Act II, sc. vii and Jaques deflatingly asks: 'Of what kind should this cock come of?' and calmly eats a grape. Even Phoebe joins her voice to the chorus of those poking fun at extravagant gesture and rhetoric when she attacks Silvius's lover's hyperbole (in Act III, sc. v).

Traditional satiric themes appear and are given set-piece treatment: the ways of court (Corin and Touchstone in Act III, sc. ii and Touchstone's solo performance on the degrees of a lie in Act V, sc. iv), the waywardness of women (Rosalind to Orlando in Act IV, sc. i), and the affectations of travellers (Rosalind to Jaques in Act IV, sc. i).

The liveliness and good-humour of all this are akin to the satirical manner of *Love's Labour's Lost* but there is one element, not touched on so far, which introduces a different quality into *As You Like It*. Jaques in his role of Monsieur Melancholy employs a darker satiric style than anything so far mentioned. His apostrophe to the wounded deer in Act II, sc. i is in a vein of social/moral satire not present in *Love's Labour's Lost*:

> Thus most invectively he pierceth through
> The body of country, city, court,
> Yea, and of this our life . . .

His account of man's life in Act II, sc. vii, the famous 'All the world's a stage' speech, reflects an ironic and critical view of the human condition. The Duke in *Measure for Measure* makes an essentially similar estimate of life in this world when he speaks to Claudio in prison:

> all thy blesed youth
> Becomes as aged, and doth beg the alms
> Of palsied eld; and when thou art old and rich
> Thou hast neither heat, affection, limb or beauty
> To make thy riches pleasant. . .

Jaques' speech comes to the same point:

> Last scene of all,
> That ends this strange eventful history,
> Is second childishness and mere oblivion,
> Sans teeth, sans eyes, sans taste, sans everything.

The difference of tone between the two speeches, however, is crucial. The Duke's words are an admonition to the young man to loosen his ties with earth and prepare for another world. Jaques' stance is the satirist's and his aim is to cut away the ground from the pride of mankind, exposing men and their works as ridiculous. Swift makes a head-on attack on human pride at the end of *Gulliver's Travels* and he invented his own 'world set apart' for Gulliver. Jaques speaks from deep in the Forest of Arden and the setting takes much of the sting from his words. All the same, they belong to the same line of thought as Swift's.

In *Love's Labour's Lost* and *As You Like It* Shakespeare tries out the range of the satiric scale. It can be clever and witty, it can be coarse and blunt, it can laugh at affectations or it can cut more deeply into the moral fibre of man, it can be light-hearted and high-spirited or it can be sombre and take a severely disillusioned view of human existence. But though he runs up and down the scale, with the exception of the intrusion of death, the ultimate satirist, into *Love's Labour's Lost*, he keeps the satiric material and its treatment essentially in harmony with the comic spirit.

Against this background one scene stands out with surprising incongruity. In Act II, sc. vii Jaques has been rejoicing in an encounter with Touchstone which has made him laugh for an hour, as he claims, and in his enthusiasm he goes on to declare that he himself covets the role of Fool—'I am ambitious for a motley coat'. Yet it is evidently not his intention to make people laugh, as the Fool Touchstone does. He would claim the Fool's licence to 'blow on whom I please' but he would use it as a severe critic of society, not for jest:

> Invest me in my motley. Give me leave
> To speak my mind, and I will through and through
> Cleanse the foul body of th'infected world. . .

The language he uses is a good deal more violent and severe than that used by any other satiric commentator in *Love's Labour's Lost* or *As You Like It* and the new tone and Jaques' ambition are alike instantly reproved by the Duke. Jaques as administrator of a moral purge to the infected world would do, the Duke says:

> Most mischievous foul sin in chiding sin,
> For thou thyself hast been a libertine,
> As sensual as the brutish sting itself,
> And all th' embossed sores and heated evils
> That thou with licence of free foot hast caught
> Wouldst thou disgorge into the general world.

With these speeches we seem to have moved into a different area altogether from anything we have been prepared for earlier. Jaques a libertine? The idea is not developed elsewhere nor is it even taken up here, for Jaques' reply to the Duke turns to a different point. He defends himself against the reproach (often made, but not made here) that satirists are motivated by malice towards individuals, and to this common complaint he makes the common defence. The satirist, he claims, identifies sins and follies: if individuals apply his comments to themselves, they confess their guilt by doing so. If the cap fits, let them wear it. He does not meet the real thrust of the Duke's attack on him and the dialogue remains curious, not only because of the weight and severity of its language, but also because of its inconsecutive, inconclusive nature.

Why then is it there? Evidently because Shakespeare was thinking about satire and more concerned for the moment with some thoughts on the subject than with character or action. *As You Like It* is the second of his plays to be activated to a considerable extent by a satiric impulse and he has exploited the possibilities with wit and vivacity. But one note in the scale has remained untouched, that of the Juvenalian satirist, the harsh castigator of mankind, dedicated uncompromisingly to do what Jacques says he wants to do: 'Cleanse the foul body of th'infected world'. The note is sounded here and produces a discord.

The Duke's comment goes to the heart of the ambiguity in the Juvenalian satirist's role. He claims, like Jaques, a moral function and asks for licence to discharge it but, in so far as he deals with pitch, he is always open to the suspicion of being himself defiled and his knowledge of and obsession with the least amiable, most ignominious and shameful aspects of humanity may suggest that his pose as moral corrector masks a diseased mind of his own. Like Wordsworth's Godwinian, he may be one of those whose 'passions had the privilege to work/And never hear the sound of their own names'. It is to make this point, it would seem, that Jaques becomes, momentarily, a libertine. The possibility of a different satiric tone, a grimmer estimate of life and humanity, is glanced at and rejected.

Jaques stands in here for the Juvenalian satirist, dedicated to scourging the world, but the play is too sunny to continue him in that role. The immediately following episode is Orlando's arrival with drawn sword, in which Jacques' cool aplomb puts the laughter on his side. The startling picture, held before us for an instant, of him as a creature of 'embossed sores and headed evils' is already dissolved and we can listen to the 'All the world's a stage' speech without too much disturbance. As has often been pointed out, Jaques has no sooner ended his chronicle of futility than Orlando enters, carrying Adam, and this spectacle at once renders Jaques' account of life invalid. Adam, old and worn, sans teeth as he is, commands a love and respect which speak well for him and also for those who offer him care and courtesy. Such things receive no recognition from Jaques.

The potentially black satiric strain in Jaques is not, then, allowed full development. Nevertheless his attitude is marked off from that of the others and he and Orlando are especially contrasted. Their antipathy, though comically phrased, is basically serious: 'let's meet as little as we can', says Jacques and Orlando agrees: 'I do desire we may be better strangers' (III, ii). Jacques, indeed, deceived by Orlando's wit, thinks for a moment that they may have something in common. There can be only one use for wit as he sees the matter: 'Will you sit down with me and we two will rail against our mistress the world and all our misery?' But Orlando's attitude is quite different: 'I will chide no breather in the world but myself, against whom I know most faults.'

The difference between them is summed up in this. Jaques shows all the arrogance of the satirist who awards himself the status of critic sitting in judgement on the world and deploring 'our misery', while Orlando shows the humility of the man whose heart goes out in loving relationships with others. 'The worst fault you have is to be in love', Jaques accuses him and Orlando answers very decisively: ''Tis a fault I will not change for your best virtue. I am weary of you.' Jaques fares no better in his efforts to strike up an acquaintance with Rosalind. Love and happiness are not the satirist's milieu and at the end of the play he will not join the dance, opting out of the relationships which it symbolises and preferring to retain his role of critical observer in company with the converted Duke Frederick.

Throughout, Jaques shows a particular interest in Touchstone and their conjunction is a significant one. The role of the Fool in literature and in life always had a satiric potential and Touchstone provides some effective examples of how it could be used. But he remains a merry Fool, a source of laughter, an enhancer of the gaiety of the play. When Jaques cries out to be invested with motley, however, and claims to long to be a Fool, the satiric potential alone is all he is interested in and he allows for no mitigating laughter. Gaiety is the last thing that he would wish to contribute to a world that he means to cleanse by violent methods. Jaques, in fact, touches on the point where satire is no longer funny, a point at which the satiric range of plays written up to this time has stopped short. The range is about to open out into these darker areas, however, and the next move will be out of the sunshine of *Love's Labour's Lost* and *As You Like It* into a different climate altogether.

Troilus and Cressida, like the two earlier plays, is constructed on a considerable ground-work of satire. Figures of heroic and romantic legend are cut down to contemptible size and the activities of love and war are held up to sardonic examination. The quality of language becomes again, as it was in *Love's Labour's Lost*, a medium of the satire. In the Greek council scenes Agamemnon and Nestor use a grossly inflated language which Ulysses mocks. The Trojans talk a good deal better at their council but the language of Helen and her court in the opening scene of Act III exposes the cheapness and triviality at the heart of the Trojan exaltation of honour.

As in the earlier plays, the satiric voice is heard in a number of accents. Ulysses and Aeneas employ it. So does Patroclus, as fully and (considering his audience) unkindly reported by Ulysses. Another parody is given to us at first-hand in Act III, sc. iii, where Thersites plays Ajax, puffed up with pride, for the amusement of Achilles and Patroclus. This is a genuinely comic performance which is aided and abetted by the stage audience and it might have belonged to a more genial figure than Thersites. Thersites has, in fact, partially the role of Achilles' Fool and in Act II, sc. iii we see him recognisably in the role, a provoker of laughter, a lightener of the mood. Yet much more consistently and continuously he plays the bitter Fool whom Jaques describes, whose only feature in common with the merry one is his licence to speak 'truth' to all and sundry. He is, in fact, for most of the time, the satirist for whom Jaques' language, 'the foul body of th'infected world', is the common idiom. His speech is full of disease and filth. He is 'a deformed and scurrilous Greek' whose constant employment it is to translate the loves and conflicts of Greece and Troy into his own terms. Touchstone offers his earthy counterpoint to romantic fervour on many occasions in *As You Like It*, but Thersites' translations of what he sees and hears bespeak a sordid mind in a sordid world:

Here is such patchery, such juggling, such knavery. All the argument is a whore and a cuckold, a good quarrel to draw emulous factions and bleed to death upon. Now the dry serpigo on the subject, and war and lechery confound all! (II, iii)

Thersites is the satirist as Duke Senior described him, full of 'embossed sores and headed evils' which he 'disgorges into the general world' (see, for example, his entry in II, i). But far from being silenced in *Troilus and Cressida*, his voice becomes more insistent as the play reaches its climax. In Act V, sc. i he has two soliloquies, one a vicious commentary on Menelaus, the other an offensive account of Diomed. 'They say', he ends: 'he keeps a Trojan drab, and uses the traitor Calchas' tent. I'll after—nothing but lechery! All incontinent varlets!'

Satirist and Fool alike are by constitution observers, detaching themselves, as far as they are able, from the situations on which they comment. By Act V of *Troilus and Cressida* Ulysses, Aeneas and the rest have been drawn into the action of the play, committed to sharing the emotions and events, and have ceased to satirise, but Thersites continues to move around only to watch and curse or jeer. In the remarkable eavesdropping scene (V, ii), so far removed in temper from the eavesdropping in *Love's Labour's Lost* or *Much Ado about Nothing* or *Twelfth Night*, he adds his typically debasing comments on the meeting of Cressida and Diomedes, a meeting which is breaking Troilus' heart. His commentary on war and policy is no more elevated than his commentary on love: 'Now they are clapperclawing one another; I'll go look on.'

The roles of merry Fool and dark satirist were split in *As You Like It* and the satirist was held within comic bounds. There is some attempt to combine the two in Thersites, though it is not altogether convincing and the foul-mouthed satirist certainly has the upper hand. Shakespeare is still seeing the two as intimately connected, perhaps as two halves of one whole, but he is giving increasing weight to the darker element. Our reactions to Thersites as satirist take us back to the discussion in *As You Like It* and the points made there. We see enough, independently, of life in the Greek camp and in Troy to believe that much that Thersites says is true. Yet we are also repelled by him. Jaques exulted in the idea of administering a strong purge to the world and Thersites, in every

way a coarser version of his predecessor, seems to revel in the muck
he rakes. But disease and scurrility hardly qualify him to be the voice
of judgement. He exemplifies perfectly that ambiguity which Duke
Senior's speech pointed to, our recognition on the one hand that the
satirist, however brutal, may speak home truths, and our revulsion
from him on the other, and questioning whether truths from such a
source are not themselves contaminated.

The line of satire has led us now as far as *Timon of Athens*, a
play more obviously organised as satiric drama than *Troilus and
Cressida*, as has already been pointed out in a previous chapter.
Towards the end of the play, the Poet is working on a new gift to
offer Timon: 'It must be a personating of himself; a satire against
the softness of prosperity with a discovery of the infinite flatteries
that follow youth and opulency' (V, i). In the world of 'youth and
opulency' of the beginning of the play lives Apemantus, 'a churlish
philosopher'. Like the Fool, he is licensed to 'spare none'. Like the
Fool also, he is an accepted part of the society, fed like a comedian
by the 'straight man', Timon, on his first appearance so that he can
show the quality of his wit. There is nothing very intellectual about
this philosopher who descends to badinage but evidently, like
Jaques in motley, he has taken it upon himself to 'Cleanse the foul
body of th'infected world'. 'He is opposite to humanity', the First
Lord comments (I, i) but at his first appearance he is not formidable.
His role grows in the banquet scene and with it his stature. Timon
rebukes him sharply, as the Duke rebuked Jaques: 'Y'have got a
humour there/Does not become a man; 'tis much to blame', but he
stays on, as the dedicated satirist must, to observe, and his observations lead him to some telling speeches. He becomes a sombre and
weighty assessor of men's deeds and motives, laying a cold finger on
Timon's happiness and his dream of brotherly love:

> Who lives that's not depravèd or depraves?
> Who dies that bears not one spurn to their graves
> Of their friends' gift?
>   (I, ii, 134–6)

Yet in spite of all that may be said for Apemantus's shrewdness,
and although he is by no means so abhorrent as Thersites, he does
not claim our admiration. Thersites' language came from a foul
mind which coloured all he looked on and Apemantus's attitudes are

suspect too, not for the same reason, but because they are too easily assumed. We see him, his separate table and his frugal diet notwithstanding, comfortably domesticated in the world he professes to challenge. He seems only just to have put aside his motley and to retain something still of the status of a member of the household. Olivia's comment in *Twelfth Night* seems to fit him: 'There is no slander in an allowed fool, though he do nothing but rail'; but he does not qualify for the second part of her sentence: 'nor no railing in a known discreet man, though he do nothing but reprove (III, i).

In Act II, sc. ii he enters in the company of a Fool who appears nowhere else in the play. Whatever Shakespeare's intentions at any stage for this Fool were, it emerges clearly from the scene that he and Apemantus are closely akin. Apemantus sustains most of the repartee and the Fool's own contribution is capped by a remark of which Apemantus says approvingly, 'That answer might have become Apemantus'.

Apemantus, so nearly a Fool himself, is paired with a 'real' Fool in this scene and in Act IV, sc. iii he is brought, as churlish philosopher, into competition with Timon. Contrasts and parallels are structural devices in many plays and Shakespeare uses them in *Timon of Athens* but he also employs the much less common scheme of discriminating difference in likeness. Apemantus has partly a Fool's role but he is not quite Fool because, like Jaques, he tips the scale towards the entirely unfunny. He is a satirist, a sardonic commentator on motive and behaviour, but not quite a misanthrope for he does not, as Timon disillusioned does, spurn mankind. He is certainly not heroic, for his way of life is compromise. He lives by the society he condemns. Timon becomes, as Apemantus has always been, a critic of man and society but he feels more, suffers more, and will make no concessions when the ideals he lived by prove to be illusions. In the magnitude of his gestures of repudiation, and his confronting of intolerable pain, he is almost but not quite, a tragic hero. The stain that Duke Senior laid on the satirist taints him, as it has tainted his predecessors, and stays with him to the end.

The dialogue between Timon and Apemantus in Act IV, sc. iii brings out more fully, and takes further, points that were implicit in *As You Like It*. Both Apenantus and Timon are by this time committed to railing upon 'the foul body of th'infected world'. As

Duke Senior does with Jaques, they question each other's motives and credentials. Apemantus accuses Timon:

> This is in thee a nature but infected,
> A poor unmanly melancholy sprung
> From change of fortune. . .

He sees in Timon no more than an affectation of misanthropy, a kind of petulance, and doubts if he has learnt any lessons from his experience. He discredits Timon's new attitudes by diagnosing him as constitutionally guilty of misjudgement: 'The middle of humanity thou never knewest, but the extremity of both ends', and he refuses to see any dignity or authority in Timon's role. Timon himself is even more abusive about Apemantus' credentials as a condemner of mankind:

> Thou art a slave whom Fortune's tender arm
> With favour never clasped. . .
> . . .
> If thou hadst not been born the worst of men,
> Thou hadst been a knave and flatterer.

Since Apemantus was born the lowest of the low, and is debased by nature, his misanthropy, Timon claims, is simply a means by which he accommodates himself to his situation. Convulsed with fury at what each thinks are the spurious claims of the other, they descend to crude insults and throwing stones.

It is a curious scene and a fact which contributes to its oddness is that *As You Like It*, a sunny comedy so obviously different in style and temper, stands clearly visible in the background.

> 'ay', quoth Jaques,
> 'Sweep on you fat and greasy citizens,
> 'Tis just the fashion. Wherefore do you look
> Upon that poor and broken bankrupt there?'
> (II, i, 54–7)

The story of Timon is the story of Jaques' wounded deer and it is this sample of man's inhumanity to man which causes Timon to follow Apemantus in piercing 'most invectively' through the body of society. Jaques' background is the Forest of Arden and the merry Fool who pricks bubbles to make people laugh is still close at hand when he makes his satirical plans. He asks for motley but, though Timon and Apemantus call each other fools, they have no figure like Touchstone in mind. A wood outside Athens was the setting of *A Midsummer Night's Dream* as it is of the meeting of Timon and Apemantus but their wood is a very different place from that where Bottom was translated and lovers learned to know their true mates. It is very different from Arden, too, where heaven rejoices: 'When earthly things made even/Atone together' (V, iv). Yet it effects a translation, of Timon from the giver of banquets to the wild man grubbing for roots, and his and Apemantus's talk is full of images of men as beasts. It brings about recognitions, including Timon's acknowledgement of the 'singly honest man', his steward Flavius. Not even this leads to love, however, and Timon's farewell to him is among the most terrible of his speeches. Yet for all the difference in tone and development, the scenes of Timon in the woods lie close to earlier handlings of pastoral so that Apemantus even borrows a speech of Duke Senior's to emphasise a point:

> What, thinkest
> That the bleak air, thy boisterous chamberlain,
> Will put thy shirt on warm? Will these moist trees
> That have outlived the eagle, page thy heels
> And skip when thou pointest out? Will the cold brook,
> Candied with ice, caudle thy morning taste,
> To cure thy o'ernight's surfeit? Call the creatures
> Whose naked natures live in all the spite
> Of wreakful heaven, whose bare unhoused trunks,
> To the conflicting elements exposed,
> Answer mere nature—bid them flatter thee.

This is a re-working, infused with far greater passion and with irony, of the Duke's bland speech welcoming the pastoral life at the beginning of Act II of *As You Like It*.

The last Acts of *Timon of Athens*, in fact, stand pastoral on its head or, to use E. M. Forster's phrase, show us 'the vision with its back turned'. The pastoral world of this play is not one set apart, for prostitutes, brigands and time-servers all come into it and none of them is converted by what they find there. It cannot be contrasted with the sophisticated life of the city for hatred, rancour and spite exist in it, only more nakedly than they might do elsewhere. Far from there being 'good in everything', the earth yields Timon the all-corrupting gold and is addressed by him as 'damn'd earth,/Thou common whore of mankind' (IV, iii). Jaques refused to accept the idyllic view of Arden that the Duke fostered and with Apemantus and Timon in their wood Shakespeare develops the black elements in Jaques as far as they will go, to the very limits of satiric possibility. Timon, in fact, goes beyond the verge of satire to a point where indignation and invective lose their hold and death, which cancels everything, becomes the only desirable condition: 'Graves only be men's works, and death their gain!' The presence of death fulfilled a satiric function in *Love's Labour's Lost* by suddenly placing the masquerade of the rest of the play in a starker context, but in *Timon of Athens* death is extinction welcomed by the satirist himself. 'Vex not his ghost', someone might have said of Timon, as Kent said of Lear:

> He hates him
> That would upon the rack of this tough world
> Stretch him out longer. . .

To trace the satiric impulse, then, from Jaques to Timon, is to unravel a strand in Shakespeare's thinking. He had always rejoiced in a Fool and he extracted the fun, good humour and good sense which may be contained in parody and mockery in some of his sunniest comedies. But in *As You Like It* he took a look at the severer kind of satire and the moral issues it raises. Jaques, in so far as he is associated with Touchstone, is a bitter Fool contrasted with a merry one but only at the end of the play does he slip himself out of the comic frame altogether. Thersites' moment of merriment in his impersonation of Ajax seems, on the other hand, incongruous and even offensive in the generally tainted atmosphere of *Troilus and Cressida*. He is the satirist of Jaques' imagination at his most scurrilous and he is presented without any saving grace of character or manner: 'As sensual as the brutish sting itself', and a thing of 'embossed sores and headed evils'. In *Timon of Athens* Shakespeare pushes his exploration of the satirical view-point yet further. Jaques and Thersites were tainted men from the start but Timon begins as an idealist and when he turns to castigate the world, he takes no pleasure in the office but in the act lacerates his own sensitive nature. With such a man to wield the lash of the Juvenalian satirist, will the satiric view of life and human nature then hold? As he does so often, when the tide appears to be flowing strongly in one direction, Shakespeare makes us aware of powerful currents running against it. Timon puts his own claims to justified misanthropy higher than those of Apemantus but Apemantus's attacks on Timon carry weight. Timon's own words to Apemantus earlier in the play stand against him: 'Y'have got a humour there/Does not become a man; 'tis much to blame', and Flavius is a witness that even after the suffering of calamity a man may retain faithfulness and generosity and 'merely love'.

At this point we come back to *King Lear* and the elements of satire which it too contains. As we contemplate the sequence of treatments of satirists and satiric material which has been traced, *Lear* begins to appear as the next and essentially the last stage, the play in which Shakespeare gives his ultimate version of the situation adumbrated in relation to Jaques in *As You Like It*, Act II, sc. vii. In *King Lear* the Fool comes back as the major figure he has not been since *As You Like It* and *Twelfth Night* and he is one in whom the satirical strain is well developed, though his licence to speak true becomes a duty he would willingly evade: 'Prithee, Nuncle, keep a schoolmaster that can teach thy Fool to lie. I would fain learn to lie' (I, iv). Like Touchstone, he translates the doings of his betters into his own idiom: 'When thou clovest thy crown i' the middle and gav'st away both parts, thou bor'st thine ass on thy back o'er the dirt' (I, iv). His jokes and his songs, however, play with fire. Danger threatens on all sides and his satirical sallies, made in consciousness of this, half dare the worst and half attempt to ward it off. On the heath the situation passes beyond his capacity. He suggests once to Lear that he should capitulate: 'Good Nuncle, in; ask thy daughters blessing. Here's a night pities neither wise men nor fools' (III, ii), but he follows Lear nevertheless and see his own role surpassed by others. Edgar, as poor Tom, satirises the sophisticated life of court and city, Lear in Act III, sc. vi, arranges a mock-trial of his daughters, a scene of wild and terrible comedy with a Fool, a mad beggar and a mad king as actors. When Lear next appears, the Fool has quite disappeared and Lear himself has donned a kind of motley. He is 'fantastically dressed with wild flowers' (IV, vi). 'I know that voice', says the blind Gloucester and Lear's reply, like the trial scene, might be Fool's humour if it were not so charged with fearful experience: 'Ha! Goneril with a white beard'. Gloucester makes the courtier's gesture: 'O, let me kiss that hand' and Lear brings it sharply to earth (in every sense): 'Let me wipe it first; it smells of mortality'. With the Fool's wit, he absorbs also his satiric function:

> Down from the waist they are Centaurs,
> Though women all above. . .
>
> Through tattered clothes small vices do appear;
> Robes and furred gowns hide all. . .

and he sees the world and men's activities in it in the same terms as Jaques:

> When we are born, we cry that we are come
> To this great stage of fools. . .

Touchstone and Jaques have come a long way from Arden to the heath and the field near Dover. Their roles have been united in *Troilus and Cressida*, split again in *Timon of Athens*, split and finally united in *Lear*. How near tragedy and comedy lie to each other is a perception that Shakespeare has often employed and his keen awareness of the two-facedness of experience led him, as he worked the vein of satire, to develop the Fool from buffoon to tragic hero. The Fool's role always included the two possibilities, of laughing at life or of criticising it and, securely placed in comedy though he usually is, the fool could border, on one side, the tragic. Feste, in *Twelfth Night* carries the shadow of unhappy things with him but Shakespeare does not choose to develop this potential sadness further. He does, however, develop the critical strand in the Fool's make-up and it leads him by another path to tragedy, through Thersites, deformed and scurrilous, to Timon 'a noble Athenian', and ultimately to Lear. The line of development seems to point to the firm conclusion that *King Lear* comes after *Timon of Athens*, not before, for, while Timon made of the satirist figure almost a tragic hero, Lear, having been both Fool and satirist, goes beyond both and claims indisputably tragic stature.

The figure of Timon can never be free from the charges that Duke Senior made against the satirist—that he brings his own defects of character and experience to colour the picture of the world that he presents. And Timon, having arrived at the ultimate point of criticism, where he wishes only for universal destruction, can himself do nothing but die, a solitary, self-willed death. Lear, on the other hand, culpable, short-sighted, misjudging as he is at the beginning of the play, goes through experiences in which his personality is broken down and reordered. When, in Act IV, he treats the satirist's common themes of sexual incontinence and abuse of justice, he speaks with a kind of impersonality as one who is a long way from the experiences which formed his views and from the immediate passions they aroused. He is therefore much less vulnerable to the Duke's (and Apemantus's) criticisms than Timon was.

In the later Acts of *Timon of Athens* Timon aspires to the role of prophet denouncing the sins of the world but, embedded within a largely satirical play as he is, he cannot escape the suspicions which attach to the satirist and his claims to prophetic authority are questionable. Lear has a stronger title and his denunciations of the 'foul body of th'infected world' are the more powerful and damaging as a result. His criticisms of life goes further than this, however. When he clasps his dead daughter and cries:

> Why should a dog, a horse, a rat, have life
> And thou no breath at all? . . .

he expresses the deepest of human anguish, when incomprehensibly, wantonly it seems, a cherished human life is lost. Jaques' sarcasms about the futility and ignominy of human life look very shallow and facile by this measure.

So, in *King Lear*, Fool and satirist are united and then transcended, as the satirist becomes first a prophet denouncing the sins of the world and then the voice of human grief exclaiming at the irremediable sufferings of mankind. As he approaches his end, Lear loses altogether the character of satirist and even in his most satiric scene he is distinguished from the professional railler. When he describes the vileness of the world in Act IV, sc. vi, he recoils from the picture he has himself painted and wishes to cleanse his own mind of the images he has conjured up:

> Give me an ounce of civet, good apothecary,
> To sweeten my imagination.

Whereas Jaques invited Orlando to sit down and 'we two will rail against our mistress the world and all our misery', Lear, who might with far more reason have spoken like this to Gloucester, does not do so. Instead the conclusion of his commentary on the ways of the world is, 'Thou must be patient'. Cordelia, who epitomises wronged innocence, true virtue deserted in favour of specious appearance masking evil, was never tempted to make a satiric response even in the freshness of suffering at her father's rejection of her. She fears the worst of her sisters but hopes for the best. When Lear is restored to her, a loving relationship becomes the most important thing in his life and he attains humility. Love and humility are the direct opposites of the satiric character, as Jaques and Orlando knew. His picture of himself and Cordelia in prison points the contrast, for in their communion of love and mutual blessing they will observe the world, not in a spirit of raillery or distaste, but with an interest which is sympathetic, albeit imperturbable:

> so we'll live,
> And pray, and sing, and tell old tales, and laugh
> At gilded butterflies, and hear poor rogues
> Talk of court news; and we'll talk with them too,
> Who loses and who wins; who's in, who's out;
> And take upon's the mystery of things
> As if we were God's spies; and we'll wear out
> In a wall'd prison packs and sects of great ones
> That ebb and flow by th'moon. . .
> (V, iii, 11-19)

With *Timon of Athens* Shakespeare took satire to its limit in the self-destruction of the satirist. In *King Lear*, the satiric view gains a new authority but Shakespeare brings Lear out of that mood. In the final scene of the play, there is disaster and deep pain, treachery, murder, suicide and heart-break. There is also love, loyalty and repentance, so that positive and negative challenge each other in dynamic conflict. The satiric point of view is ultimately too one-sided a response to the mingled yarn of life as Shakespeare has so subtly woven it. As a dramatist he worked through its possibilities and considered its psychology but *King Lear* seems to show that in the end he found it exhaustible. After this, there are no more satirical plays and scarcely any satire. Antonio and Sebastian indulge a sour-flavoured wit in *The Tempest* but, whatever disappointments may cloud the working out of Prospero's plans, their view of life is accorded no status at all.

King Lear can be considered, then, as the culmination of a long line of satirical writing and, however limited the description may be, it has its usefulness. From time to time there are renewed bursts of critical argument about the tendency of the ending of the play, whether towards religious hope or secular despair. The force given to satiric attack and the movement away from satire may give ammunition to both sides and this ambivalence is a quality deeply rooted in the play, like the characteristic pushing beyond expected limits which was discussed earlier. We observe the ambivalence, for example, in the treatment of pastoral motifs. The golden world of the forest of Arden gave way to the bitter landscape of *Timon of Athens* and in *Lear*, the king himself, Edgar and Gloucester are all driven out of society to encounter, beyond the walls of court and castle, a fearful storm. The heath is reductive. The revelation it makes is of 'unaccommodated man' stripped of his 'lendings', but it is not the only pastoral landscape in the play. There are also the fertile acres of Kent, 'high-grown' with corn, and the cliff with life busy upon and around it, which Edgar imagines to cure his father of despair. Disintegration and regeneration face each other in these pastoral images as they do elsewhere in the play and the treatment of satirical themes and attitudes is part and parcel of the same complex.

This perhaps was the effect which, once created, Shakespeare was content to leave. What may well appear on analysis (as it appeared to Nahum Tate and, more disturbingly, to Tolstoy) a defective structure becomes, by the immense creative imagination which is poured into it, an intensely imagined representation of the two poles between which our judgement of human experience may stand— one, that its pains and joys, triumphs and failures mean 'nothing', and the other, that the fight of good against evil is important and that in some dimension, somehow, ground painfully won for virtue matters.

Conclusion

What ever is said about Shakespeare, there remains always a great deal still to say and critical judgements based on quite contrary premises can sometimes claim equal assent. This book has suggested that Shakespeare's management of his stories is sometimes mis-management and that it produces problems which a purely efficient organiser of narrative would have avoided—'a very slight considera-tion may improve them', Dr Johnson said of the stories of the plays. But to suggest this is at once to invite a counter-statement to the effect that Shakespeare's techniques as a dramatic story-teller are in fact highly skilful and subtle. In support of this contention there is the evident truth that the story-based plays are susceptible of the most refined exposition and interpretation. I have tried to present the case for the first kind of comment and have stressed the advan-tage of the approach it represents in that it throws emphasis on to the creative energy which is actively engaged in the course of compo-sition. To take a broadly Lawrentian view of the 'work of creation' in relation to the plays is not to deny to Shakespeare what Rossetti called 'fundamental brainwork'. It is, however to doubt whether the brainwork involved is of the Pricean kind, 'a strict intellectual construction developed from point to point'. It is, above all, to resist some of the critical developments stemming from Price's attitude, which deaden the plays by imposing upon them schemes of ideas which effectively smother the breathing life that is in them. The account suggested in these pages is certainly not a plea for the revival of an old view of an artless, unsophisticated Shakespeare. When his stories gave him trouble, the methods he adopted to deal with his problems are invariably highly intelligent in themselves and, moreover, Shakespeare is quick to see how what has been adopted as an expedient can be used to enhance the whole play. On occasions, the expedients are adopted because a surge of creative energy has taken hold of the original story and necessitated a re-shaping; at other times, the expedients, required for other reasons, themselves produce a burst of powerful imaginative activity. When the activity is intense enough, as it is, most notably of all, in *King Lear*, the new energies released diffuse themselves by sheer power and concentration throughout the whole play.

Shakespeare's handling of his stories reveals also other aspects of him as a superb creative artist. There is the Shakespeare whose resourcefulness in an emergency is always capable of endowing a play with another dimension and there is also Shakespeare the good husbandman who works carefully to test and explore all kinds of material which may be capable of generating dramatic interest. To watch him at work on historical sources, or following out reconciliation as a story-line, or opening out, step by step, the possibilities of satire, is to see a professional writer of high expertise and commitment to his calling. But as the improvising Shakespeare asserts control over his structures in the end, so the Shakespeare who husbands and carefully assesses his material retains the capacity for free invention. The different habits of composition as he works on his stories intersect and penetrate each other. It is a pity to cover up the geological evidences of the creation of his worlds by smothering the whole with an overlay of themes and lessons.

There was little about story-telling that in the end Shakespeare did not know and he was fully capable of seeing the weaknesses at the heart of the whole narrative endeavour as *The Tempest* in particular, suggests. Twentieth-century writers have made their own protests at the conventions of narrative and have devised their own accommodations. Virginia Woolf is among those who have thought most penetratingly about the subject and some of her acute comments have been quoted in this study. But the last word should not be about stories themselves but about the creative imagination which presents, distorts, deepens, twists and generally transforms them and this last word can be, as it should be, with Shakespeare. 'A rare talent', says Sir Nathaniel, in admiration of the poet's fertility of invention. To which Holofernes replies, superbly accepting the pedant's tribute to his extempore verses:

> This is a gift I have, simple, simple; a foolish extravagant spirit, full of forms, figures, shapes, objects, ideas, apprehensions, motions, revolutions: these are begot in the ventricle of memory, nourished in the womb of *pia mater*, and delivered upon the

mellowing of occasion. But the gift is good in those in whom it is acute, and I am thankful for it.

The joke mocks even those who praise Shakespeare's 'gift' with the lightest touch but nevertheless we must still echo Holofernes and, when he tells us he is grateful, respond, 'So are we all'.

Index

Footnotes are indexed only when they contain material or a reference independent of the text.